# Person-centred communication:
# Theory, skills and practice

# Person-centred communication: Theory, skills and practice

*Renate Motschnig and Ladislav Nykl*

Mc Graw Hill Education Open University Press

Open University Press
McGraw-Hill Education
McGraw-Hill House
Shoppenhangers Road
Maidenhead
Berkshire
England
SL6 2QL

email: enquiries@openup.co.uk
world wide web: www.openup.co.uk

and Two Penn Plaza, New York, NY 10121-2289, USA

*Konstruktive Kommunikation: Sich und andere verstehen durch personenzentrierte Interaktion*, First edition by Renate Motschnig and Ladislav Nykl, copyright © 2009, Klett-Cotta – J.G. Cotta'sche Buchhandlung Nachfolger GmbH, Stuttgart.

Revised English language edition of *Konstruktive Kommunikation: Sich und andere verstehen durch personenzentrierte Interaktion* by Renate Motschnig and Ladislav Nykl, translated by Renate Motschnig, copyright © 2014 by Open University Press

A catalogue record of this book is available from the British Library

ISBN-13: 978-0-335-24728-8
ISBN-10: 0-335-24728-8
eISBN: 978-0-335-24729-5

Library of Congress Cataloging-in-Publication Data
CIP data applied for

Typeset by Aptara Inc., India

# Praise for this book

*"This book shows the incredible value of person-centred communication to educators, psychologists and leaders, anyone interested in effective, helpful and growthful human relationships will find this an excellent resource."*

Stephen Joseph, Professor of Psychology, Health and Social Care,
University of Nottingham, UK

*"No matter what your field or context, Person-centred Communication offers a path to a more meaningful, successful life. As researchers and practitioners with a wealth of experience, Renate and Ladislav share their communication expertise in management, information technology, education, psychology, psychotherapy, and everyday life. They find beautiful and time-tested ways to share how communication can be enhanced to help you live a more satisfying life. The book is easy to read, with rich content and helpful organizers, such as text boxes and hands-on activities to help transfer your learning into all areas of your life."*

Jeffrey H. D. Cornelius-White, Professor and Graduate Program
Coordinator of Counseling, Missouri State University, USA

*"This book presents a very good understanding of theory and practice of the person -centred approach and I believe it can be helpful for the professional and student interested in person centred communication. The authors' presentation of live case examples, personal experiences, questions asking the reader to reflect and the connections they make with other sources pertaining to subjects outside the Person Centred way, makes for an enjoyable and valuable reading."*

Antonio Monteiro dos Santos, Clinical, Coaching & Counseling
Psychologist, USA and Brazil

*"The authors bring together modern scientific data, practice and everyday experience to reveal the depth and power of person-centred communication. In a continuing dialogue with the reader they inspire and guide through case scenarios, suggestions for reflections and exercises - to develop one's own unique person-centred way of communication."*

Veniamin Kolpachnikov, Associated Professor, Higher School of
Economics, National Research University, Moscow, Russia

*"Carl Rogers was the greatest influence on our culture of interpersonal communication in the past century, as the originator of what we now refer to as active listening. One of the most ardent and sincere advocates of explaining Rogers to the current generation is Renate Motschnig. In this book, she and her colleague, Ladislav Nykl, do an excellent job of illustrating the importance of the person-centred approach, with moving stories and systemic applications. This is a great book at the right time for all those interested in avoiding power struggles, communication breakdowns and even those little personal wars that constantly wear us down. This book, in other words, can change your life for the better!"*

David Ryback, President of EQ Associates International and
author of Putting Emotional Intelligence to Work, ConnectAbility
and over 60 professional articles

*"The authors demonstrate how the person-centered approach is universally applicable and confirm its effectiveness in both the therapeutic and non-therapeutic context."*

Eva Sollarova, Professor of Psychology and Dean,
Constantine the Philosopher University, Nitra, Slovakia

Dedicated to our mentor Carl R. Rogers, and equally to all who want to grow from his, our, and their own experience

# Contents

# Part III: Experiential learning

# Foreword

I am delighted to write this Foreword for this revised English language version of a text that was first published in German.

Renate and Ladislav have been co-operating together for many years now from their adopted city of Vienna. Both of them are originally of Czech origin, a subject they wrote about in the *Handbook of Transcultural Counselling and Psychotherapy*. It is interesting to note that, despite their apparently divergent fields of professional endeavour, Renate being a professor of computer science and Ladislav a psychotherapist and lecturer, their joint commitment and passion for the person-centred approach, and the promise it holds for enhanced sensitivity and communication between people has united them once again in the production of this very fine and very practical text.

In the preface to this book they introduce their concern for the development of 'co-actualisation' potential in and amongst people. Here they have taken one of Carl Rogers' theoretical ideas initially generated in the early to middle decades of the last century for the practice of psychotherapy, (originally referred to as the 'actualising tendency') and developed this concept for our post-modern, post-structuralist world. As they argue: "*we need flexible psychological equipment that allows us to experience each situation comprehensively and enables us to tune our understanding of others*". It is surely no accident that both colleagues, who work in academic settings geared towards facilitating the educational and personal growth of young people, are dedicated to the pursuit of educational methodologies that contribute to "*the building of a flexible organized inner world in which mind, feeling and intuition are in frequent interchange with each other... this is the most meaningful and necessary investment each of us can make for our own and other's benefits.*"

Divided into four parts spanning thirteen chapters which cover theory and skills, practice and experiential learning, and two concluding chapters, this text constitutes a comprehensive and practical guide for the development of enhanced communication style informed from a person-centred perspective.

In reading this text, I have particularly enjoyed and valued the very accessible nature of the text which is so helpfully structured to make explicit each chapter's intentions and contents, exposition of theoretical principles (derived from an impressive international body of authorship), the inclusion of case examples and clear summaries.

Great clarity of writing enhances the reader's capacity for understanding a wide range of important issues and one essential value of this book (of which there are many for me) is that it is rooted in real everyday examples.

Additionally there is a chapter towards the end of the book looking specifically at groups and communication. I was pleased to see this additional context taken so seriously, as I personally believe that this is the medium which deserves much more developmental attention in society, from the dynamics of youth groups to work teams, from national association proceedings to international negotiations. Any moves to enhanced 'co-actualisation' in these areas will reap dividends in our co-existent potentialities.

This is a text that can be used as a personal and professional development tool for individuals. I am sure it will also prove of considerable value to teachers and lecturers alike across many subjects and disciplines. It is a considerable resource of ideas, theoretical perspectives, exercises and case examples for use in all arenas where communication and relationship are of importance... and what area of human activity, I must add, is there where these values are not important? Education, business, politics, human services, health delivery, the judicial system and so on are all locations in which enhanced, sensitive communication capacity by all involved can only be to the overall, as well as individual, good.

This is an ambitious book with noble intentions. Renate and Ladislav are to be congratulated on its creation.

*Colin Lago,*
*Sheffield, UK.*
*November 2013*

# Preface

Be it by phone, mobile, email, meeting, conversation, class, child care or sharing with friends, many of us tend to spend much of our lifetime in direct or media-supported communication with others. The humanistic psychologist Dr. Carl Rogers writes: 'As a result of the interaction with the environment, and particularly as a result of evaluational interaction with others, the structure of self is formed...' ([1951] 1995: 498). Hence, it is the interaction and thus communication that adjusts our inherent, human species-specific, potential through which we, in turn, influence our environment. This reciprocity is nicely expressed by a popular German saying which can be translated as: 'How you call into the woods is how the echo responds.' It is the 'woods' in which we live that co-construct our calls, our needs and our potentials. If we interpret the woods symbolically as environment, family, culture, the reciprocity becomes evident. This may help us to grasp that we're always just part of a bigger scenario. Yet, at the same time, we influence that whole scenario and contribute to its everlasting change.

This book is about highlighting and motivating those interpersonal attitudes that enable our communication to affect personal development – ours and that of our environment. Let's call it 'co-actualization' in interaction with others. This can happen only if we perceive ourselves and our environment in an encompassing way, engaging our mind, heart, feelings, intuition, and only if we manage to integrate our original equipment of intuition and feeling with the evolutionary, much more recent, capacity of rational thought and reflection. If we fail, we estrange ourselves from our inner self without having developed a reliable substitute for it. The consequences of that are too well known: people suppress one another, follow ideologies that make them fight and try to outdo their peers, because they see their mental constructions threatened and are not capable of empathizing with others.

Some readers may now ask: 'Is it the case that interpersonal attitudes are sufficient in our knowledge society and culture of professionalization, continuous assessment and striving for excellence?' This question can't be responded to easily. For sure, numerous professions require professional knowledge and action. Nevertheless we believe that professional communication and interpersonal relating that miss the core attitudes of appropriate openness and transparency, positive regard towards self and others, and the deep desire to comprehensively understand the other are only empty façades. In the longer term, they break down under ongoing motion and change. This can lead to power struggles, the collapse of relationships, and even, in extreme cases, war. In a time of dynamic and continuing change, from our perspective, codes of conduct and communication techniques are not enough when encountering new situations and tasks, and reacting to them in a way that is appropriate and creative. Such new situations bring the limitations of conventional training or conditioning and learning-by-rote to the forefront. Hence, we need a lot more than traditional learning and training – we need flexible psychological equipment that allows us to experience each situation comprehensively and enables us to tune our understanding to that of others. This is why, in our view, putting untiring effort into building a flexibly organized inner world in which mind, feeling and intuition are in frequent interchange with one another is the most meaningful and necessary investment that, day by day, each of us can make for our own benefit as well as the benefit of others. This book is intended to accompany you in your own process of uncovering your resources and talents. We don't intend to teach you or to set up rigid rules. Rather, we offer Rogers' as well as our own insights and experiences and we invite you to find out how far they turn out to be meaningful for *you*.

For our insight, we express gratitude to our mentor, Carl Rogers, even though he can't hear us directly because he hasn't been physically present in this world since 1987. Nevertheless, his books, thoughts, videos and theories motivate and impress both of us deeply and always anew. We also feel enriched and thankful for being able to provide each other with a climate of person-centred attitudes, even though we don't claim to manage this completely in our own lives at each and every point in time. We would also like to express our sincere thanks to the large number of individuals whom we don't list by name, in particular our students, participants in person-centred encounter groups and workshops, and friends/colleagues in this country and abroad who have provided us with innumerable experiences in the process of forming our thinking.

To us, the person-centred approach offers vast, perceivable potential for constructive personality development in *any* relationship – far beyond that of psychotherapy. This development typically proceeds in mindful interaction between people. Hence, we take the liberty of referring to communication in the realm of the person-centred approach as 'person-centred communication'. Now we invite you to form your own opinion and formulate your own experience.

Please feel free to contact us as you like – your view matters to us very much:
renate.motschnig@univie.ac.at
nykl@aon.at

*Vienna, September 2013*

# PART I
# Theory and skills

# 1 Introduction

*I have learned, however, that realness or genuineness, or congruence –*
*whatever term you wish to give it – is a fundamental basis for the best*
*of communication.*

(Rogers 1980: 15)

---

**In this chapter you will learn about:**

- The authors' motivation to write this book

- The psychological foundations of person-centred communication

- The vital function of our inner state: our body can express inner states without us being aware of it

- The criteria that are necessary for person-centred communication to fully unfold

- The circumstances under which person-centred communication is strongly compromised

- The purpose of the examples in the book and how to optimally benefit from reading the book

- The fact that person-centred communication is 'applicable' across cultures

- The specific intentions and unique features of the book

---

Inadequate mutual understanding, premature devaluing of another's opinion and talking at cross-purposes are frequent everyday experiences that can be painful, exhausting, time-consuming and, as a consequence, costly. Hence, successful, fluent communication is one of the major unresolved challenges for today's society. Person-centred communication offers the valuable, scientifically-founded paths illuminated in this book (Rogers 1959, 1961; Cornelius-White *et al.* 2013a, 2013b). Our primary objective in this effort is to contribute to a better understanding between people.

Our complex world makes it urgently necessary to develop a better perception and more mindful attitude towards each other, based on an encompassing sensitization and harmonization of our personal resources or dispositions (Nykl 2005). This means that we first must free ourselves from rigidly-held mental and behavioural models as well as prejudices (Senge 2006). Subsequently we need to extend our awareness of feelings to develop rich, flexible interconnections between our cognitive and emotional capacities. In a nutshell, we aim for a versatile, *ordered and flexibly adaptable* experiential landscape ('inner world') that can unfold if the proper conditions are provided.

Person-centred communication is based on the person-centred approach developed by the renowned American psychologist, Carl Rogers (1902–87). Rogers held the 'becoming' and 'growth' of every person in relation to other people in high regard. He was convinced that people develop constructively if they encounter an appropriate interpersonal climate. We intend to give continuing support to his groundbreaking theories and experiences that have made and are continuously making their way into numerous works, even in our time. To the best of our knowledge, however, none of these works is devoted explicitly and in the first place to communication – as the direct expression of the person-centred approach – in *any interpersonal relationship.* In this area, we elaborate the meaning of constructive, healthy communication in everyday- and work-related situations. We provide several examples, many of which are borrowed from the well-known and perhaps most widespread human relationship – the partnership or family. Other examples come from counselling and psychotherapy, and are intended to illustrate person-centred communication it its original 'pure' form, which needs to be sensitively adapted for situations in everyday life. Aiming for more than a passive understanding of the basic principles, we provide inspiration and calls for personal reflection in the form of examples from experience, invitations to reflect, case scenarios and student comments.

We have also included discussion of the person-centred approach in relation to new media such as email and the internet. Naturally, direct personal presence can't be substituted by computer-mediated communication. Nevertheless, technology is offering almost endless opportunities for contact, any time and anywhere. We are amazed by the degree to which the sensitization towards feelings and perceptions of the other can lead to better computer-mediated communication and cooperation and thus to greater economic efficiency.

A further reason for writing this book lies in the desire to consider communication not as an analytical object or a subject of inquiry, but rather as a way of living, as an integral, perceivable way of being oneself in any given experiential situation. In order to let readers connect to this holistic approach and the resulting novel approach to perception, we ask the question: 'What, after all, is the purpose of communicating?' The response depends on the context and the relationship. A conversation with our partner will be different from a scientific presentation, and the presentation will be different from a team meeting with our colleagues to arrange a joint event. However, all these situations share things in common: the influence of our own attitudes, our attitudes toward the other party in the specific situation, our inner world, how we feel, what we expect and what we want to offer in this moment. This complex state exists only *within* us and is accessible only *to* us. We can willingly influence it to some degree, but never completely. This is because numerous processes operate unconsciously and are determined by former complex experiences and structures.

Consequently, we can consciously co-determine which parts of our inner world we want to communicate to our communication partners and the environment, but most of the time we can't entirely control this. For example, we can make a conscious decision to either hide or express our anger or joy, our conviction or our uncertainty. Yet, we tend to have only partial control over our non-verbal language, tone of voice, gestures, etc. that may reveal our feelings or inner state even if we have decided not to express them explicitly. There are also states, feelings and emotions that we are not (yet) conscious of because, being unconscious, we can't articulate them. Interestingly, in this sphere our body is quicker to communicate than our consciousness, which means that sometimes others can perceive something before we become aware of it ourselves.

Recently, neuroscientists such as Antonio Damasio (2003, 2012) have confirmed that our body can express inner states without us being conscious or ever becoming conscious of these inner states and their expression (Rogers 1959; Nykl 2005). Person-centred communication inherently includes all these subtle but often essential experiences. They are practically alive and clearly formulated in the theoretical framework of the person-centred approach. The following example is intended to illuminate the importance of attending to moment-to-moment experience. Perhaps you have experienced something similar in your family or work context?

**Example from experience**

I was becoming restless because I knew that my son Tomas would have a vocabulary test the next day but he didn't show any signs of doing something about it. While walking by, I shouted into his room: 'Tom, you need to revise for your vocabulary test!' I didn't care at all what Tom was engaged with and at that moment I was neither prepared nor had the energy to assist him in learning the vocabulary. I heard from his room: 'Yes, later!' Then for quite some time nothing happened. After some arguing in the meantime

I asked him some words before he went to sleep. The whole situation was a strained and unpleasant experience for both of us. A few days later a similar situation came up. I reminded Tom about learning his vocabulary using the same words, but at a point in time only when I felt that the situation was appropriate and that I'd be prepared to support him in his task. His spontaneous response was: 'Now?' I replied, with my eyes meeting his: 'Sure, let's do it now, why not?' And both of us even managed to have some fun in this common activity.

Of course, things don't turn out so successfully every time but from this example from experience I discovered that perceiving the momentary situation as well as my own inner world can make a huge difference to how we affect others and whether certain activities succeed or not. Once I had gone through this key experience, similar situations in my work context often became obvious. In the literature on organizational development, Peter Senge (2006) calls the process of thoroughly 'putting yourself' into a whole situation (sensing) and considers it to be an essential precondition for strategic action.

Person-centred communication is oriented towards offering a clear and facilitative relationship to ourselves, others around us and any given whole situation. It is not intended as a 'hook' or 'instrument' with which to drive or manipulate others. In this spirit, this book is intended to support you in bringing some of your inherent potential to the forefront, to reflect on it and to make use of it in a way that is in utmost tune with your own personality. It is not our primary goal to have you learn new, external facts but rather to strengthen your self-determined, self-organizing influence on your implicit, often unconscious experiencing and its expression.

Person-centred communication tends to refrain from teaching others or influencing them in a directive manner. Most probably you know very well the difference between an activity that you yourself decide to engage in and an activity directly (or covertly) imposed upon you. We feel there are oceans of difference between the two modes. This difference is grounded in our inherent motivation for self-organized experience in contrast to other-directed activity, the former being based on the actualizing tendency[1] (Rogers 1959).

[1]In his later work, Rogers (1980) extends his thinking by assuming a 'formative tendency' in the universe. This is in tune with recent system-theoretic considerations (Kriz 1998; Natiello 2001; Senge 2006, etc.) that include whole systems and relationships (Barrett-Lennard 2005). We plead for moving away from the simplistic view, which says that in human beings each reaction results from exactly one cause. This move can facilitate our understanding of versatile, multidimensional connections. For us it entails the motivation for countless unfolding possibilities for relationship formation and problem-solving. Rogers, too, rejects the linear cause–effect relationship perspective that he believed to underlie most social science research.

This basic source of motivation is inherent in each living organism and is directed towards the actualization, maintenance and enhancement of the organism. Our knowledge about the direction of the actualizing tendency inspires us to respect the sensation and valuing of our experience and to trust the orientation we derive from it (Rogers 1980; Sheldon *et al.* 2003; Sheldon 2004). Perhaps you have already experienced the great value that can result from freely sharing your thoughts? Recently, Renate experienced how meaningful and worthwhile it can be to be listened to by another truly supportive person, as outlined in the next example from experience.

**Example from experience**

A colleague with whom I had shared my research activities in the field of person-centred learning asked me what meaning the results had for me personally. 'What do the results show you? What influence do they have on you? Why are you conducting this kind of research?' This gave some aspects of my work a greater weight while I suspended others. Moreover, the conversation encouraged me to be in deep contact with my own thoughts, perceive them more clearly and organize them. The individual 'bricks' started to fit together and form something greater.

## A comment on the examples

As you will already have seen, this book includes what we have called 'examples from experience' (examples from the everyday) and 'examples from therapy', and so on. At this point, we need to emphasize that the examples are not intended to produce rigid response patterns. Also, we can't evaluate which responses are right and which are wrong. Such evaluation is not possible because each time only a fraction of the respective complex situation can be described. Any analysis is destined to lack important information and hence would be incomplete. Nevertheless, with these examples we hope to motivate readers to recognize similar situations in a more conscious, more mindful way and to reflect upon them.

## Starting point, delineation and potential

Person-centred communication has its source in a thoughtful, respectful attitude towards the other person. It is targeted towards interpersonal contact, the sharing of experience and a deep understanding of self and others. In an ideal case, both partners share this basic attitude.

Consequently, in situations dominated by manipulation, authoritative guidance or commanding demands, person-centred communication can be practised only marginally. Also, the free 'breathing' in person-centred communication can't be experienced if interaction is used for establishing dominance, or where one partner – be it a person or an organization – claims to have the only truth in the sense of: 'But everybody knows that...' We are aware that in real life this imposes considerable limitations. However, we also see the immense potential of people unfolding their capacities, given a person-centred climate, and the enormous strength and immediacy inherent in this way of being. Therefore we focus our energy on this promising area with the intention of awakening and strengthening upcoming opportunities.

Furthermore, in our view, there is almost always an opportunity to influence a situation through one's own transparent presence and action. Sometimes change doesn't come immediately but needs time to happen. We do not always succeed in sensing and using an opportunity at the right moment. However, often a fitting and transparent sharing of one's clear message, arising from the 'whole substance' of a person, affects the other and can move the whole situation forward.

Every person has in them the potential to influence their human environment through their being and acting and thus to leave their trace. What is needed is one's own transparency, thought, courage and precise perception of the respective situation. This can most clearly be observed in person-centred encounter groups (according to Carl Rogers), to which we devote a complete chapter. It is important to note, however, that person-centred communication can't be 'acquired' merely through training (or by reading a book about it!). Despite this, reading this book and/or participating in a person-centred workshop *can* inspire readers to seek experiences in their lifelong process toward better understanding and more consciously perceiving their environment. As a result there is a better chance that one's 'inner wisdom' and genuineness will not be overshadowed by trained, rigid communication patterns, following a set of given rules.

## Objective

The objective of this book is to speak to readers through examples and dialogue from everyday situations and through explicit prompts to practise reflection (via the 'invitation to reflect' panels, among other things). In this way, readers will be challenged to perceive their own experiences in communication, along with their feelings, more consciously and clearly. If, as a consequence, we are in contact with our inner world, we can express ourselves more in resonance with our core and hence be better perceived and understood.

Another objective of this book is to open up the principles of the person-centred approach to communication to a broad audience and thus to manifest person-centred interaction as a constructive phenomenon in inter-personal development, far beyond psychotherapy. If the experiences and basic theoretical approaches we share in this book have any effect on you and help you to move forward, then the main purpose will have been fulfilled. The book is targeted at everybody who wants to understand others better and, vice-versa, be better understood. Readers interested in scientific aspects will gain insight into theoretical findings and our own research in individual chapters.

## Basics and core attitudes

The foundation of the person-centred approach is the actualizing tendency that is oriented towards the maintenance and enhancement of the organism. Under the influence of the actualizing tendency, humans tend to develop optimally if they are provided with a climate that is characterized by three supportive, interacting attitudes, referred to as 'Rogers variables'. These three attitudes of *acceptance, empathic understanding* and *congruence* – which are the subject of Chapter 5 – are also referred to as 'dispositions' by Nykl (2005). They co-determine our communication in so far as they are an inherent part of every expression and resonate with each.

In our view, a sufficiently balanced inner world as the basis of one's personality is the foundation on which to build. When this foundation is absent, any inducement and optimization of the effect of one's expressions through special training (such as in negotiation, rhetoric, leadership, etc.) is questionable. We do not doubt, however, that demanding professional challenges, like organizational consulting, crisis intervention, psychotherapy, etc. require specific skills, education, practice and knowledge *in addition to* a balanced inner world. Hence, one of the major challenges here is the *concurrence of personal and professional competence.*

## Intercultural validity

Since we humans react relatively similarly on the level of dispositions (the level of attitudes), this level has the potential to establish a connection between people (as well with nature). For example, we tend to perceive positive regard as pleasant but have a negative response when we feel misunderstood. Regardless of our origin, job, discipline or culture, as human beings we share the conditions under which we tend to develop constructively and interact in a way that is mutually supportive.

Rogers' overarching contribution to better interpersonal understanding consisted in his proposing and researching the dispositions of acceptance, empathic understanding and congruence. He introduced these attitudinal conditions in thousands of interviews and group sessions to people from many different cultures. Hence, the quality of communication that is in the foreground of this book can also be considered as a key competence that transcends disciplines and cultures and is ever more needed by our intertwined and networked society (Fischer 2005; Lago 2011).

At this point we don't want to leave our readers with the impression that we always excel in private, interdisciplinary and intercultural communicative situations only by understanding the interrelationships described above. What we are increasingly capable of, however, is an improved capacity to perceive communicative situations more consciously and comprehensively. For example, we would suspend a conversation that appears hopelessly entangled before becoming completely frustrated. We might say: 'I fear we are passing each other by and not making any progress. What about trying to clarify this issue later?' Our experience has revealed that communication – like any other behaviour – tends to mature during one's lifetime if space is devoted to it.

## The path being the goal

Every conversation, whether successful or not, first of all provides a source of opportunity to derive experience. More precisely, the felt interpersonal relationship enables us to learn something about ourselves and our feelings such that we become able to adapt our behaviour. In this context, one goal of this book is to stimulate, support and encourage you to enjoy moving forward in the direction of conversations that you will sense as being successful and meaningful – to perceive in a more vivid way in order to better understand and sense yourself and those close to you.

It fascinates us to witness how we ourselves are changing and which new 'elements' our relationship is acquiring. Differences surface and occasionally give rise to conflicts and difficult communicative situations. Some can be resolved quickly, others take a bit of time, still others endure and keep changing their importance and weight. If, however, we gradually find solutions after having mindfully expressed the problem and listened to the other person, the solutions tend to be more fitting than any one of the initial opinions. Moreover, we feel that these situations allow us to learn significantly, be it in a painful or in a constructive, enriching way. Experiences and insights of this kind fit nicely into the theoretical framework that Carl Rogers left us as his legacy, such that we want to share some of them with our readers. We consider that Rogers' framework remains highly applicable in the modern world and indeed essential at a time in which communication occurs almost round the clock and is becoming increasingly important. Integrating the theoretical with the practical, and the personal with the work-related, gives us a sense of enrichment comparable to 1 + 1 equalling not just 2 but a great deal more. We will be very pleased if we manage to succeed in persuading you to participate in such a new integrative adventure!

In summary, for the speaker, person-centred communication means: 'How can I express myself constructively? How can I perceive and give expression to what is going on in me, my thoughts, opinions, questions, feelings, in a way that you can empathize with and through which our relationship becomes clear?' For the other person it means: 'What does the received message trigger in me? What effect does it have on me? What did I understand and what is left unclear? Where am I now and how and when am I going to share with the other person such that he or she can hear me and perceive the relationship that I'm offering?'

If you now think that these are too many aspects to be kept in mind consciously, we'd fully agree. This is why good communication has to be 'intuitive' and 'controlled' from within in order to be natural and effective. From this we can infer that getting along within oneself and the unimpeded, floating perception of one's environment lies at the very heart of conducive communication.  If we express ourselves clearly and in a way that is appropriate to the current situation and thus provide an opportunity for the other person to understand us clearly, this 'being understood' and understanding of the respective inner worlds will enrich both us and the other person. In other words, we become more actualized. This applies within the context of one's own culture, family and work, as well as cross-culturally, since person-centred dispositions (Nykl 2005) tend to foster understanding, even across cultures (Rogers 1970, 1980; Santos 2003; Lago 2011, 2013).

Now, if basic, constructive attitudes are inherent in the core of humans, why are there so many problems and so few people who really understand one another? Why are so many relationships characterized by strong deficits in person-centred communication? We think that our fast-paced culture and hectic way of living (striving for power, information overload, the often one-sided achievement-orientation) stand in the way of facilitative communication that needs our undivided, full commitment as well as time (Ryback and Motschnig-Pitrik 2013). Also, we believe that the constructive core attitudes need to be renewed again and again and to mature, in order to be able to unfold. Would it be too odd to presume that in infancy very few of us were lucky enough

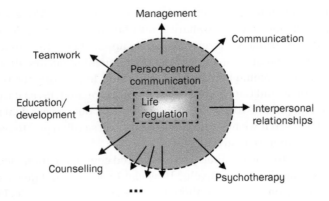

**Figure 1.1** Tier-model illustrating person-centred attitudes being allocated immediately above autonomous processes of life regulation (proceeding without conscious control). They affect cognition and emotion and influence various areas of life (as indicated by the arrows)

to have sufficiently experienced relationships that supported the sustainable development of the core conditions?

Figure 1.1 illustrates the central role of person-centred attitudes – congruence or genuineness, acceptance and empathic understanding for the human species. They interface with processes that regulate the basic life functions (such as body temperature, digestion) without conscious control. So, person-centred attitudes are inherent in both intuitive as well as conscious psychic processes (Motschnig-Pitrik and Nykl 2003, 2013; Nykl 2005) and act as catalysts of behaviour in various situations. One of these situations – person-centred communication – lies at the heart of this book. May it serve as a starting point or a continuation of a path that leads to mindful, non-directive, constructively-oriented communication that is geared to the development of the whole person.

## Primary goals of this book

### Experiential level

- Provide motivation for person-centred development
- Provide paths and hints for getting closer to oneself and others for fuller understanding
- Provide inspiration for creating and offering a facilitative climate

## Knowledge level

- Show how basic principles of the person-centred approach apply to communication
- Argue for the importance and scientific grounding of person-centred communication
- Accurately describe the nature of person-centred communication, its potentialities, strengths, and constraints

## Scientific grounding and contribution

- Formulate the theoretical basis of person-centred communication
- Provide illustrative studies from application areas such as learning and encounter groups
- Compare person-centred communication with dialogue (according to David Bohm)
- Transfer, thoughtfully adopt and mediate Rogers' theories to the field of everyday (including computer-supported) communication in the twenty-first century

# 2 Communication basics and neuroscience

*I discern more sharply the concern of my life as having been built around the desire of clarity of communication, with all its ramifying results.*

(Rogers 1980: 66)

---

**In this chapter you will learn about:**

- Everyday communication by studying a case example with a variety of reactions

- The notion of openness and its vital role in interpersonal relationships

- The ways in which conditions of worth can compromise your openness

- What neuroscience reveals about our inner world and communication

---

## Influence of our inner world

Each communicative exchange has aspects of our inner state taking part. We reveal part of us whether we want to or not, whether we are aware of it or totally unaware of it. Our 'inner state' or 'inner world' or, in Rogers' terms, 'experience' (1959: 197) means all that is going on within the organism at any given moment, all potentially available to awareness. In the following, we devote our attention to the notion of 'inner state' and its influence on (or flowing into) our communication.

In each moment we radiate feelings or 'signals' that reflect our inner state. In so doing we have an effect on those we communicate with. Depending on how sensitive another person is, they receive some or all of the 'signals' we are radiating. However, the quality, quantity and level of 'filter' with which another person perceives our message depends on the state in which they reside at any given moment. Moreover, the perception of the radiated message, in turn, changes the inner state such that a reciprocal interchange is set in motion. Most probably you will have experienced how you react to the to go, but I'll try to be home soon.' He may then say, 'Just take your time, and have a successful meeting! See you later.'

The conversation emerges at a slower pace because the underlying feelings and their meanings need to form and unfold incrementally. Such a conversation can't proceed in a stereotyped way, it arises from the inner worlds of the two people. The ensuing paradox is that the effect would be lost if the conversation were studied or conditioned/learned.

---

**Invitation to reflect**

*What do you infer from the four options given above? Which one resonates most with you? Do you think that the other options are justified too? Can you confirm this from your own experience?*

*Try to recall a very good – in the sense of very beneficial and enriching – conversation. Who participated in it? How was it for you? What did you feel? Did you have the chance to express what you felt in that situation/relationship?*

*What is it that makes you remember this conversation as a very positive one? Is there anything from it that has been living on in you since then?*

*Have you been torn between alternatives recently? Which words would you use to describe your feelings in that situation? Was there anything in the situation that you were aware of but could not or did not want to express?*

*Did you ever think about such issues? Did you share them with your friends? Why or why not?*

---

The conversational options described above are intended to show what influence the inner world – our organized and also unorganized attitudes and habits – tends to have on communication as well as relationship and style of expression. Perhaps now you are thinking about which conversational options you adopt most often and which ones you'd aspire to?

We'd endeavour to avoid Options 2 and 3. However, it would be an exaggeration to say that we're always successful. In some relationships we experience situations in which we don't succeed in being genuine or transparent.

**Congruence versus incongruence in one's expression**

Let us now make an effort to formulate the consequences of the observations described above. If what is going on in my inner world and what more or less shines through to the outside are in tune with my conscious, say verbal, communication, then my whole expression is in accord, transparent, genuine. It is also referred to as *congruent* if, in addition, I accept the *other* person and try to understand him or her (Rogers 1959). If, however, the impression I leave doesn't concur with my verbal expression then the whole communication is *incongruent* – not genuine, not transparent – and can cause tension or mistrust in me and my interlocutor. Hence, the full and uncompromised understanding of me as a person will be facilitated – sometimes even made possible – in the first place by my *congruent* expression. The less congruent (i.e. the less in tune with *my* inner world) my expression is, the more difficult it will be for the other person to understand me and, in turn, express himself or herself congruently.

A *congruent* communicative exchange consists of the concordance/consistency between my inner world (experience) and my perception (awareness) of it (e.g. I am disappointed) as well as the transparent expression of the whole situation (e.g. my disappointment *about* something). The precondition for this is an inner world that is free from rigid constructs that would hamper perception. Hence, *incongruence* can happen in two ways. In the case of an *inner incongruence*, we don't perceive ourselves accurately, for example, because of fear, anxiety, defence or protective mechanisms. So it might happen that disappointment doesn't fit into the self-concept of a successful person and hence the perception of disappointment is 'censured' or distorted before it can unfold at all. In the second case, *incongruence in expression*, we perceive the inner state but refrain from expressing it transparently. This means that we cheat, lie or conceal something, whatever the reason might be. For example: 'I don't care at all about what you're doing,' even though one actually feels very strongly about it. The reaction is not real and often leads to conflict. In such a case, the other person doesn't have a chance to learn about my real feelings and to derive experience from them, learn from them, and find out how his or her behaviour has affected me. The other person is left in doubt, perhaps also in a state of puzzlement and insecurity, as a consequence of this lack of transparency. It is easy to imagine that any follow-up conversation won't be constructive. Only in an exceptional situation will the other person express his or her puzzlement or doubt about the speaker's message in a way that is beneficial to the relationship, and the original speaker is sufficiently open to perceive it and to consider it.

Much of the time we are not even aware of the processes taking place, even though our body is, allowing others to see something we cannot (Damasio 2003). In this context, Carl Rogers (1961: 344) formulated a 'tentative statement of a general law of interpersonal relationships' as follows:

> Assuming (a) a minimal willingness on the part of two people to be in contact; (b) an ability and minimal willingness on the part of each to receive communication from the other; and (c) assuming the contact to continue

over a period of time; then the following relationship is hypothesized to hold true:

The greater the congruence of experience, awareness and communication on the part of one individual, the more the ensuing relationship will involve a tendency toward reciprocal communication with a quality of increasing congruence; a tendency toward more mutually accurate understanding of the communications; improved psychological adjustment and functioning in both parties; mutual satisfaction in the relationship.

This means, in essence, caring for the relationship and meeting the other with respect. Rogers (1961: 345) continues:

Conversely the greater the communicated incongruence of experience and awareness, the more the ensuing relationship will involve: further communication with the same quality; disintegration of accurate understanding, less adequate psychological adjustment and functioning in both parties; and mutual dissatisfaction in the relationship.

Although we're going to deal with incongruence, its development and resolution in Chapter 5, we will continue our short introduction here (Rogers 1959, 1961, 1983; Nykl 2005). Inner incongruence develops due to so called *conditions of worth*. These can hinder us in being open to experiences and perceiving them congruently, i.e. without distortion.

## Openness to experience versus conditions of worth

If a child is repeatedly told that they have to get good marks at school and is only accepted, loved and well regarded by their parents if they are performing well, this could be interpreted as meaning: 'I accept you only if you learn and work.' Acceptance, love or regard is placed under a *condition*. This child is likely to develop into a person who finds fulfilment only in work, overworks often, and discards all other activities and social contacts. This person isn't consciously aware of the fact that his or her behaviour is driven by the fear of being accepted by others only under the condition of working hard and performing well (condition of worth). The desire for activities that don't result in achievement is repressed; the child or person is no longer open to such appeals or feels guilty when following them. Rogers (1959: 206) writes:

When the individual is in no way threatened, then he is open to his experience. To be open to experience... signifies that every stimulus, whether

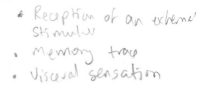

originating within the organism or in the environment, is freely relayed through the nervous system without being distorted or channelled off by any defensive mechanism. There is no need of the mechanism of 'subception' whereby the organism is forewarned of experiences threatening to the self. On the contrary, whether the stimulus is the impact of a configuration of form, color, or sound in the environment on the sensory nerves, or a memory trace from the past, or a visceral sensation of fear, pleasure, or disgust, it is completely available to the individual's awareness.

Rogers (1959: 209) characterizes conditions of worth that reduce openness to experience as follows:

> A condition of worth arises when the positive regard of a significant other is conditional, when the individual feels that in some respects he is prized and in others not. Gradually this same attitude is assimilated into his own self-regard complex, and he values an experience positively or negatively solely because of these conditions of worth which he has taken over from others, not because the experience enhances or fails to enhance his organism... It is an important specific instance of inaccurate symbolization, the individual valuing an experience positively or negatively, as if in relation to the criterion of the actualizing tendency, but not actually in relation to it. An experience may be perceived as organismically satisfying, when in fact this is not true. Thus a condition of worth, because it disturbs the valuing process, prevents the individual from functioning freely and with maximum effectiveness.

At this point, interested readers might ask when, actually, are we open to experience? For sure, not in a state in which we feel pressured, embarrassed, fearful or rejected, but rather more if we feel we are moving forward in some way, trust the other person, feel understood and received exactly the way we are. These feelings and attitudes are the carriers of transparent communication or, in other words, in their absence open communication most likely won't happen.

## What neuroscience research tells us

Part of our transparent expression, namely the expression of our inner world, is anchored in our physiology. For example, we yawn when we are not challenged or we turn red when we're ashamed. In the 2000s, so called 'mirror mechanisms' were discovered in higher creatures. It is assumed that they enable us to perceive aspects of another person's inner world (Damasio 2003;

Rizzolatti and Craighero 2004; Lux 2007, 2010). Mirror mechanisms are assumed to be located in the frontal cortex but have since been discovered in other areas of the brain. They allow us to receive subtle bodily signals and movements of the person with whom we are in contact and to re-enact them in our body without ever making a conscious decision to do so (Marci *et al.* 2007). Thus, we can infer that nature, through evolutionary development, is supporting our transparent communication with each other. Of course, we can pretend and put something else into the foreground, as is, for example, practised by actors, but in each case this consumes extra energy and obscures intuitive understanding.

Even though nature supports our transparent communication, the relationship between the affective and the evolutionary, much younger, cognitive system needs – to a significant degree – to be established throughout one's lifetime (Damasio 2003). To fully experience feelings and to perceive the accompanying meanings, at least to some degree, is something that we can/have to develop and that requires experience in/from relationships. From this, one can imagine the utmost value of meaningful, significant relationships (Barrett-Lennard 2005, 2013b; Nykl 2005, 2012) and ensuing communication for both our thinking and feeling.

The fact that our organism is able to react to stimuli that we are not (yet) aware of had been known for some time under the term subception (Rogers cites McLeary and Lazarus 1949; Rogers 1959) and more recently was confirmed by researchers in neuroscience (Damasio 2003). We are particularly thrilled by the fact that subceptions most likely can be perceived by others through the above-mentioned 'mirror mechanisms' even before the experience unfolds within one's own organism. This means that others can perceive some aspect of a person's inner world without that person being – or ever becoming – aware of that aspect (Iacoboni *et al.* 2005). The emphasis here lies on the word 'aspect', since the whole meaning-context of an experience is accessible only to us and only to a certain degree (Rogers 1959). In the context of an email exchange about the meaning of congruence and its deep roots in our organism, a colleague made the following telling comment:

> In good relationships it is really something beautiful. I need not even [make] an effort to reveal what is going on in me, the other senses it simply and his resonance can help me to find out more about myself. In my view, a problem in this scenario is that I want to hide part [of] what is going on in me from others and also from me because I might fear [rejection]. The other then senses that something isn't in tune, he/she senses the incongruence but isn't clear about what is causing it and this, I believe, often results in conflicts.

## Implications for the significant value of constructive communication and relationships

The psychological and neuroscientific arguments given above let us derive the following insight for the field of communication: communication with another person can help us to gain more complete access to our own experience than we can manage on our own. This happens if the other person – through mindful and transparent reactions – allows us to perceive those aspects of our experience that we have not been previously aware of. This happens *only* if we are open to the experience and don't (unconsciously) ignore, deny or distort it to protect our inner world from undesired, threatening experiences.

Let us illustrate the effect of learning more about oneself by sharing with a sensitive other person – in this case a therapist (referred to as 'Int' for interviewer, while the client is referred to as 'D'). The complete version of the interview can be found in Rogers ([1951] 1995: 373).

---

### Example from therapy

**D:**  . . . I think there is something. Whether it is in a group relationship or personal relationship, I hold back something of me. And I have – and I think when I say, 'What do your friends think of you' and so on, that would be one thing that would occur to me. My friends have said, 'You don't give at all of yourself.' Well, I think that is right – or consciously think so. I can't figure out what I don't give, but I think this has pointed out, they're probably right.

**Int:** One of the learnings might be, now, a little more sensitivity to the fact, that perhaps there is some truth to that.

**D:** I think there is.

**Int:** As I get your feeling, you're not real sure what it is that you're holding back–

**D:** That's right. I'm not.

**Int:** That's why it's kind of puzzling.

**D:** Yes, I'm not at all sure what it is.

**Int:** You're much more sure that perhaps this thing is true, but you're not just sure what aspect of yourself is being held in check.

**D:** I think that is right. It's a definite desire to please and not to get into something that might not please. I like to please. And apparently I have gotten a great deal of satisfaction in being a nice little girl and so forth and so on, and that I enjoyed.

**Int:** And you can even perhaps see some origins of this that you do have the feeling of wanting people to like you and like the things you do.

**Invitation to reflect**

*What, in your view, is special about the conversation between the therapist and the client?*

   *What is it that 'D' finds out? Do you think she is open to her experience? How would you respond if you were the interviewer?*

In Rogers' words (1961: 330):

> The task of psychotherapy is to help the person achieve, through the special relationship with the therapist, good communication within himself. Once this is achieved he can communicate more freely and more effectively with others. We may say then that psychotherapy is good communication, within and between men. We may also turn this statement around and it will still be true. Good communication is always therapeutic.

Such considerations show how important and helpful it can be to share oneself with others in a trustful atmosphere. Furthermore, readers will now probably understand that direct, personal contact is needed to allow for this kind of immediate, sensitive reacting, and that such contact is severely constrained in written text or electronic media.

## Summary

So far we have argued that our inner world is the basis of all communication. To a large degree its expression happens unconsciously and immediately. This can either support us, or – in the case of incongruence – be a hindrance, since we don't appear authentic. Hence, it isn't difficult to imagine how vital a rich, well-organized and flexible inner world is for any communication. Furthermore, it follows that conscious access to our inner world contributes significantly to our making sense of it and aspiring to a form of organization that is fluid rather than rigid. This in turn facilitates congruent communication. If we consciously feel our happiness or attraction, it is easier for us to express it. Since this is an essential aspect of expressive, congruent communication we're going to revisit it in later chapters and describe how access to one's experience (self-experience) can be fostered and facilitated. The focus is on raising awareness of the fact that congruence is a must for successful communication and thorough understanding. Thereby a regardful and empathic attitude is conjoined with congruence. Furthermore, congruence is rooted in one's inner world. Any improvement of our access to it, in other words the capability to be able to 'listen to oneself', is a step towards its clear, fluent organization.

· Congruence  ➞ empathic, regardful attitude  ➞ communication

### Invitation to reflect

*Do you occasionally try to attend to what is going on inside you during or after certain communicative experiences?*

*Do you attend to your feelings and where in your body you feel – for example, tensions, heaviness, 'thick air', ease, warmth, flow, heartbeat, breathing? Are there situations and feelings that recur frequently? What meanings do you derive from your experiences? Do they give you some orientation?*

*Do you intend to try to be more deeply in contact with yourself and to attend to the processes that are going on within? Why or why not?*

Various opportunities exist for listening to oneself, such as meditation, focusing (Gendlin 1978) and the 'inner team' (Schulz von Thun 1998/2001), to name just three examples. However, there also exists a (let's call it) 'attitude' – that everybody can freely practise every day: *active listening*. Now, if you protest and respond that active listening, naturally, refers to contact with another person then, of course, you'd be right. Sure, it stems from attentive, unbiased, unconstrained listening to another person. But it quickly leads further to the practice of your improved capacity to listen to yourself in this deeper way. Active listening and listening to oneself can unfold in a clear and pure way in person-centred encounter groups (Rogers 1970; Barrett-Lennard 2003; Nykl and Motschnig-Pitrik 2005; O'Hara 2013). More on this follows in Chapter 11.

# 3 What is person-centred communication?

*...a helping relationship might be defined as one in which one of the partners intends that there should come about, in one or both parties, more appreciation of, more expression of, more functional use of latent inner resources of the individual.*

(Rogers 1961: 40)

---

**In this chapter you will learn about:**

- What the term 'person-centred communication' stands for

- The effects of person-centred communication

- The features that characterize person-centred communication and why it indicates a 'way of being'

- The direction in which people develop in a person-centred climate

---

There are almost as many attempts at defining person-centred communication as there are experts in the field of the person-centred approach. Such definitions, however, convey the impression that what is being defined – in our case a way of communicating – is something fixed, 'prefabricated' like some object, something that can be taught and learned. This again tempts one to build constructs and to apply or deploy them.

We think that there is no one person-centred communication per se. It is rather a multitude of personal developmental paths towards autonomy, supportive community, empathy, acceptance and congruence that form person-centred communication. The communication of an individual indicates the particular phase in which that person and his or her relationship is at any point in time. Hence, what is at stake is the person's nature, environment and partnerships, including interrelations with others. The communication that thus emerges will be explored from the outside regarding its nature and characteristics. This happens with the steady awareness that any attempt at describing a phenomenon that is constantly evolving and thus in motion can only lead to an approximate description of its nature. Thus, it is not our intention to pinpoint fixed constructs.

## Person-centred communication and the iceberg model

To highlight a characteristic feature of person-centred communication, we borrow the 'iceberg model' that is attributed to communication psychologists. It is employed to illustrate that only a small fragment – comparable to the tip of an iceberg – of the whole communication between people is visible. The major part, the remainder of the iceberg, remains hidden underneath the waterline (see Figure 3.1). This part of the iceberg is its foundation. According to the communication psychologist Kurt Watzlawick (Watzlawick *et al.* 1969), the visible part is referred to as the *factual level* ('*Sachebene*') and comprises all that is *explicitly* expressed or shared. The major and typically by far more influential part, that hidden under the surface, is the *relationship level* ('*Beziehungsebene*'). It encompasses implicit, unexpressed assumptions, feelings, emotions, expectations, attitudes, values, wishes, needs, etc., and is based on the personality structure. While communication psychologists tend to use the terms 'factual' and 'relationship' level, these labels can be confusing when a relationship is the explicit subject of discourse. This is why we propose to refer to the visible part as the 'explicit level' and to the hidden part as the 'implicit level'.

The iceberg model implies that the explicit, visible parts of communication are just expressions of the invisible, implicit foundations. Let's

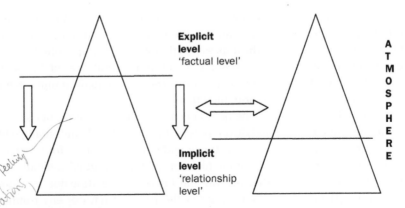

**Figure 3.1** Tendency towards an extended and more transparent expression of a person and their relationship in person-centred communication (based on the 'iceberg model')

now depict the increasingly more transparent, understandable and congruent expression of a person communicating in a person-centred way in terms of the iceberg model. The gain in transparency and clarity can be imagined as a hypothetical dropping of the waterline such that more of the whole communication becomes visible: we reveal more of ourselves and perceive more of the other person, as long as this feels appropriate for the relationship and situation. Aspects that otherwise would remain hidden under the surface will rise to become perceivable or visible. In this way, a better or, in the true meaning of the word, 'deeper', understanding becomes possible.

It is not surprising that a well-organized, inner world is of the utmost importance in enabling deeper understanding. In person-centred communication the inner world is more visible, more accessible than in a more obscure, distanced, or masked communication style, where it could be announced that 'the steering committee has decided that...' or 'statistics say that...' and further questioning of meanings and reasons is suppressed.

Of course, more openness or honesty requires courage and often brings about some risk. In order not to behave naïvely, not to 'run into a trap', it is important to sense what I am ready to offer and to reveal in a particular relationship. Where am I and where are we – my communication partner and I – going? Am I aware of my opportunities *and* limitations? Can something happen that, sooner or later, wouldn't happen anyway?

Rogers (1961: 345) writes:

> To communicate one's full awareness of the relevant experience is a risk in interpersonal relationships. It seems to me that it is the taking or not taking of this risk which determines whether a given relationship becomes more and more mutually therapeutic or whether it leads in a disintegrative direction.

Rogers (1961: 51) conveyed his experience regarding transparent sharing as follows:

> Now, acceptantly to be what I am, in this sense, and to permit this to show through to the other person, is the most difficult task I know and one I never fully achieve. But to realize that this is my task has been most rewarding because it has helped me to find what has gone wrong with interpersonal relationships which have become snarled and to put them on a constructive track again. It has meant that if I am to facilitate the personal growth of others in relation to me, then I must grow, and while this is often painful it is also enriching.

# Characterizations of person-centred communication

Recently, in a letter to the authors, Reinhard Tausch shared his view on the optimal conditions for communication. He wrote:

> If people respect other persons, value them, empathize with their mental world without judging it and if they are genuine and honest and support the other in a non-commanding way, then an optimum of conditions for good communication and action for one person in relationship to another is provided.
>
> (22 July 2007)

In order to describe person-centred communication, let us first investigate how the notion of communication can be captured. In the psychological dictionary, communication (latin: *communicatio*: connection, note) is described as 'the most important form of social interaction' (Häcker and Stapf 1994). It 'happens through speech, visuals, mimics, gesticulation, writing, etc.'. The *Lexicon of Practical Psychology* describes communication as 'interpersonal message and accommodation' (Knoll 1991): 'It depends on the capability of one person to convey their wants and feelings as well as on the other to receive this expression and to construe it... One would need to learn anew to articulate oneself and to listen.'

In the following we describe person-centred communication from the point of view of a particular person.

## A way of being

The core of person-centred communication as an expression of the person-centred approach lies in an ongoing, developing inner approach to a way of being that is based on genuineness, acceptance and empathic understanding, and aims at a balanced disposition of these three attitudes (dispositions) in each life situation. Their well-balanced, sensitively tuned offering fosters a climate that supports the development of facilitative relationships. In such a climate, people can unfold optimally and learn significantly in the intellectual, personal and social spheres (Rogers 1980, 1983; Barrett-Lennard 1998; Nykl and Motschnig-Pitrik 2002).

Rogers (1980: 115) captures the basic idea underlying the person-centred approach in one sentence: 'Individuals have within themselves vast resources for self-understanding and for altering their self-concepts, basic attitudes, and self-directed behaviour; these resources can be tapped if a definable climate of facilitative psychological attitudes can be provided.' Rogers proceeds by stating the relationship between three attitudinal conditions:

- Genuineness, realness, congruence
- Acceptance
- Empathic understanding

These conditions apply in any relationship and communication that is growth-promoting. Thus, person-centred communication is characterized as communication that builds upon the core attitudes of genuineness, acceptance and empathic understanding. From the point of view of the process of communication or of a relationship, the communication will be referred to as person-centred if one person experiences the person-centred core attitudes of the other person at least to some degree.

One participant in a congress on the person-centred approach in Stuttgart (2005) shared the following with us, which we found very appropriate in characterizing person-centred communication. He said: 'Person-centred communication means to encounter your partner person-to-person at eye-level with appreciation of the differences in your views while endeavouring to understand them.'

Nevertheless, a verbal description can draw a rough contour at best and only the practical and personal experience of such communication gradually allows one to grasp its full character. This experience tends to be pleasant but occasionally can also be painful. It will, however, not be indifferent.

## Extended conception

When comprared with person-centred psychotherapy, person-centred communication can be said to have an extended scope. First, there is an extension from 'conducting' therapeutic interviews in the realm of psychotherapy to the typically 'mutual sharing' in personal communicative exchanges. Second, person-centred communication includes various forms or contexts of communication such as interaction in teams, management, negotiation, moderation, knowledge communication, etc. and also extends to computer-supported communication. The goal of person-centred communication is the integration of intellectual and experiential perceptible experiences in a facilitative atmosphere that fosters the holistic, transparent understanding of all who are involved (Motschnig-Pitrik and Nykl 2004, 2005). Thereby the path towards person-centred communication coincides with its goal.

## Developmental direction

If both or all people provide each other with a mutually facilitative climate, then their relationship can develop in a direction that, in each moment, is guided by the actualizing tendency. Rogers (1961: 37–8) describes the direction of development in a person-centred atmosphere as follows:

> If I can create a relationship characterized on my part:
> by a genuineness and transparency, in which I am my real feelings;
> by a warm acceptance of and prizing of the other person as a
> separate individual;
> by a sensitive ability to see his world and himself as he sees
> them;

Then the other individual in the relationship:

> will experience and understand aspects of himself which
> previously he has repressed;
> will find himself becoming better integrated, more able to
> function effectively;
> will become more similar to the person he would like to be;
> will be more self-directing and self-confident;
> will become more of a person, more unique and more self-
> expressive;
> will be more understanding, more acceptant of others;
> will be able to cope with the problems of life more adequately
> and more comfortably.

Often an essential consequence of the person-centred approach is forgotten. The development of a person can also be recognized by a better sensing of oneself and one's environment as well as by one's ability to intuitively understand others, to react appropriately to others' hidden sensations and to make mature decisions. Such a mature person is less often helplessly exposed to their environment without ever aspiring to having power over it.

## Summary

In this chapter the most essential features that distinguish person-centred communication from 'usual' communication have been identified and described, most notably the increased transparency, whenever it seems appropriate. Furthermore, the scope of person-centred communication has been established as reaching far beyond that of person-centred therapy: it is any interpersonal relationship in which personal growth and a constructive interpersonal climate is the goal. As such, communicating in a person-centred way can be considered as a 'way of being', aiming at mutual enhancement in collaborative relationship(s) with others.

In conclusion, the effects of such relationships and equally the consequences of the lack of this kind of relationship in everyday life will be illustrated experientially by quoting an excerpt from a therapeutic interview – a

*Or even beyond that?*

pure 'showcase' of constructive communication – between David Cain (2010: 115–16) and Sabina. Sabina, a woman in her late forties and of African-American descent addressed a core issue she had wrestled with over three years of therapy. Dr Cain writes (p. 115): 'It was as if we encountered the storm together, with her leading the way while I accompanied and supported her courage in wrestling with her most challenging issues.'

We selected this excerpt not only to provide an illustrative example of person-centred communication in a therapy context but primarily since it so vividly shows how we as human beings, regardless of cultural background, may want to be heard by those whom we are close to.

---

### Example from therapy

**C:** . . . I've been feeling better about not calling my mother. My heart just isn't in it. And I call her one night . . . it was a reach out call on my part. I was not feeling myself. I couldn't exactly put a grasp on it. I called [my mother] and we did the formalities and I said 'You know, I'm not feeling myself,' and then she goes, 'We're all like that sometimes. You need to go to talk to God or you need to go to talk to your therapist.' And I felt what she was saying was 'Don't tell me about it.'

**T:** In other words you're hearing, 'If you're needy and troubled, go find somebody else to cry on their shoulder, not mine'.

**C:** Yeah! That's what I interpret it. And it could have been just me. Like I said, I wasn't feeling myself. Maybe I was more sensitive, and I haven't been calling her.

**T:** What you were hoping for was . . .

**C:** 'Tell me how you feel. What's wrong?'

**T:** You wanted your mom to be sympathetic.

**C:** Yeah. [just ask] 'What's wrong?'

**T:** Just show that you're there so I know you care and that you'll support me.

**C:** Yeah! And she basically told me about [how] she's been dealing with pain and when she asked about me, I told her, 'I don't feel right. I'm not exactly myself.' And she basically told me, 'Go away' and then she said, 'Got to go. Bye.' End of conversation.

**T:** So you felt abandoned, I imagine.

**C:** Rejected would be the word.

**T:** More rejected [and] pushed away.

**C:** Yeah, 'You have a problem today and I don't care about it.' You know what I mean.

**T:** 'I don't care about it' feels like 'I don't care about you.' [C: Uh. Huh.] So that hurts.

**C:** So that hurts! And um it's just been like weird. This pain has just been just devastating.

**Invitation to reflect**

Do you think a similar conversation would be possible between close friends?

Can you identify therapist responses that are unlikely to be part of an exchange 'out there'?

# 4 Attentiveness, listening, understanding, sharing

*I would like to propose, as a hypothesis for consideration, that the major barrier to mutual interpersonal communication is our very natural tendency to judge, to evaluate, to approve or disapprove, the statement of the other person, or the other group.*

(Rogers 1961: 330)

---

**In this chapter you will learn about:**

- Why good listening isn't a passive activity

- The function of a person's self-concept in communicative exchanges

- What you can do to improve your listening as well as the listening competences of people around you

- What you can do when speaking or sharing to facilitate the other person's listening and thus improve understanding

- Ways of 'listening to yourself'

- Frequent barriers to communication

- The fact that there exist guidelines and helpful, though only partial, techniques for listening and articulating

- The fact that, to listen well, techniques in themselves are not sufficient, rather, effective listening and sharing need to be grounded in a person's attitudes and basic values if mutual understanding is to be improved

---

Listening and sharing – isn't this something we do all the time? Sometimes we've even heard, 'You learned this already in kindergarten, so what's the problem?' Nevertheless we dare to ask: 'How often does someone *really* listen to you, wanting to understand you?' This question often leads to some deliberation – it seems that good listening is not as self-evident and widespread as it may seem at first glance. We have experienced big differences in the quality of listening and sharing and think that both can continually be advanced. Since listening and sharing are omnipresent, it seems particularly relevant to work at them. We see every step forward as particularly worthwhile, even if the moving forward seems to be relentless. Relationships gain in immediacy, vitality and real presence, and we understand more of the whole structure we're part of. In this sense, this chapter may motivate you to seek your own path. Carl Rogers, the authors and many people worldwide have found it inspirational in their search to be accompanied by person-centred encounter groups (Rogers 1970, 1978, 1980), and this will be explored as part of the chapter.

## What does it mean to listen well?

### Contact and participation

Have you ever asked yourself why you listen at all? Wouldn't the most evident objective be to make contact with others and understand what's happening around us – to receive and explore something that isn't yet within us and to internally participate in a conversation? In order to do this it is essential to grasp the message and the context as completely and accurately as possible. Schulz von Thun (1989) explains that the message that reaches us carries with it the sender's inner world – the person shares himself or herself with us. Therefore, in order to be able to orient oneself and behave appropriately, the goal is to understand as much as possible from the message – not just its content, but its context as well.

Some messages focus on sharing a fact or an association that we need to grasp correctly. For example, consider the sharing of the code you need to type in order to switch off your alarm system. Another example is given below.

### Example from experience

A colleague explains to me how to work with a computer program. I need a small, specific piece of information; however he explains a lot and uses an instructive tone. It takes a long time and I become impatient. He doesn't get to the point, he is stubborn and continues explaining. He ignores the knowledge I already have. I want to know the answer to my specific question and then engage with the matter myself, independently, so as to explore further on my own and, when finally successful, be proud of myself. After half an hour I'm thoroughly instructed but also rather frustrated. He has ignored all my efforts to stop him and to share myself. I thank him but, in effect, I'm glad he's gone. I'm left with a feeling of gratitude but equally with feelings of frustration and anger.

On other occasions it may primarily be part of the inner world that a close person wishes to share – for example their current sorrows, what they have succeeded in doing in their life so far, how furious (with us) they are right now, or how thankful to us. In all these cases we want to understand this person as accurately as possible in order to adjust our reaction to what has been shared. Through listening we become part of something larger that we create together, or *co-determine* (Isaacs 1999).

## Preconditions

If we are not satisfied with superficial contact with another person, but wish to understand that person (or situation) in depth, then it helps to first establish access to *ourselves*. This means perceiving the tones, melodies and motions in our inner core, to accept them, to understand them and, should we decide to listen, to be able to let go of everything disturbing and put it to one side.

William Isaacs (1999: 101), the founder and president of DIAlogos Inc., Cambridge, Massachusetts, and consultant to renowned organizations, shares a picturesque metaphor:

> By being still in ourselves, quieting the inner chatter of our minds, we can open up to a way of being present and listening that cuts through everything. Think of this as calming the surface of the waters of our experience so that we can see below to the depths. As we learn to lift ourselves out of the net of thought, the conclusion we jump to, the disturbances of our heart and resistances of our mind, this surface sea of reactions can calm down. We discover that there is another world of possibility for listening. We can listen from silence within ourselves.

Isaacs thinks that it is possible to listen in such a way that we manage to recognize the resistance within us to the statements of others and to suspend that resistance so as to better perceive and experience the reactions of the other person. If we become consciously aware of the fact that our own opinion hinders us in perceiving the viewpoint of another without distortion, then we will also understand that we tend to impose some of our tones (moods, prejudices, behavioural patterns, etc.) on the other person. We have to try to consider only what *really is*. Along with this 'access to ourselves', openness and impartiality are also needed in order to listen well. If my attitude is that I'm not interested in the concerns of the other person, that I don't have time now, or that I know everything anyway, I'll tend to close myself off to the other person's messages and experiences, and downplay them.

Openness to messages from other people, however, isn't enough to allow for our understanding. If, for example, we mistrust the person or group with whom we are communicating, we'll tend to reject the message rather than accept it, in order to maintain our own mental models and constructs. If, for some other reason, we're dominated by a rejecting or patronizing attitude – for example, that our younger colleague can't write project proposals or can't deal with children properly, or whatever – we'll tend to dismiss messages or experiences that suggest otherwise. Such 'premature devaluing', in turn, reduces our openness and makes understanding more difficult, if not impossible. Consequently, besides being open, complete and accurate, understanding calls for a basic attitude that prevents us from premature devaluing and hence is often referred to as *acceptance*. In this context let us share what a female student who participated in a person-centred encounter group experienced.

> What occurred to me was that I should not encounter other people with prejudice. In other words, I should not prematurely judge another person or take my first impression too seriously. It happened to me frequently that my first impression of someone totally disappointed me. Therefore I'm now taking the view that one can simply meet others regardless of first impressions. There's nothing to be lost for me, except for a few minutes. Another thing I learned was not to take feedback as criticism about oneself or as an attack. This impressed me and while I was thinking about it I realized that this had often been a source of misunderstanding. I learned to accept statements at their pure value and not to defend myself against them.

At this point we want to emphasize that it is not our intention to encourage readers to ignore their experiences and to blindly and naïvely trust everyone. This would obviously be inappropriate. We do intend, however, to point to the consequences of prejudice and rigid valuing (or devaluing) of others, which almost always results in yet more rigidity.

## Potentials

What opportunities arise if we perceive others as part of a process of becoming? If we encounter them without prejudice and with a basically trustworthy attitude? If we *accompany* them instead of limiting them through our own judgements? If the person who shares feels they are being listened to attentively and are not being judged, that person is more likely to share openly and honestly, to openly perceive his or her own doubts, and not pretend something in order to appear in a good light, or hide something to avoid being criticized. This in turn increases that person's congruence in the relationship and leads to better understanding. This understanding and being understood, in turn, raises the feeling of 'being received', thus facilitating further sharing. Experiences are expanded and called into awareness and the organization of experience and knowledge gets supported. In the next example from experience, a student describes his impression of sharing himself and being attentively listened to in a person-centred encounter group.

> I explained [to the group] my momentary situation regarding the lack of acknowledgement I got at the university and in sports. Although I didn't arrive at a solution – since it didn't even exist, and I just had to wait for a while until my leg had healed – all of a sudden an understanding of the whole situation opened up in me. I could see the connection between individual problems such as my impatience, lack of acknowledgement of my good grades, financial problems at work and sport injury, thus gaining an aggregated view of all that. This helped me a lot and I really felt lighter.

It's interesting that intensive listening tends to bring about mutual development, which means that both the speaker and the listener can unfold and grow psychologically. Also, any third person who listens silently but attentively can gain important experiences from this process. A student who participated in a person-centred encounter group mainly by listening reflects in the next example from experience.

> Several problems that were shared in the group addressed me as well and I was somehow glad that others had similar feelings or thought about similar concerns that I have, such as starting to study an additional subject, what we are going to do after we've finished studying, challenges in life, etc. Since I consider myself to be part of the group of people who talk little, I'd like to point to the fact that several thoughts came to my mind in the evenings after and during the group sessions and this process has lasted until now.

Unprejudiced, deep listening can be perceived as pleasant but also as painful. For example, when we try to be open toward the anger or disappointment that another person expresses regarding us, and not 'shoot back' with counterarguments or feel offended and withdraw. The next example from experience comes from Renate herself.

### Example from experience

Shortly before my husband left for a weekend in Carinthia – I had a seminar in Vienna – he said: 'I thought you would have packed the bags for the boys!' From his tone I sensed a reproach and was close to asking him whether I had some special talent for packing bags, but then I felt that Herbert was already stressed about leaving on time. So I just said: 'Hmm, I see, you expected the bags to be done. [pause] Can I help with something right now?' Herbert said, 'Yes, please check that we haven't forgotten something important. The boys packed their bags mainly on their own.' I added a few things and, in any case, perceived the situation as intensive and formative. After initial pain and anger, I felt we were being a good team. Then I just said, 'Okay, done, have a good trip and see you soon.'

### Invitation to reflect

*How do you perceive Renate's scenario? Do you feel some reservation about the whole 'story'? If so, what is this reservation, how does it feel?*

Having briefly explored the idea, preconditions for and objectives of mindful listening, we're now going to go into more detail and use examples to help readers experience it themselves, at least in part. Of course, in this book we can only write *about* it and share experiences. Readers wanting to experience the effects of active listening for themselves must actually try doing it.

The following section draws heavily on Carl Rogers' and Richard Farson's article on 'Active listening' published in the journal *Communicating in Business Today* in 1987. A short version of the article is freely available on the internet. Our characterization closely matches the writings of Rogers and Farson; it is, however, complemented by our own examples and ideas. If we compare the style of this article with other works by Rogers, we find an unusual 'recipe-like' style that may be due to the target audience – management.

## Active listening

Rogers (1980: 12–13) explains what active listening means to him personally:

> When I have been listened to and when I have been heard, I am able
> to reperceive my world in a new way and to go on. It is astonishing
> how elements that seem insoluble become soluble when someone lis-
> tens, how confusions that seem irremediable turn into relatively clear
> flowing streams when one is heard. I have deeply appreciated the
> times that I have experienced this sensitive, empathic, concentrated
> listening.

For Rogers and Farson (1987), active listening in everyday situations doesn't
necessarily mean spending long periods of time just listening to other people's problems. It is, rather, a constructive path of approaching issues that
result from everyday situations at the workplace or at home. In order to be
really effective, active listening must be grounded in the basic attitudes of the
listener. We can't just use it as a 'technique' that we can switch on and off. If
our basic attitudes contradict the principles of active listening, our behaviour
will appear artificial and those we communicate with and listen to will soon
realize this.

To become an effective listener, it is necessary – as argued above – to
suspend one's *own* view for a time and be able to consider the perspective of the person who is sharing *their* view. In addition we must be able
to trust the other person to be self-organizing and able to move forward.
We understand that suspending one's own thoughts can be a difficult
endeavour and will not always be successful. But almost every time it
*is* successful, it provides us with new, valuable insight. In his book, William Isaacs (1999) observes and describes the importance of suspending one's own opinion. In his view, this releases an enormous amount of
energy. Isaacs writes: 'To suspend is to change direction, to stop, step
back, see things with new eyes. This is perhaps one of the deepest challenges human beings face – especially once they have staked out a position' (1999: 135).

In the literature one often finds tips or 'behavioural rules' that prove
useful when listening, and active listening is also promoted as a technique
to be learned in groups (Schulz von Thun 2005). However, we consider this
to be an enormous oversimplification. We believe that the primary activity
in active listening is demonstrating and experiencing genuine and active
interest in the person who is sharing with us, and allowing that person consciously to perceive this interest. This means becoming aware of our wish to

explore the perspective of the other person, being interested in perceiving parts of the inner world of that person and trying to understand them (Faber and Mazlish 1980). This active participation has the potential to validate the other person in his or her existence. Not doing this, however, can result in the relationship becoming shallow, or not even being established, or turning into a feud.

According to Rogers' and Farson's writing (1987), directed primarily at managers, active listening is an important way of bringing about changes in people. Contrary to the popular notion that listening is a passive activity, research clearly shows that sensitive listening is a most effective agent for individual personality change. This is because it influences people's basic attitudes toward themselves and others. People who have been listened to sensitively become more emotionally mature, more open to their experiences, less defensive, more democratic and less authoritarian. They tend to listen to *themselves* with more care and to make clear exactly what they are feeling and thinking. Because listening reduces the threat of having one's ideas criticized, it is easier to see those ideas for what they are. In a 'meeting culture' that embraces active listening, team members, for example, tend to listen more carefully to one another, become less argumentative and more open to incorporating other points of view.

Rogers and Farson point out that a worthwhile result of listening is the change that takes place within the listener himself or herself. Besides providing more information than any other activity, listening builds deep, positive relationships and tends to alter constructively the attitudes of the listener. Listening is a *growth experience*. But how do we become active listeners? Before addressing this question, let us look at how the individual personality develops.

### Development of personal attitudes

How do we see ourselves? From childhood on, we have learned to think of ourselves in very definite ways. We have built up images of ourselves. Sometimes these self-images are fairly realistic, but at other times they are not. For example, if we think of ourselves as reliable and dutiful, and succeed in finalizing our tasks reliably and fulfilling our duties responsibly, then we perceive such an experience precisely and accurately. It is consistent with our self-image and nurtures it. It is, however, much harder to accept experiences that do not fit our self-image. Such experiences tend to be distorted or not admitted at all if it is very important for us to defend our self-image.

---

**Case scenario, part 1**

A good example of distortion in defence of self-image is that instead of admitting that she has forgotten to buy something important during a shopping trip and thus acknowledging that her reliability isn't 100 per cent, a woman instead argues that, for example, she met a neighbour who talked to her and irritated her, making her forget what she needed; or that the store was about to close, making the search for the important item impossible; or that the important item wasn't in stock, etc.

---

To communicate effectively it is important to understand that people tend to maintain their self-image and to defend it. They tend to perceive every statement that might change their self-image or demonstrate that it isn't (fully) accurate as a threat or an attack.

---

**Case scenario, part 2**

Let's assume the woman who forgot to buy an important item at the shops considers herself to be reliable and someone who doesn't make mistakes. If nevertheless a mistake does happen, she feels guilty, like a bad person, and looks for ways to defend herself against this guilt. The guilt is therefore projected onto another circumstance or person (e.g. the shop itself, the annoying neighbour).

Let us now say that the woman failed to make her purchase because the shop had closed by the time she got there. Her partner says to her, 'You should get used to leaving to go shopping on time if we need something important.' This remark is *meant* as a helpful tip, but our shopper will, in all likelihood, react by defending herself since her self-image is threatened. She might, for example, reply: 'Well, why don't you go shopping yourself if you're that clever,' or 'If you had put away the dishes from breakfast, I definitely could have left earlier.' The fault is being shifted to the other person, be it covertly or overtly. This tends to lead to meaningless back and forth arguments – accusation and defence. It demonstrates why direct attempts to change another person, to teach them, or to change their self-image, are perceived as particularly threatening.

---

To maintain their self-worth, a person is forced to defend themselves or to completely deny the experience. This defence of self-image tends to bring on rigidity of behaviour and creates difficulties in personal adjustment. Active listening has a different effect. It does not present a threat to our self-image, hence we don't have to defend it. Rather, we are able to explore it, see it for what it is, and make our own decision about how realistic it is. Then we are in a position to make those changes that we consider necessary.

Let us look at our shopper once again, this time in a more constructive version of the scenario.

---

**Case scenario, part 3**

If the woman's partner remarks, on her return from the shops, 'You look worried; what's happened?' (which means he is aware of his partner and shows interest in how she feels), then she might respond, 'Yes, I couldn't buy the halogen bulb for our living room. The shop was closed, damn it.' He says, angrily: 'So we're heading toward a weekend in darkness.' She replies, 'What you say is true. But I have another idea. I can drive over to the superstore that's open 24 hours.' We believe that this conversation has a better chance than the previous one to be followed up constructively, to lead to a path towards personal development, and to find a 'solution'. However, the result doesn't depend so much on the spoken words, perhaps only to a minor degree, but rather on the genuine attitudes and on the momentary constitution of the two people, both mindful of their overall expression.

---

**Invitation to reflect**

*Optimally, the scenario above will help you understand some of your own experiences and allow you to perceive them in a wider perspective. Try to think about a situation in which you didn't succeed in managing something. What did you feel, think, say? How did your partner react? How does your 'failure' and its consequences fit with your self-image?*

## Preventing and supporting a facilitative climate

If we want to help a person reduce their defensiveness and become more adaptive, we must try to remove the threat of ourselves being seen as a potential 'changer'. The other person should not get the impression that we want to communicate to them they are doing something wrong, unsatisfactorily, or even perfectly, if this runs counter to their opinion. As long as the atmosphere is threatening, there can be no effective communication. If, however, we manage to create a climate which is neither evaluative nor moralizing, and an atmosphere of equality, freedom, permissiveness, understanding, acceptance and warmth, then the person will feel safe enough to incorporate new experiences and new values into their self-image and to keep this flexible.

Rogers and Farson (1987) point out that when we encounter people with a problem, our usual response is to try and change their way of looking at things – to get them to see their situation the way *we* see it or would like them to see it. We plead, reason, scold, encourage, insult, prod – anything to bring about a change in the desired direction, that is, in the direction *we* want that person to travel. What we seldom realize, however, is that, under these circumstances, we are usually responding to our *own* needs to see the world in certain ways. It is always difficult for us to tolerate and understand actions which are different from the ways in which we believe we should act. If, however, we can free ourselves from the need to influence and direct others along our own paths, we enable ourselves to listen with understanding and thereby employ the most potent available agent of change. There are several ways to develop solutions, while at the same time respectfully *including* the other person rather than *teaching* them.

A big enemy of free expression is judgement, be it positive or negative. Judgement is inflexible, hinders any evolution, blocks anything new from coming up. Statements such as: 'The article/proposal is perfect, boring, overloaded, etc.', take away any opportunity for the author to form their own view and to advance the work. The judgement is spoken, the result is frozen, and there is no point in following up further thought.

We all have a tendency to process experiences rapidly, and without even realizing it, derive conclusions. This is why we often regard these conclusions as facts and, on that basis, form our opinion, stick to it and want it confirmed. As a result we tend to overlook other evidence and thus deprive ourselves of developmental options that could accrue from considering the perspectives of others.

*Advice* and providing *information* are often seen as efforts to change another person or to lead them in a certain direction. They are barriers to the person's self-expression and the development of a creative relationship. Moreover, advice is seldom taken if it is not desired or appropriate. The eager young trainee will probably not become patient just because he is advised that 'the road to success in business is a long, difficult one, and you must be patient'. It is a difficult lesson to learn that *positive evaluations* are sometimes as stultifying as negative ones. For example, it is almost as destructive to free expression in a relationship to tell a person that he is good or capable or right, as to tell him otherwise. To evaluate him positively may make it more difficult for him to talk about his faults as he perceives them.

*Encouragement* may be seen as an attempt to motivate a person in a certain direction or cut him off, rather than as support. 'I'm sure everything will work out OK' is not a helpful response to someone who is deeply discouraged about a problem. In general, most of the techniques and reaction patterns common to human interaction are of little use in establishing a facilitative relationship, a relationship that enriches our inner worlds.

What does active listening entail, then? Essentially, it requires that we get inside the speaker, that we grasp, from their point of view, what it is they are communicating to us. More than that, we must convey to the speaker that we are seeing things from their point of view (Rogers and Farson 1987).

In the following we emphasize some basic aspects of active listening with the objective of allowing readers to experience them in a form that is adapted to reflect a situation from everyday life. To listen actively and to establish well-functioning interpersonal relationships, then, means including the following behaviours as frequent aspects of your communication (Rogers and Farson 1987).

**Listen to all levels of a message.** Any message a person tries to get across usually has a content-level *plus* the feeling or attitude underlying this content. The relationship between the people communicating is also influential. All this calls for awareness that it is this *total* meaning of the message that we must try to comprehend.

---

### Case scenario, part 1

A team member says to his colleague, the manager, 'Now I'm done with the data input.' This message has a content component that reveals that the person is ready for a chat or a further task. Let us assume, however, that he says, instead, 'At long last I'm done with this damn data input.' While the content of this message is the same, the whole meaning has changed in a way that is important for both the team member and the manager. In this case, sensitive listening can help to build the relationship.

Imagine that the manager responds to the first utterance by immediately assigning the next task: 'By tomorrow we need to submit the financial report. I've made a start but there's still more to do.' Would the team member feel that his total message had been received? Would he feel free to talk to his manager? Would he enjoy working in such a team and be particularly motivated to complete the report?

Now suppose the manager responds to the second utterance with, 'Glad to have that tough task over with, huh?' or 'Had a pretty hard time with it that you'd have preferred to spend otherwise?' or 'I guess you don't feel like doing anything like that again,' or just simply 'Oh, great!' This tells the team member that the manager has heard and *understood*.

It doesn't necessarily mean that the next task assignment needs to be changed or that the manager must spend an hour listening to the team member's complaints. She may do a number of things differently in the light of the new information she has from her colleague – but not necessarily. It's just that extra sensitivity on the part of the manager that can transform an average working climate into a good one.

**Respond to feelings.** In some instances, the content is far less important than the feeling which underlies it. To catch the full flavour or meaning of the message, it is helpful to respond particularly and appropriately to the feeling component.

### Case scenario, part 2

If, for instance, our colleague had said, 'I'd like to blow up this whole system by inputting arbitrary numbers; that would be better,' responding to this content would obviously be absurd. However, responding to his disgust or anger recognizes the meaning of this message.

There are various aspects to the components in the meaning of any message. An attentive listener will try to remain sensitive to the total meaning the message has to the *speaker*. What is he trying to tell me? What does this mean to him? How does he see this situation? What difference is there when we say: 'I agree,' rather than uttering sensitively, 'You seem to be angry; that must have been a tedious task.'

**Note all cues.** The speaker's words alone don't tell us everything a person is communicating. Hence, sensitive listening requires that we become aware of several kinds of communication besides verbal. For example, the way in which a speaker hesitates in his speech can tell us much about his feelings. So, too, can the inflection of a speaker's voice. She may stress certain points loudly and mumble others.

**Communicating regard through active listening.** Since listening tends to be considered as mainly passive, most people feel that listening does not affect the speaker. In fact, nothing could be further from the truth. By consistently listening to a speaker, we are conveying the idea that 'I'm interested in you as a person, and I think that what you feel is important. I respect your thoughts, and even if I don't agree with them, I know that they are valid for you. I feel sure that you have a contribution to make. I'm not trying to change you or evaluate you. I just want to understand you. I think you're worth listening to, and I want you to know that I'm the kind of a person you can talk to' (Rogers and Farson 1987). The subtle but more important aspect of this is that it is the demonstration or 'living' of the message that works. While it is very difficult to convince someone that you respect them by telling them so, you are much more likely to get this message across by *really behaving* in a way that demonstrates respect. Listening achieves this most effectively.

**Checking your understanding.** Because understanding another person is actually far more difficult than it at first seems, it is important to test constantly your ability to see the world in the way the speaker sees it. You can do this by reflecting in your own words how you received the speaker's words, expressions and actions. His or her response to this will tell you whether or not he or she feels understood. A good rule of thumb is to assume that you never really understand until you can communicate this understanding back to the other person, to their satisfaction. As Rogers ([1951] 1995) noted, it is only the other person who can really know and evaluate what he or she means and feels.

**Like other behaviours, listening behaviour is contagious.** This has implications for all communication problems, whether between two people or within a large organization. To ensure good communication between associates up and down the line, we must first take responsibility for setting a pattern of listening. Just as we learn that anger is usually met with anger, argument with argument, and deception with deception, we can learn that listening can be met with listening. Every person who feels responsibility in a situation can set the tone of the interaction. The important lesson in this is that any behaviour exhibited by one person will eventually be responded to with similar behaviour in the other person.

Listening is one of these constructive behaviours, but if one's attitude is to 'wait out' the speaker rather than really *listen* to him or her, the behaviour will fail. The person who consistently listens with understanding, however, is the person who eventually is most likely to be listened *to*. If you really want to be heard and understood by others, you can develop them as potential listeners, provided you can first develop yourself in these ways and sincerely listen with understanding and respect, sense the personal meaning of the other and react accordingly.

### Becoming an active listener

Active listening is not an easy skill to acquire, even though everybody inherently has the potential capacity for it. It demands work and the whole personality. Perhaps more important, it may require changes in our own basic attitudes. These changes come slowly and sometimes with considerable difficulty (Rogers 1961). Let us look at some of the major preconditions for active listening and what can be done to meet them.

To be effective at all in active listening, one must have a sincere interest in the speaker. Rogers and Farson (1987) use the picturesque expression of us all living in glass houses as far as our attitudes are concerned. They always show through. And if we are only pretending to have an interest in the speaker, he or she will quickly pick this up, either consciously or unconsciously. And once this happens, the speaker will no longer express themselves freely.

> ### Example from experience
>
> I [Renate] remember an impressive statement that affected me deeply when I was at school and that I still recall vividly. During a church service the minister said to the congregation: 'Remember, you can learn something from everyone. For each person you encounter, ask: "What is it that I can learn from this person?" You'll see that in each case you're going to find something worthwhile that you can experience from that person or encounter.' Perhaps this statement also has some meaning for you?

Active listening carries a strong element of personal risk. If we manage to accomplish what we are describing here – to sense deeply the feelings of another person, to understand the meaning their experiences have for them, to see the world as they see it – we risk being changed ourselves. To get the meaning which life has for the other, we risk coming to see the world as they see it. We are faced with giving up, even momentarily, what we believe and starting to think in someone else's terms. It takes a great deal of inner security and courage to be able to risk one's self in understanding another.

Developing an attitude of sincere interest in the speaker is thus no easy task. It can be developed only by being willing to risk seeing the world from the speaker's point of view, receiving them, and understanding them empathically (and not just factually). This does not in any way diminish the importance of understanding the subject matter. In fact, a *complex understanding* of all facets is called for. If we have a number of such experiences, however, they will shape an attitude which will allow us to be truly genuine in our interest in the other and experience a surprisingly deep and balanced relationship.

# Barriers to active listening

## Rigid thought constructs

Every communication includes all of a persons' features, whether or not we are conscious of it – we react as an organized whole. We can't, however, always recognize or control which of our features are in the foreground of our attention and which reside in the background. Often, the major part of our reaction is based on experiences, mental models or constructs that underlie the way we perceive new situations or ignore some of their features. Due to this way of thinking we need to become aware of the fact that – regardless of how hard we try – we perceive in others only those features that correspond to our cognition. Isaacs expresses this in the following way: 'The challenge is to become aware of the fact that especially when we try hard to listen, we will often still have a part of us actively failing to do so' (1999: 108). The more we focus our attention, the less we perceive the situation as a whole. One way to escape this bottleneck can be found in groups, in which more people listen and gradually become able to complement one another in their perceptions, thus helping to make personal constructs and rigid thought patterns more easily perceived and even resolvable.

## Unclear relationship, missing trust

We think that active listening is possible only in the areas in which the relationship is clear or congruent. If there is strong and sustainable hurt, ignorance, arrogance or malicious jealousy, then it is hard to imagine that active listening can happen.

From the speaker's perspective, a lack of trust in the listener (and oneself) is a notable barrier. Will the listener be able to understand what I'm sharing, will she interpret it accurately, keep it to herself and not use it against me? Or, will I be able to cope with it if any of these things happen anyway, and thus can I consciously take the risk? It isn't fun to be laughed at or imitated as a result of opening up to someone. However, it is highly questionable whether staying silent or fleeing can avoid a confrontation or the collapse of a relationship in the long run. In this context Rogers (1961: 345) writes:

> To communicate one's full awareness of the relevant experience is a risk in interpersonal relationships. It seems to me that it is the taking or not taking of this risk which determines whether a given relationship becomes more and more mutually therapeutic or whether it leads in a disintegrative direction.

## Wanting to share

In everyday situations and in particular those in which time is limited, another problem arises. Many of us will know from our own experience that it is not possible to listen actively all the time because often we want to be the one sharing our own experience and fear that we will run out of time before we can speak.

## Explaining, justifying

However helpful explanations can be in various situations, they often do not lead to the goal when used for the purpose of clarifying issues in a relationship. Circular explanations are not helpful; they cause impatience on the part of the other person. They tend to evoke many issues that, when addressed, blur the central concern of the conversation. In the case of confrontation, justifications heat emotions and lead to senseless quarrels. It can be difficult to really listen in such situations and engage deeply with the other person.

## Confrontation

This is a particularly challenging situation for active listening since the feelings and utterances of the speaker are directed against us. This makes it difficult to stay with the other person and accept their feelings and meanings without justifying oneself, talking back or explaining. In the first phase, it is important to listen precisely and actively. Then the listener often becomes the speaker and shares his or her thoughts and feelings. It depends on both people whether the confrontation will turn into a conflict or a dialogue with a great opportunity for personal growth. There also exist situations that are inherently conflicting and in which differences are hard to overcome or be bridged. In our view an unavoidable conflict with genuine expression of anger, while simultaneously respecting the other person, can at times be a necessary path to bring about change and a resolution.

## Expression of anger

Anger is one of the basic emotions that can be triggered if something runs counter to our own direction, hinders us in moving forward or hinders our development. Who doesn't know the feeling when something goes wrong or, after numerous requests, asking a favour, taking chances, etc., something that matters to us doesn't happen?

> **Invitation to reflect**
>
> *When was the last time you were really angry? What happened? What did you feel, think, say? How do you think and feel about that situation now? Has something changed since then?*

We think that it is hardly possible to listen actively when angry. We tend to 'cook' in our own feelings and hence are unable to empathize with ourselves or even the other person. Once the anger passes, or we take a moment to pause and breathe deeply, the situation/person can be experienced afresh. Perhaps we can then establish better contact with our unmet needs, become more aware of them, articulate them more clearly, and, consequently, gain more understanding or at least some clarity.

All this throws up the question of how anger can be expressed such that the other person can perceive it as an open, genuine expression of feelings. If this is accomplished then there is a change that the other person can react to based on their own experience, or just pause. If, however, the anger is combined with a reproach or an accusation – for example: 'You make me furious when you . . .', then immediately a barrier is created and is often followed by defence against the 'attacker'. Then we're no longer open to the messages and feelings of the other person and tend instead to be flooded with our own feelings. Any kind of logic or reasoned argument hits a concrete wall. In the fight with words, anything is used that is available, so issues surface that we would otherwise have kept to ourselves or guarded better. Whether this openness of expression will turn out to be supportive or hindering will, finally, depend on the particular situation and, primarily, the two people involved and their relationship with one another.

We believe it is important to distinguish between anger, fury and aggression. Anger subsumes a number of unpleasant feelings with varying degrees of distinction. The strongest form is fury, which is usually impossible to hide from another person. Anger, as such, is neither good nor bad – and hence is not to be valued morally. Aggression is the act of making an unprovoked attack, engaging in a hostile action or hostile behaviour (Webster 1990). Before sharing our own thoughts about the expression of anger, let us see what some renowned authors from the field of communication say regarding this theme.

Marshall Rosenberg (2003), the originator of 'non-violent communication' (NVC), believes that anger rests always in me and is always *caused* by my thinking and never by anybody else. While another person can trigger my anger, he or she can't be its cause. Rosenberg thinks that every judgement must be translated into an unmet desire and proposes four steps to expressing anger (Rosenberg 2003: 149):

1   Stop. Breathe.
2   Identify our judgemental thoughts.
3   Connect with our needs.
4   Express our feelings and unmet needs.

Rosenberg suggests training in these steps until they become an attitude and proceed without conscious thought. As much as we appreciate the feature of non-violence in communication, we can't help questioning this schematic, trained procedure that, to us, can't be reconciled with person-centred principles, according to which each situation can be experienced afresh and creatively. In our view, no construct – even though it might help to deal with certain situations appropriately and supportively – can ever substitute for substantially experiencing new situations.

Schulz von Thun ([1989] 2002: 134, our translation), a renowned German communication psychologist and best-selling author, writes:

> Whereas Bach and Wyden in their book *Streiten verbindet* [*Quarrelling Unites*] accredit fundamental meaning to furious attacks as a means of providing real intimacy and mental health, others (such as Tausch and Tausch ([1963] 1998) or Gordon (1972)) consider aggressive impulses directed against others as signifying that the furious person hasn't yet reached clarity within himself or herself. From this conception there results the...suggestion to take upcoming aggression as a signal for self-exploration: 'What is it in *me* that means I can hardly stand the other person at this moment?'...As much as I agree with this approach in its fundamental tendency, at this point I want to doubt whether fury and aggression are always 'feelings of a second class' and whether it is always a sign of personal maturity to be able to discover and express the underlying first-class feelings.

In the course of characterizing the positive features of an aggressively-devaluing personality style, Schulz von Thun argues that readiness for conflict and the capability for direct confrontation are helpful in coping with anger and thoughtlessness in others.

If, in an instance of disagreement, it is possible to react quickly and express yourself clearly, before the disturbance or dissatisfaction – the roots of anger – give way to *real* anger, then one has the opportunity to perceive the opinions and concerns of the other party. In such a case, moving forward in that situation or relationship is in the foreground. As a result, it may be easier to develop a willingness to see the problem from the other person's perspective. If this in turn leads to an understanding of the interests or position of the other, then anger is less likely to escalate. Nevertheless, we are aware that in some cases a difference (e.g. of opinion) may surface less distinctly and be 'swallowed' or disregarded prematurely – i.e. before all relevant aspects and their impact can be perceived clearly. This can cause a blurring of issues, but it can also lead to fearless dealing with differences.

Even if a conflict seems insolvable, it can help to 'switch' from one's anger or fury and focus on the positive aspects of the relationship. This, of course, takes a lot of effort, and sadly it is also true that some conflicts can never be resolved.

Our 'conclusion' is that there is no fixed rule about whether or not to express anger and that only the particular situation and the feelings and needs of the participants can reveal what is appropriate and helpful in the long run. We see a potential for development in becoming more conscious of every situation. If I interpret the inner message and situation appropriately, I can experience, for example, that I am snivelling, I am wrong, or I can assert myself. I disclose something. Often we hear: 'I'm not going to tell you what's wrong, you'll have to work it out on your own.' But how can that other person know what is wrong if I don't share anything with them? If there is no reaction that they can perceive and interpret? Some questions we can ask ourselves in such situations are: How far can I tolerate the opinion or behaviour of another without neglecting myself? How can I show my dissonance without raising any doubt about the fact that, basically, I do respect the other person?

There are situations in which anger can't be expressed because the relationship doesn't allow for it. For example, I can't express my anger towards an incompetent superior without risking my job in the organization. It is a great art and requires courage to communicate anger while at the same time not causing harm to a relationship.

We think it is desirable to create a climate in which differences can be expressed and explored, and there is space for different personalities without stress and aggression being on the agenda. When anger develops it then has a special effect. One objective is to create a culture which – for as long as possible – considers differences to be opportunities for developing individual perspectives and personalities; in other words, empathically balancing the weights of respect and authenticity.

To sum up, the perception or expression of anger can bring about clarity and contact, in particular if anger is not *expressed* as an attack and/or is not *perceived* as an attack on one's personality. In this way, feeling angry can trigger the sensing of unfulfilled needs and help us establish intense contact with our own, genuine needs and feelings, such as, for example, disappointment about the behaviour of a close friend, or frustration about an action that has failed. In person-centred communication, the confluence of congruence, acceptance and empathic understanding guides our behaviour even when we are angry. The key is to give it a chance for a few seconds: first take a deep breath, then continue breathing, pause, receive and sense what is there.

So far we have summarized individual perspectives in order to demonstrate their overlaps and differences. This illustrates the importance of one's own experience of a situation and the ensuing feelings – including anger – with their meanings for an appropriate and constructive communication – inwardly as well as outwardly.

## The other person asks for advice or help

'What would you do if you were me?', or 'Please, can you explain that to me?' Only our perception of the whole situation can enable us to decide whether in these cases a direct response might limit the other person's creativity. Even with questions such as those given above it *can* be helpful to accompany the person back to themselves and include them in solving the problem. 'Do you perhaps already have an initial idea?' Where facts are the issue, a precise explanation can often resolve the problem very effectively. Regarding the issue of giving advice, a student once commented: 'For sure, giving advice is not always appropriate. When we talk about everyday situations, though, I wouldn't generally discard giving advice.'

### Invitation to reflect

*How do you deal with advice? Do you like to give advice or tips in order to help someone? What is your main feeling in such situations? Are there other feelings or thoughts involved? How do you feel if someone gives you advice? How do you react? Do you tend to follow the advice?*

## I'm losing the 'thread'

One of the fundamentals of listening is to give the other person the opportunity to express their thoughts completely. How annoying is it to be interrupted in the middle of one's sharing, when the essential part of the message hasn't yet been expressed? Being interrupted is usually an unpleasant experience, however, there are nevertheless situations when interrupting is justified. For example, if while listening we have lost the 'thread' and feel we're impatiently waiting for the end, it is probably more helpful to interrupt and admit this in an appropriate way. In such cases it *can* be preferable to own up as soon as you sense you're 'losing the thread': 'Let me see whether I've understood you so far. You said…' or 'I fear I can't follow you precisely any more. Can I ask you a question to clarify things?'

It makes sense to try, intuitively, to decide whether it is more important to understand the message or accompany the speaker in formulating his or her thoughts, expressing them and organizing them, without requiring full clarity. In such cases it can help not to interrupt the other person's process and to wait for the result of sharing before seeking any clarification.

---

**Invitation to reflect**

*Have you experienced how the sharing of vague thoughts or ideas contributes to clarification or change? Have you experienced how another person's questions helped your own process or actually slowed it down?*

---

Occasionally the speaker loses track of his or her core issue, circles around it, or searches for it. In this case it is helpful if the listener tries to lead the speaker back to the core message as far as possible.

### I have severe difficulties myself

A colleagues turns to me with a problem but I myself have a problem with issues such as a death, an illness, a separation, etc. – in such cases I can't concentrate on the other person because I'm too distracted. At times, it can turn out to be impossible; at other times it needs a lot of energy to nevertheless listen to the other person if their concern is a serious one.

### The speaker appears to have rigid, apparently distorted patterns of thought

When talking with a person who appears to have rigid attitudes and distorted patterns of thought, it is difficult to establish good communication because that person sticks to these patterns and tries to argue according to them. Thomas Harris (1970: 96) writes the following in the context of rigid attitudes (prejudices), where the 'Parent' and the 'Adult' are two of the three ego-states in transactional analysis:

> …yet the Parent in these people steadfastly dominates a position of the Adult, and they will surround their prejudiced cases with all kinds of

irrelevant arguments to support their position. As illogical as their position may seem, the rigidity of their position is in its safety...Therefore, one cannot eliminate prejudice by an Adult discourse on the subject of the prejudice. The only ways to eliminate prejudice are to uncover the fact that it is no longer dangerous to disagree with one's parents and to update the Parent with the data from today's reality.

These are only a few out of numerous blocks to active listening. Gordon (1970) deals with some of these in detail and introduces further barriers to communication.

## Listening to oneself

To us, an integral element of person-centred communication is the ability to 'actively listen' to oneself, to sense one's own inner world. In many ways this is a precondition rather than an integral element.

A good way of acquiring an empathic perception of our inner world is to be listened to attentively and deeply by another person. In this section we're going to summarize various options in order to illuminate 'listening to ourselves' as a capability of the utmost importance for our development. However, first we want to highlight that, in the case of difficult, personal problems, it may be more helpful to talk to a person who is particularly 'trained' for such situations. His or her congruence can empathically strengthen the direction toward one's own congruence.

First, have a look at the next example from experience.

---

### Example from experience

I [Renate] shared with my colleague that I had left a decision regarding the design of a workshop to the highly experienced organizers who had carefully prepared for it. My colleague asked me with a softly empathic voice: 'And how was that for you? How did you feel?' I responded that in this particular case I didn't want to be solely responsible for the programme of this well-prepared event and that I had had very mixed feelings, creating a tension between 'I was untrue to myself, I didn't communicate my own experience well enough' and 'I behaved cooperatively, I didn't rigidly follow just my idea'. My colleague listened to me attentively and then asked: 'And how do you feel about your decision now?' This set free a stream of 'listening to myself' and further thought. In this context we had a highly fruitful exchange that let me discover the sensitive 'listening to myself' that I wouldn't give up any more.

## Listening to yourself

Useful questions while listening to yourself include:

- What does this whole situation/project/relationship mean to me?
- What is it that matters to me most?
- How do I feel right now?
- Why do I feel discomfort now? How does it feel? Where do I feel it?
- What is it that makes me nervous/impatient/(un)satisfied?
- What could I do to feel better?

At this point let us present a descriptive, well-structured model by Schulz von Thun ([1998] 2002), which, while not part of the person-centred approach, nevertheless aims to support us in perceiving various aspects of our inner world in a mindful and transparent way.

Schulz von Thun introduces the metaphor of the 'inner team' as an explicit way of discovering one's inner world. In order to distinguish and consciously listen to the diverse voices that reside in us ('inner plurality'), he suggests calling an 'inner team conference' to deal with upcoming issues such as the planning of a trip. First the individual participants or voices are identified and named evocatively. Examples are the 'dutiful sister', the 'adventurous colleague', the 'exhorting mother', etc. In this phase it is important not to exclude anybody and, in due course, to also include those voices that announce themselves later on. Then we listen individually to what each participant has to say. For example, the adventurous colleague might think that the upcoming trip could bring fascinating experiences, whereas the dutiful sister thinks it will be a waste of time and there are more important things to be done. In the next step the participants share freely, and then the conversation is specifically moderated. Next there is a brainstorming phase using consecutive, focused questions such as: How far can the trip also contribute to work-related promotion? Is it possible to postpone the trip, etc.? At the end, the team leader proposes an integrated statement that combines the wisdom of the team members.

These individual voices can influence conversations and make communication more precise. For example: 'If I let the critic in me have his turn then he'd say that...' or 'My very first, immature reaction is... but I'd prefer to sleep on it...' or 'I feel two different tendencies in me. On the one hand I'd like to start the project immediately; on the other hand I first have to make space in order to be able to better concentrate on it...' All these statements show that there is more than one point of view to be taken into account.

In the metaphor of the 'inner team', Schulz von Thun combines two schools: humanistic thinking and systemic thinking. He emphasizes the originality of the model, which is derived from his extensive experience as a communication psychologist.

In the USA, Eugene Gendlin (1978), a colleague of Carl Rogers, created and researched a well-founded approach to 'listening to oneself' that substantially includes the world of feelings. He called his approach, or method, which was derived from thousands of interviews, *focusing*. Here, the emphasis is on establishing contact with one's feelings in order to perceive their signals more precisely and include them consciously in one's decision-making.

Gendlin starts from the fact that we can feel every problem and situation in our body. The perceived sensation, referred to as *felt sense*, is labelled with a *referent* – for example, 'agitated'. Once a fitting word is found, you ask yourself: 'What is it that makes me so agitated?' While you keep switching between the felt sense and its referent (resonance), the former can change with a so-called *shift*. The thoughts you have during the shift and during the whole process allow you to understand yourself more deeply. Interested readers will find a description of focusing and contacts for professional focusing support at this website: www.focusing.org.

## Appropriate sharing

Now that we know that sensitive listening isn't something passive, and can in fact lead to constructive, self-determined changes in the speaker as well as the listener, we ask the question: Is person-centred communication more than active listening? We think it is.

In everyday situations, of course, expressing oneself, sharing one's perceptions, thoughts, feelings, opinions, meanings, objections, ideas, etc. is important. Often we need to decide whether we prefer to listen or to share something. Hence, if we are interested in communication processes between friends, colleagues, peers, etc. being on (approximately) the same level, then an essential aspect of helpful communication is the sharing of oneself depending on the situation. This is what we shall address below. Many aspects appear as reciprocal to what has been said regarding listening and we can say that helpful sharing should support active listening such as to optimally exploit its conducive potential.

We anticipate a question that frequently comes up in this context: When should I listen, and when should I speak? This question represents an essential decision that needs to be made anew in each situation by being suitably sensitive to it. By illustrating a few typical situations, we hope to sharpen your awareness of which ones call for such a decision. We invite you as a reader to critically think about the following situations and compare them with your own experience.

## Balance

Occasionally people are so appreciative of having someone who listens to them that they fail to let the other person have their turn. If this happens frequently it leads to an imbalance in the relationship. One person will be known to the other far less well and hence also be perceived and understood less well. Or, they won't be able to infer/transfer their concerns or inputs. As a likely consequence, this person and their field/concern will lose weight in the relationship. This can even be intentional, as might be the case in some hierarchic relationships, but is more often inadvertent – as for example in symmetrical relationships – and hence should be addressed so that there is an approximate balance between giving and taking over time.

## Don't let the other stand in the rain

A bad but often encountered habit is jumping to one's own experience as triggered by another person's 'story' before actually 'hearing' or perceiving what the other person actually wants to convey. The next example from experience highlights this.

### Example from experience

Imagine that my colleague complains about a snowstorm while driving home and is about to share how he managed to prevent an accident. I promptly grab the word 'accident' and say: 'Oh, that's something I know all about. You won't believe it, but last time I drove back from our skiing vacation, a crazy driver . . .' , and it's hard to stop my flow of words. Naturally, my colleague can't be expected to have much enthusiasm for my story and there is a danger that he might even lose the willingness and energy to share his own story.

In a slightly different scenario, my acquaintance has already been sharing her perspective about a theme we are both interested in for quite some time, and I feel that any opportunity for dialogue will drift away forever if I don't bring myself in. As one after another opportunity to contribute vanishes, I start feeling pushed away. In such a situation, it can be helpful to address the problem or make a note in order to be able to listen attentively and contribute one's thoughts later on. It is important to consciously perceive one's inner world and to share it with the other person, if appropriate. Thereby, both people can share their perceptions and try to mutually respect each other's feelings regarding the conversation. However, at times, situations like this can be really difficult and their resolution may require considerable time and personal development.

### Transparent sharing

In person-centred communication, sharing is directed primarily toward mutual understanding and acceptance. This does not mean agreeing to everything. Blind agreement, whether one really agrees or not, causes incongruence and hinders understanding. Ideally, an optimal mix of openness, respect and empathic understanding is needed. Even if you are really angry, try not to lose your basic respect for the other person; or, when agreeing with the other person and feeling affection for them, you still need to stay with yourself and not completely lose yourself in the other person. The basis for this lies in a respectful, non-directive attitude that allows the other person to understand where you both are in the relationship and that they are free to make their own personal decisions. In the context of understanding, you shouldn't overlook the fact that sharing yourself significantly contributes to a better understanding of yourself and makes it easier to organize your thoughts and feelings. Whereas in everyday communication this aspect may be considered as a 'byproduct' and a fundamental understanding of one's personality is assumed at the outset, a better understanding of self is one of the objectives of person-centred psychotherapy. Indeed, good conversations can have therapeutic effects, as has been scientifically confirmed by Reinhard Tausch (2007).

### Invitation to reflect

*Do you know someone who excels at expressing themselves? What does this depend on? What is it that you observe in that person?*

The more we facilitate another person's active listening endeavour, the better we will be understood. Achieving this means not speaking for too long, occasionally asking whether we have been understood, and catching and keeping the listener's interest by actively involving them. The perceivable inclusion of the other signals acceptance and can be achieved in various ways, both verbally and non-verbally. Acceptance can be communicated by an honest look or by resorting to shared experiences, using a common vocabulary or language, actively showing interest in the other's feelings and meanings, checking whether they have understood our message or whether something remains unclear, can be improved, or whether the other person would like to add something, etc. We support listeners also by our body language, gestures, emphasis, the modulation of our voice, and, in general, our overall expressions, used to differentiate the weight of individual aspects of our communication and thus allowing for a complex and rich perception. If, for example, something isn't clear to us, we can say that in advance and let the other contribute in the clarification process rather than confusing them. It is always inspiring to hear someone say, 'Let me think aloud, perhaps we can manage to arrive at a solution,' instead of getting lost in an ocean of unclear utterances and confusion.

Despite the importance of acceptance of the other person, Rogers (1980: 160) underlines that acceptance does not mean ceasing to have and express our own reactions. Furthermore, he emphasizes the importance of an open, congruent expression of one's own inner world in order to facilitate the other person's emotional orientation:

> In the ordinary interactions of life – between marital and sex partners, between teacher and student, employer and employee, or between colleagues or friends – congruence is probably the most important element. Congruence, or genuineness, involves letting the other person know 'where you are' emotionally. It may involve confrontation and the straightforward expression of personally owned feelings – both negative and positive. Thus, congruence is a basis for living together in a climate of realness.

## Summary

Even though listening actively to someone can facilitate the personal growth of the person who is listened to and the one who listens, person-centred communication wouldn't be complete if it did not also include 'listening to oneself' and expressing oneself. All these activities have a common objective: living and experiencing person-centred attitudes for maximum mutual understanding and improved interpersonal relationships.

What follows is a summary of the practices that are frequent components of active listening. If I want to be there for someone and am prepared to risk that I potentially may be changed, and I'm willing to listen to what the other person has to say, then the following will be useful:

- Suspending intruding thoughts and making inner space
- Taking on the perspective of the other person
- Putting my opinions to one side for a time

- Listening attentively to the other person without wanting to guide them in some direction
- Not interrupting the other person but accompanying them
- Trying to receive the whole message including its content and associated feelings
- Taking into account the words, signals, body language, gestures, composure and expression of the other person
- Checking understanding by summarizing what has been said in my own words and reflecting it back
- Asking whenever something is unclear to me
- Feeding back, in my own words, what I have heard in the context of the whole meaning but not judging it

Now let us see what two students have to say who tried to listen actively and had thoroughly read Rogers and Farson (1987).

To show respect is the largest innovation in my thinking since I read the article. I had never had the idea that through pure listening you can express more respect toward the other person than through articulating respect. This theory by Rogers explains this very intuitively and understandably. I'm quite sure that in the future I'll consider this again and again.

Many issues can directly influence one's daily practice, however, we have to watch out against too rigidly adhering to some technique since this, in my view, can rapidly lead to an unfavourable ending of the conversation. To me, an essential issue is to retain the freedom of the speaker, not to devalue them and not to judge their ideas and thoughts. The more I open myself to listening to what the other has to say the better I can understand them. To me it is vital that the speaker can retain the space that they need to completely express themselves. It is of little help if you immediately start searching for solutions or showing alternative paths. Often it really is better to take the time and listen to the other person and to understand them.

# 5 Characteristics of person-centred communication

*To understand another person's thoughts and feelings thoroughly, with the meanings they have for him, and to be thoroughly understood by this person in return – this is one of the most rewarding of human experiences, and all too rare.*

(Rogers 1961: 323)

**In this chapter you will learn about:**

- The basic assumption regarding the *view of the human being* underlying person-centred communication

- The grounding of *essential features* of person-centred communication, in Rogers' person-centred approach

- The practical consequences of person-centred communication in fields like partnership, work, creativity, decision-making, etc.

- The validity of person-centred communication across national cultures

- The ways person-centred communication can contribute to intercultural understanding

The objective of this chapter is to view person-centred communication from the perspective of person-centred attitudes and the value system that is based in these attitudes, and to use this perspective to derive a number of characteristics. The three main sections of the chapter concern our characterization of person-centred communication as attitude-based, relationship-driven and development-process-oriented.[1] These sections mutually depend on each

[1]These three features can immediately be aligned with three categories distinguished by the American philosopher Charles Peirce: firstness, secondness, and thirdness. 'Firstness' as the property of entities (concepts of thought) maps a person's attitudes. The property of being relationship-driven is clearly a relational quality, hence a 'secondness' property that typically establishes a relationship between entities. The goal, intention, or result of the association of firstness and secondness properties brings about a 'thirdness' quality. In the case of the person-centred approach, the tendency toward further development can be seen as an example of thirdness.

other and overlap to some degree. Furthermore, we explore how far person-centred communication facilitates communication between nations and how it qualifies as providing a meta-level for constructive communication across cultures.

The 'carriers' of person-centred communication are people who have within them the attitudes of congruence, acceptance and empathic understanding to a maximum possible and well-balanced degree. Hence, person-centred communication can be characterized as *attitude-based*. However, to become effective, the attitudes that a person holds need to be lived or set free in a relationship with at least one other person. In other words, for their actual unfolding, the attitudes need a climate that has to be provided by the social environment. This leads us to characterize person-centred communication as *relationship-driven*. The word 'driven' emphasizes the significance of the interpersonal relationship as the essential path to the enhancement of self. As the goal of a person-centred way of being and hence also communicating, Carl Rogers discovered and specified a developmental process that can be observed and confirmed. The orientation in this developmental process that grows out of the synergy between attitudes and relationship provides us with the third feature of person-centred communication: *development-process-oriented*.

After thorough characterization we consider arguments and evidence that point to the intercultural, or, more appropriately, culture-transcending validity of person-centred communication.

## Humanistic view of the person

The person-centred approach is based on a particular view of a person – a special anthropological concept. As opposed to Freud, Rogers was convinced that the human organism is trustworthy and that in every person there are vast resources that can be tapped for self-understanding and constructively altering one's self-concept (Rogers 1961; Cain and Seeman 2002). In the person-centred approach the person is seen as always changing and equipped with an innate capacity to develop in the direction of increased maturity. This view gets support from social- and motivation-psychological studies, in particular 'self-determination theory' (SDT) (Deci and Ryan 2000; Sheldon *et al.* 2003). In his own words, Rogers (1961: 194) characterizes the basic trustworthiness of human nature as follows:

> It will be evident that another implication of the view I have been presenting is that the basic nature of the human being, when functioning freely, is constructive and trustworthy. For me this is an inescapable conclusion from a quarter-century of experience in psychotherapy. When we are

able to free the individual from defensiveness, so that he is open to the wide range of his own needs, as well as the wide range of environmental and social demands, his reactions may be trusted to be positive, forward-moving, constructive. We do not need to ask who will socialize him, for one of his own deepest needs is for affiliation and communication with others. As he becomes more fully himself, he will become more realistically socialized.

Thus, based on his long experience, Rogers was convinced that the human being, when functioning freely (i.e. under the necessary and sufficient conditions that comply with the human species), is basically trustworthy and constructive. According to Rogers, the human need for affiliation and communication are so strong that the development toward being oneself also leads to maturing along the social dimension.

**Invitation to reflect**

*Under what conditions or in which relationship do you feel that you behave constructively? Are these the same or different situations or relationships in which you feel encouraged to grow personally?*

*What, for you in particular, are the major blocks that hinder you in being the way you would like to be, or acting in the way you consider to be right?*

*Are there situations in which you act aggressively? If so, think about a recent one and reflect upon the potential positive and negative consequences. What do you think about that situation now? Was there any variable missing in that situation?*

Gisela Steenbuck (2005: 84) expresses the interrelation between autonomy, community and relationship as follows:

The foundation of human development [and also communication] is binding and contact as well as autonomy and self-determination. The human being is an autonomous and distinctive individual and at the same time depends on the community of persons. The human being has in himself or herself the energy to develop from within oneself. But he/she depends on relationships that enable this development to actually take place.

Communication has a primary function in interpersonal relationships in so far as it facilitates the interaction of ever-changing people and thus co-determines the development of their relationships as well as their ways of being. Rogers succeeded in identifying a way of being which was based on three attitudes that bring about a climate of growth. It is communication and behaviour that allow us to express as well as pass on all three interrelated attitudes or variables.

One consideration regarding the way we construct reality (compare also proposition 1 in Rogers [1951] 1995) particularly underlines the necessity and helpfulness of the presence of person-centred attitudes in communication. Rogers notes: 'There are as many "real worlds" as there are people!' (1980: 102). He derives this from his cognition by observing that: 'The only reality I can possibly know is the world as *I* perceive and experience it at this moment' (1980: 102). This reality he also acknowledges for the other person. Consequently, following this thesis means that by accepting and trying to understand the 'reality' of the other, we can arrive at another perspective of 'reality'. This enables us to react to the 'whole situation' in a more adjusted way. Thus, through the other person, we tend to understand more about ourselves and our environment. Hence it is not surprising that clear and understandable communication offers further perspectives and benefits that – from the mere way a person is built – they can't reach alone.

## Person-centred communication is attitude-based

Communication that is appropriate to the situation at hand is directed toward mutual understanding, and is not distracted by any inner blockages or imposed coercions. For reasons of exactness we stick to Rogers' own definitions and descriptions even though almost every person-centred writer introduces his or her own characterizations. In this sense we invite everybody to search for and propose their own meanings and associations.

Rogers postulated three necessary and sufficient conditions for the process of a growth-promoting relationship. These conditions, or attitudes (or 'ways of being') need to be lived by at least one person and be perceived by the other person(s):

- Congruence or genuineness, realness (transparency)
- Acceptance or unconditional positive regard
- Empathic understanding (sometimes briefly but imprecisely termed 'empathy')

Rogers (1980: 115) writes that these attitudes must be present in any situation in which the development of the person is the goal. Congruence, unconditional positive regard and empathic understanding, the so-called three Rogers variables or, as Nykl (2005) refers to them, dispositions, form the basis of a constructive climate. Such a climate enables a comprehensive, extensional perception of any situation, optimal personal development and, as Rogers calls it, *significant learning*. If these attitudes are perceived at least to some degree, then people can freely develop toward their personal optimum (Rogers 1961).

The objectives of the following characterization are to:

- Mediate an initial understanding of the three attitudes or dispositions
- Allow readers to explore the interrelationships between the three attitudes
- Help readers to become more aware of the influence of the three attitudes in everyday communication
- Provide incentives to allow the three attitudes to influence readers' conversations

We emphasize once again that the three attitudes are neither techniques nor methods that can be *applied*. Rather, they are the basis for an interpersonal approach that has its core in our inner world and radiates it to the environment through interaction, such that it is present in every relationship and every contact. By living the attitudes and expressing them in our behaviour we pass them on to our environment. If, step by step, the attitude is perceived as helpful, we assimilate it as an integral component – attitude – into our inner world and also our communication.

The triangle in Figure 5.1 is intended to suggest that attitudes build the basis or foundation of communication processes. It is neither knowledge nor trained skills that are *decisive* for person-centred communication, although both may play a considerable part. These are the (inter)personal attitudes that constitute the fertile soil for person-centred communication.

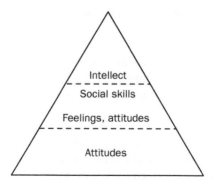

**Figure 5.1** Attitudes as a basis of person-centred communication

Therein the task is not to train patterns of communication, but rather to find a path to letting one's own dispositions unfold in a way that, in our relationships, we are able to both perceive and provide the conditions of a climate of growth.

### Distinction from psychotherapy

In the context of the theory of a therapeutic relationship, the assumption is always that at least one side of the dialogue – the therapist – is close to being in an ideal psychological state, meaning that he or she is largely free from valuing conditions and other rigid constructs and, furthermore, he or she stays congruent in the relationship. This is the result of a long path of personality development and training.

Moreover, there exist significant differences between everyday communication and psychotherapy. In everyday communication, offering a deep therapeutic relationship is seldom the goal. Each time there are totally different and changing constraints as compared to therapy, such as, for example, various demands, wishes, problems and needs, other relationships, lack of time, etc. Hence, most of the time we can't offer a therapeutic relationship to our own partner, because the whole relationship is built on different ground. However, many situations can still be handled totally differently if only we were to listen actively and to share ourselves. It is nevertheless the case that advanced milestones of personal development need to be reached and experienced, before a kind of intuitive receptiveness and behaviour can unfold that match a given situation most appropriately. Such milestones are often those unforgettable personal encounters that you can experience intensively if you choose the path that leads in that direction.

In the following, we stick to the formulations given by Rogers in the context of the therapeutic relationship because the constraints are quite clear. Rogers uses the terms 'therapist' and 'client'. However, when citing him, we also have in mind other possible relationships such as counsellor–client, pedagogue–student, facilitator–participant, project manager–team member, father–mother–child, etc.

### Congruence

Some synonyms for 'congruence' are: *realness, transparency, genuineness, authenticity.* Rogers (1961: 33) characterizes congruence as follows:

> I have found that the more that I can be genuine in the relationship, the more helpful it will be... Being genuine also involves the willingness to be and to express, in my words and my behaviour, the various feelings and

attitudes, which exist in me...It is only by providing the genuine reality which is in me, that the other person can successfully seek for the reality in him. I have found this to be true even when the attitudes I feel are not attitudes with which I am pleased, or attitudes which seem conducive to a good relationship.

At a different place, Rogers establishes the connection to bodily feeling in stating that congruence means that the therapist is consciously aware of what they experience or feel in their body and that these feelings are available to them such that they can share them with their clients, if appropriate (Rogers 1975).

More precisely, Rogers writes, 'Thus when self-experiences are accurately symbolized, and are included in the self-concept in this accurately symbolized form, then the state is one of congruence of self and experience' (1959: 206). Thereby the term 'symbolization' is used synonymously with consciousness or awareness of some portion of our experience, and this symbolic representation of some of our experience may take on 'varying levels of sharpness or vividness, from a dim awareness of something existing as ground, to a sharp awareness of something which is in focus as figure' (Rogers 1959: 198).

In order to facilitate understanding of what has been said so far, we observe that congruence – as a state, viewed at one point in time – can be seen as consisting of two partial states or aspects, whereby the second aspect depends on the first. First, we recognize the congruence (match) between the inner experience and the conscious access to it. We are open to our experience in that we feel what is happening inside of us and what meaning unfolds from it. We become aware of our feelings without their perception being falsified through defence or distortion. The second aspect is the candid, congruent communication or expression of what is going on inside us, our inner experience. The communication of this aspect depends significantly on what we consciously want to let the other person know, thus what we consider conducive in the given moment. This may depend on the specific relationship and situation.

In a counselling relationship what the counsellor shares with the client depends on whether it is deemed conducive to the client or the relationship. In a relationship between partners, both are more strongly present with their own needs, experiences and, in general, also conditions of worth – so there is a lot more that has an influence on what is shared. Nevertheless, we think that a high degree of congruence facilitates mutual understanding most prominently. If I don't even know what the other person is feeling, how can I respond to his or her needs?

There are innumerable examples for being present with one's own needs that are counter to those of the other person. Imagine, for example, a partnership in which one partner is rather conscious about spending money and wants to save it for some large investment, while the other person can enjoy life only when he or she can freely spend money on something enjoyable, again and again. Or, one partner wants to relax and watch TV while the other prefers to talk. Or, in an organization/at a school there are different opinions as to which strategy or research orientation seems most promising and should be supported. In all these cases it is a major challenge to get along with the differences, to sense one's own needs as well as those of the partner, and to act appropriately.

Another difference between a counselling relationship and a partnership lies in the considerably larger behavioural repertoire with which partners can reveal themselves to each other. Besides using words, it is primarily our behaviour by which we affect each other and through which our genuineness or façade comes through in our interaction.

### Invitation to reflect

*What is it that you derive from your relationship(s) based on what you read here?*

*Do you think that it is easier or more difficult to be congruent and communicate in a person-centred way in direct, close relationships or in relationships in which there is more distance? In which way(s) does the difficulty or ease express itself in one of your relationships that currently means a lot to you?*

We are genuine, or congruent, whenever our inner experience corresponds with the perception, as well as the communication, of this experience. If we consciously express something differently from what we feel then it is a lie, cheating, or deceit. If we don't perceive our feelings straightforwardly, then our perception is distorted, we are blinded, or we don't admit a range of experiences to our awareness in order to maintain our self-structure. For Rogers, the development of congruence is a lifelong process and complete congruence in each situation may never be reached.

In his book *A Way of Being* Rogers (1980: 115) re-addresses the key issue of openness. He clearly states that the open reaction is shared only if this is deemed appropriate. Schulz von Thun ([1981] 2002) introduces an analogous aspect of openness which he calls 'situational fit' ('*Stimmigkeit*') and refers to the work of Ruth Cohn. He writes: '"Fitting" means: In coherence with the character of the situation (as I define it).' We think that 'situational fit' captures exactly the quality of appropriate openness that Rogers describes in the context of the interdependence of the three core attitudes.

While characterizing the basic attitudes for a facilitator in the context of learning, Rogers (1983: 121) writes that congruence is perhaps the most basic of these essential attitudes:

> When the facilitator is a real person, being what she is, entering into a relationship with the learner without presenting a front or a façade, she is much more likely to be effective. This means that the feelings that she is experiencing are available to her, available to her awareness, that she is able to live these feelings, be them, and able to communicate them if appropriate.

### Invitation to reflect

*Do you remember a good teacher? How would you characterize them? Were they a real, authentic person? How did you come to realize this? What influence did they have on your further education and/or life?*

The better we perceive the job-related, private, organizational, cultural, etc. situation and the more precisely we can manage to 'feel ourselves' into a person and their whole context, the more precisely we will know and feel what is appropriate in a given situation. This little excursion in thought is intended to illustrate the relationship between congruence and empathic understanding, namely that a part of the congruence of the facilitator is the experience of empathic understanding (Rogers 1959: 215). Another consequence is that congruence that encompasses the experience of acceptance and empathic understanding is the basis of highly appropriate behaviour. Rogers (1959: 206) refers to this kind of behaviour/perception as *extensional* and characterizes *extensionality* as follows:

> If the person is reacting or perceiving in an extensional manner he tends to see experience in limited, differentiated terms, to be aware of the space-time anchorage of facts, to be dominated by facts, not by concepts, to evaluate in multiple ways, to be aware of different levels of abstraction, to test his inferences and abstractions against reality.

From the social point of view, congruence results in psychological adjustment. According to Rogers (1959: 206), optimal psychological adjustment is 'synonymous with complete congruence between self and experience, or complete openness to experience'. As described earlier, it requires the absence of conditions of worth.

The way a congruent person behaves is characterized as mature. According to Rogers (1959: 207), a mature person would tend to perceive realistically and in an extensional manner, not be defensive, accept the responsibility of being different from others, accept the responsibility for their own behaviour, evaluate experience in terms of the evidence coming from their own senses, change their evaluation of experience only on the basis of new evidence, accept others as unique individuals different from them, prize themselves, and prize others.

How do these different aspects of congruence relate to communication? We think that they reflect themselves immediately – though not only – in our communication behaviour. For example, a congruent person would be aware of the consequences of his or her utterances and ways of expression and would feel responsible for them. Also, increasing congruence will reveal itself in more willingness – based on a comprehensive understanding – to take certain risks in communicative exchanges such as to integrate new experience.

Specific, professional situations will – besides congruence including the experience of acceptance and empathic understanding – often require further knowledge and competences in order to allow for constructive and competent behaviour. In this sense, a highly congruent instructor will necessarily require subject-specific knowledge in order to pass it on to students effectively, and a lawyer will need to know exactly the laws and legal state of affairs in order to optimally represent a client. However, congruence as the basis of professional action can optimally support every person to behave appropriately, even in new, unknown situations. We think that in particular in highly complex real-world situations, a congruent, undistorted inclusion of all inner resources is essential for constructive behaviour (Rogers 1983; Damasio 1994, 2000; Nykl 2005). Gisela Steenbuck (2005: 81–6) writes:

> When I aim to be real, I can't hide behind a façade, can't bury myself behind a professional role, rather I try to be myself and let my self shine through to the other person... What I share reflects my self-revelation (for example: 'I can't listen attentively because the noise distracts me') as well as my description of what I observe in the other along with the way it is affecting me.

Reinhard Tausch thinks that the person-centred attitude of realness significantly differs from:

> ... viewing realness as a charter to voice oneself without respect of the partner, in particular, expressing animosity and acting without empathy and consideration of him or her, for example, staying passive and not making an effort in hearing them. On the contrary, a facilitator who is

real in a helpful way expresses his feeling and thinking with clear regard and consideration of the feelings and thought of the other person. This means he chooses a form that would hurt the other as little as possible and respects him/her as a person. At the same time, he empathizes with the other and hence perceives how they feel and what his expressions mean to them.

(Tausch and Tausch [1963] 1998: 91, translation by the authors)

Rogers points out that different counsellors and therapists establish contact in a broad variety of ways. He considered those as successful who, at the relevant moments, managed to stay genuinely themselves as much as they were capable at their deepest conscious level. To Rogers, there is nothing else that is of equal importance. To emphasize the difference between revealing one's own perceptions to the other person versus judging them, he writes that, in any case, the counsellor shares his or her sensing or perception but not a fact or judgement about the situation. The statement 'I feel bored at the moment' must not be confused with the judgement that the other person is *boring*. It only expresses the feelings of the counsellor in the relationship. Through revealing the feeling of boredom and estrangement to the client, the counsellor's feeling state changes: he or she would definitely not feel bored while sharing his or her feelings (Rogers 1975).

The following is an example of congruent communication illustrating the process as Rogers (1962: 91) shares his sensations with a student:

So if I sense that I am feeling bored by my contacts with this student, and this feeling persists, I think I owe it to him and to our relationship to share this feeling with him. But here again I will want to be constantly in touch with what is going on in me. If I am, I will recognize that it is my feeling of being bored which I am expressing, and not some supposed fact about him as a boring person. If I voice it as my own reaction, it has the potentiality of leading to a deeper relationship. But this feeling exists in the context of a complex and changing flow, and this needs to be communicated too. I would like to share with him my distress at feeling bored, and the discomfort I feel in expressing this aspect of me. As I share these attitudes I find that my feeling of boredom arises from my sense of remoteness from him, and that I would like to be more in touch with him. And even as I try to express these feelings they change. I am certainly not bored as I try to communicate myself to him in this way...I also feel a new sensitivity to him, now that I have shared...this feeling which has been a barrier between us. So I am very much more able to hear the surprise or perhaps the hurt in his voice as he now finds himself speaking more genuinely because I have dared to be real with him.

Realness in one partner allows the other partner to be real too (Rogers 1961). We often experience that openly addressing an unresolved issue, a weakness, a mismatch, a momentary feeling toward the other person, or equally 'letting the other look into your hand of cards' stimulates an analogous reaction from the other person. They tend to reveal their thoughts, feeling processes, reservations, and be more open and understanding. Hence, more of the whole situation becomes accessible. Openness facilitates trust. Somebody is willing to show themselves, to encounter us without hiding. At the same time that person takes the risk of being attacked, so they trust that their revelations won't be used against them. Should that happen anyway, the other person will naturally react by closing down. Mistrust takes over and the free flow of communication is hindered if not interrupted. Here is an example from Renate's own experience to evoke your own reflection.

---

### Example from experience

**R:** Tommy, please get on with your packing, I don't want to get home too late, I need to get up in the morning early.

**T:** I don't care.

At first, I felt totally ignored and was disappointed about the lack of empathy in Tom – and I was angry. Several different responses came to my mind like: 'Rude boy, you will care if . . .' but then the following thought entered my mind: 'He's being honest; from his perspective the situation justifies his response.' I looked into his eyes and replied briefly and with determination.

**R:** Hmm, I feel it's a pity that my concerns are of so little concern to you.

Then I continued packing and tidying up the room. At first, Tom didn't react at all, but after a while he started slowly packing his stuff. However, he also teased his younger brother such that we arrived home only after midnight. The next morning the following conversation came up.

**T:** Mum, I imagine you just might not care at all, but nevertheless, could you please try to fix my zipper? Otherwise the rain will get into my rain jacket?

**R:** You said it. [Pause] So pass me your jacket and I'll see what I can do. [The action is successful and I pass the jacket to him.] Here you go. The zipper was stuck, I was able to fix it.

**T:** Perfect, thank you for doing that for me. You saved me from getting soaking wet in this bad weather.

**R:** I'm glad I could help, and I appreciate that you realized that I could have just not cared at all.

In both of us and in our relationship something has changed. Even if 'it' can leave me untouched, it is 'you' about whom I still care.

**Invitation to reflect**

*Let us reflect on the three core attitudes in the interaction between T and R. At which places do congruence, acceptance and empathic understanding enter the conversation and what effect do they have?*

*What effect does the lack of individual attitudes have? In particular, how is realness expressed that lacks acceptance and empathic understanding? Have you ever experienced a similar situation?*

*Do you think that the conversation shared above could give way to producing an interaction pattern that the participating parties could misuse? What effects might this have? What can be done to prevent the creation of such a pattern?*

## Acceptance, unconditional positive regard

Synonyms here include: *respect, caring, prizing, acknowledgement, warmth.*
Rogers (1961: 34) describes acceptance as follows:

> I find that the more acceptance and liking I feel toward this individual, the more I will be creating a relationship which he can use. By acceptance I mean a warm regard for him as a person of unconditional self-worth, of value no matter what his condition, his behaviour, his feelings. It means a respect and liking for him as a separate person, a willingness for him to possess his own feelings in his own way.

We can feel unconditional positive regard toward another person or toward ourselves (unconditional positive self-regard). The experience of unconditional positive regard from a significant other person is a precondition of feeling unconditional positive self-regard (Rogers 1959: 209). This relationship shows clearly how important our interpersonal relationships are to our self-perception and how strongly our communication and dealing with others can influence their feeling of self-worth. Most probably you will know how pleasant it feels to be accepted by others exactly the way you are – not needing to distort, disguise, perform or hide anything but freely being yourself in a given situation. To express our inner world and feel from the other person that he or she is trying to understand us from our perspective does not, however, mean that the other person has to agree with our opinion or our behaviour. That person merely perceives us with all our potentials and limitations.

Rogers defines unconditional positive regard in the counselling relationship as follows: 'If the self-experiences of another are perceived by me in such a way that no self-experience can be discriminated as more or less worthy of positive regard than any other, then I am experiencing unconditional positive regard toward this individual' (1959: 208). Since this definition builds upon the one of positive regard, we include that one too: 'If the perception by me of some self-experience in another makes a positive difference to my experiential field, then I am experiencing positive regard for that individual' (1959: 207).

The consequence of unconditional positive regard is a non-judgemental, accepting attitude toward the other person (Rogers 1983). This contributes to the loosening of conditions of worth and to strengthening one's orientation via the organismic valuing process. If others don't judge us then we can better follow our own direction of actualization and tend to move toward higher levels of congruence or mental health (Tausch and Tausch [1963] 1998; Sheldon *et al.* 2003) – in other words, our optimum and also optim*al* communication – in a self-determined way. The fact that this is not a simple path is confirmed by the difficulty of finding one's own direction, following it and making far-reaching decisions.

Acceptance means that development or change will be likely, if the two people hold a positive, accepting attitude towards each other – or, more precisely, towards what/where the other person is at this moment. It is a mutual appreciation of each other that does not depend on any conditions. This attitude gives us the safety to subscribe to the feeling that is present in us at this moment – fury, confusion, anger, courage, love or pride, animosity or softness, protest or yielding, self-trust or self-devaluation. The acceptance of the other in the relationship doesn't have any possessive or devaluing component. To accept the other also means to trust his or her direction. As a consequence our behaviour in communicative exchanges and in the relationship will be non-directive while leaving to the other the maximum possible space for self-directed development, without ever giving up our own congruence. Consequently, acceptance must not be confused with a laissez-faire style where we don't care about the other person and don't regard him or her at all.

Rogers states that a non-judgemental attitude does not mean ceasing to show reactions. On the contrary, it may grant the freedom to react without having to fear the judgement of others. In Rogers' words (1961: 358):

> ...to cease evaluating another is not to cease having reactions. It may, as a matter of fact, free one to react. 'I don't like your idea (or painting, or invention, or writing)', is not an evaluation, but a reaction. It is subtly but sharply different from a judgment which says, 'What you are doing is bad (or good), and this quality is assigned to you from some external source.'

This is because the first statement permits individuals to maintain their own locus of evaluation. The second statement, however, tends to put the person at the mercy of the evaluator's forces who judge from their authority.

**Invitation to reflect**

*Do you have a preferred pattern along which you react in response to being positively/negatively judged by others? How do you feel in such situations? How do you express your reactions?*

*Note: encounter groups provide excellent opportunities for perceiving one's own reactions as well as the reactions of other people to some particular expression, statement or situation.*

We think that in some situations it may be worthwhile to perceive judgement as a sort of reaction and not to let oneself react to the evaluation but rather to stay with oneself. 'I see, there's some truth in…' With such an attitude we can creatively influence the course of the conversation more often than we think.

Rogers formulated an interesting relationship between receiving positive regard from another person and one's own need *for* positive regard. The need for positive regard 'is reciprocal, in that when an individual discriminates himself as satisfying another's need for positive regard, he necessarily experiences satisfaction of his own need for positive regard' (1959: 223). We conjecture that this relationship explicates the roots of social behaviour – it enriches me to contribute to a positive experience in you. In a conversation, acceptance – if admitted – raises trust and creates a connection. Real acceptance, however, can only consist of a confluence of congruence and empathic understanding. Acceptance that would only function to 'serve the other' and thereby ignore one's own person ('at any cost') tends to hinder or cause a deterioration in interpersonal relationships.

**Invitation to reflect**

*On which recent occasion did you feel genuinely accepted? How did you feel afterwards? What did that particular relationship trigger in you? When do you remember feeling ignored, overlooked, or judged? How did you react and what was the consequence of the situation?*

The enormous importance of acceptance can be recognized in situations in which we are *not* accepted. Two kinds of non-acceptance are most prominent. The first is *ignorance* or *exclusion*, whereby we or our interests are not perceived. It is accompanied by the feeling that we don't exist at all, or that our work is a complete waste of time. The second kind is a premature, unconsidered *judgement*, mainly devaluing our opinion or behaviour without an effort to understand our intention, situation or relationship. This often evokes the feeling of talking to a wall. Such feelings aptly demonstrate our strong, deep need to be accepted by others.

### Invitation to reflect

*Do you have a preferred way in which you express acceptance/positive regard toward others? Do you think you express positive regard too often, too rarely, or just often enough?*

Acceptance and neglect are often expressed through behaviour and can be felt intuitively without needing to be put into words. For example, we can express acceptance by including people or groups in activities or decisions, by giving them space, inviting them, embracing them with a hug, expressing affection through bodily closeness, trusting them and letting them know and experience that they are important to us. Acceptance as well as ignorance and judgement are always dynamic components of the atmosphere of an exchange, and thereby determine the tone. Regardless of the way they are expressed, these elements, together with the other person's level of congruence, co-determine the potentials and limits of any exchange (compare also the case study in the beginning of Chapter 2).

In counselling situations, positive regard means that the counsellor respects the client as a person and that he or she cares for them in a non-possessive way as having individual self-worth (Rogers 1961). Sometimes holding the other person in regard can be challenging, in particular if he or she expresses negative feelings toward the counsellor or listener. Mearns and Thorne (2007: 96) address this challenge as follows:

> The client feels that the counsellor values him consistently throughout their relationship despite the fact that he may not value himself and even if the counsellor does not approve of all the client's behaviour. It is possible to accept the client as a person of worth while still not liking some of the things he does.

Rogers describes his attitude as one in which he doesn't take on any *role*. His attitude is that of positively approaching the client without constraining or judging them in any way. If he manages to provide that climate, clients tend to be able to speak about issues that really bother them. Rogers accepts the way the client is and not what he or she should be like. One client told Rogers he could simply always be himself, without having to care whether he behaved properly. And whenever he left, he felt more creative – and that feeling persisted thereafter (Rogers and Wood 1974). We include the above description because it nicely captures the feeling or state of mind that we tend to experience after having participated in person-centred encounter groups: a being full of potential, energized, always up to something, trying to accomplish something positive, knowing oneself better, living constructively.

### Empathic understanding, empathy

Empathic understanding means a deep understanding from the perspective of the other person. For Rogers, empathic understanding unfolds from feeling a continuing desire to understand the other person. He writes (1961: 35):

> ... I feel a continuing desire to understand – a sensitive empathy with each of the client's feelings and communications as they seem to him at that moment. Acceptance does not mean much until it involves understanding. It is only that I understand the feelings and thoughts which seem so horrible to you, or so weak... – it is only as I see them as you see them and accept them and you, that you feel really free to explore... your inner and often buried experience... There is implied here a freedom to explore oneself at both conscious and unconscious levels.

Rogers (1959: 210) defines empathy as follows:

> The state of empathy, or being empathic, is to perceive the internal frame of reference [i.e. the realm of experience which is available to the awareness of an individual at a given moment] of another with accuracy, and with the emotional components and meanings which pertain thereto, as if one were the other person, but without ever losing the 'as if' condition.

In order to empathically understand other people we listen to them attentively and try to understand them as well as we can, which means that we perceive the meanings of their feelings and memories. We sense their experienced personal meanings and reflect our understanding of them. It is not only the conscious, symbolized contents that we understand empathically while delving deeply into the inner world of the other, but sometimes also the content that is just below the threshold of consciousness. This does not happen continuously since such content rises only rarely and on special occasions of 'success'. The decisive factor is the perception of a part of the private sphere of the other person as if the facilitator were that person. Thereby the facilitator has to distinguish between the perception of both feeling spheres (his/her own and that of the other person) in a differentiated way (Watson 2007). This can't be achieved through training alone but requires the whole personality and many years of experience.

Recently, Reinhard Tausch suggested that this book could profit from practical examples and sent us some of his material for exercises. We are pleased to present a sample of these exercises for the purpose of illustrating empathic and less empathic responses in physician–patient conversations.

---

**Case scenario, part 1**

The patient says: 'When I hear the word "hospital" I always immediately think of something very upsetting.'

1) Less-empathic responses:
   'Aren't you exaggerating a little?' (judgemental)
   'Why's that? There must be something to it.' (diagnosing, analysing)
2) Empathic response-variants:
   'You are immediately overcome by upsetting fears.'
   'Just the word makes you anxious.'
   'So you would like to run away.'

---

**Case scenario, part 2**

The patient says: 'I always think that the doctors look down on me.'

1) Less-empathic responses:
   'Many patients experience this, but you'll get used to it.' (generalizing)
   'This is not true. Here nobody is looked down upon.' (teaching, instructing)
   'Oh, don't take it seriously, the best thing you can do is to ignore it.' (giving advice)
2) Empathic response-variants:
   'You would like to be taken seriously.'
   'You feel patronized.'

---

**Invitation to reflect**

*What would your response be to the following statement? 'It always affects me so badly!'*

In the following, we follow a conversation that is intended to give an impression of empathic responses with a view into the client's world of experience. While 'T' stands for 'therapist', it could equally be another empathic person. The client, 'C', is full of fear. The therapist responds not only to the words but also to the perceived feelings of the client, which remain hidden in the textual presentation.

---

**Example from therapy**

**C:** When I hear the word 'hospital' I always immediately think of something very upsetting.

**T:** You are instantly overcome by upsetting fears. Just the word makes you anxious.

**C:** Yeah, I would like to run away immediately, but this won't help.

**T:** Uh, I feel your fear, I sense it.

**C:** And the doctors look down on me.

**T:** As if they aren't taking you seriously.

**C:** Yes, sure, but the surgery can't be avoided.

**T:** You want to recover and without surgery this is not possible.

**C:** Yes, my wife urges me to finally have it done.

**T:** You like your wife, don't you, and she is concerned about you. And you appreciate that it could help you.

**C:** Yes, that's right; she's a wonderful woman; I like her very much and in some ways she's right.

**T:** So this means a lot of courage and also trust on your side.

**C:** Yes, this is still lacking in me a bit.

**T:** So, tell me, is the surgery dangerous?

**C:** No, not very much. After five days I'm supposed to return home again.

**T:** And you look forward to being healthy again, don't you?

**C:** Yes, very much, indeed. [Pause]

**T:** And how are you now; how do you feel?

**C:** A lot better; I sense that I'm becoming relaxed and I feel more trust and desire to live.

---

Godfrey Barrett-Lennard (2003: 36), who is intensively engaged in empathic understanding, writes that:

> One's expressed empathy aids that person in their expressive-exploratory engagement and process, such that this can unfold and not circle around repetitively. It is as though this response helps an inner door to open in the other person, and what lies beyond that door is now

visible or accessible to them. As they examine and share this vista, and experience the listener following and seeing with them what they now perceive, another door swings open. Such companioning, step by incremental step, can be powerfully enabling to the person in finding their way.

Barrett-Lennard (2005: 53) emphasizes an essential aspect of empathic understanding to be a lived attunement to the whole life situation of the other person.

In direct conversations and through several emails, I (Renate) experienced the influential effect that Godfrey Barrett-Lennard's active and versatile interest in my worlds of engagement had on me. There was a systematic approach to information and knowledge, a strong attraction to the person-centred approach, my family, professional relationships, activities, a conflicted relationship, research regarding team competence, publications, travelling, etc. – everything flowing naturally into the conversation. This reflects and clarifies the importance of all these worlds to me. I sensed that Godfrey's honest and vivid interest in whatever part of me made a significant contribution to my 'own' capacity for better integrating in me. Recently, the personal integration of the versatile worlds of engagement gave scientific expression to an integrated view of the person-centred approach as an overarching paradigm (Motschnig-Pitrik *et al.* 2013).

**Moments of meeting.** In special, quite rare moments that cannot be affected by pure willpower or intention, the people in a conversation can meet each other. Referring to the philosopher Buber, Rogers (1961: 202) calls such moments 'I-Thou moments' and describes them as follows. 'In these moments there is, to borrow Buber's phrase, a real "I-Thou" relationship, a timeless living in the experience which is *between* the client and me.' Rogers (1980) thinks that a deep, mutual, personal meeting is quite rare but he is convinced that we can't live as human beings unless it happens at least occasionally.

From our own experience, a moment of meeting is a spontaneous, impressive experiential process not comparable with anything else. It is triggered by some real sharing that awakens some particularly meaningful, deep experience in a person. A moment of meeting attracts one's full attention for a brief period of time, as if each cell in one's body fits itself into the relationship with the other person and allows a stream of experiencing within us as well as between us. Such moments – if we allow them to happen – are unforgettable and we can return to them at some later point in time. Ladislav Nykl (2005: 25) describes a moment of meeting as follows:

A moment of meeting most often is an intensively felt experience between two persons being in contact. It is the meeting of the emotional worlds at the same level, as if in immediate vicinity, so to speak, in me but enriched by the other. It is a tiny but significant feeling, 'I exist', and I feel the other. I sense his or her potentialities and their experiencing – I let their experience grow – and this is exciting as well as risky; it satisfies me and it also means a little friendship between us. Such a meeting flows in a sensed stream of experience of genuine giving and receiving in an unlimited, but often brief timeframe, even frequently without the one or the other even realizing it. The special issue about this experience is the increasing intensity that we understand as a sort of growth.

Such moments of meeting have the potential to lead to a holistic experience or the solution to a problem, though not necessarily on the rational level (Mearns and Cooper 2005). In a relationship this peak experience must not be destroyed through an explanation. In everyday relationships it is mostly a short experience that goes unnoticed by the other person.

In psychotherapy as well as in everyday relationships, empathy is a complex phenomenon composed of attitudes, values, skills and behaviours (Cain 2010: 92). Thus, empathic responses can take on a variety of forms. David Cain identified various simple and complex ways of expressing empathy. Based on his description (Cain 2010: 95–100), we summarize the straightforward forms in the below box. Readers interested in the complex forms are referred to Cain's book or may wish to follow examples from therapy. They tend to illustrate a whole range of ways to communicate empathy and thus lead the other person to explore what is present for him or her.

---

### Varieties of empathy

- *Empathic understanding* responses attempt to grasp and accurately communicate the other person's basic message. Example:

  **C:** I am just dragging today.
  **T:** Just no energy for anything.
  **C:** No, I just feel like staying home and avoiding everything I have to do.

- *Clarifying* responses attempt to articulate clearly what the other person is trying to say by struggling to find words, or offering just a vague expression. Example:

  **C:** I'm really out of sorts.
  **T:** You seem angry.
  **C:** I guess I am. Nothing is going right today.

- *Affective* empathic responses focus on the other person's emotions or bodily felt sense of a problem, going beyond the content of the message and articulating the feeling being expressed or implied. Example:

  **C:** I just can't believe my mother is dead.
  **T:** You're feeling sad and lost that she's no longer with you.
  **C:** Terrible.

- *Explorative* empathic responses engage a probing and tentative style as the therapist attempts to assist the other person to locate, explore, unfold, examine and reflect on unclear or hidden aspects of experience. Example:

  **C:** I can't quite put my finger on it, but I feel anxious about my upcoming wedding to Jim.
  **T:** So there's some vague sense of doubt or fear about marrying Jim?
  **C:** Yes. Like I'm not sure that he and I have the same hopes for our life together.

- *Affirmative* empathic responses validate the other person's experience of sense of self, whether positive or negative. To be effective, they require credible evidence from mutual knowledge or sharing. Examples:

  **C:** I am so proud of how my children are doing. I think I'm a good mother.
  **T:** You are a good mother.
  **C:** I think I've been neglectful of my husband.
  **T:** From what you've said I can see that you have been neglectful lately.

**Invitation to reflect**

*Consider some of the examples of therapeutic interviews and everyday conversations given in this book. Can you determine which kinds of empathic responses were given? Can you identify empathic responses that do not fit into any of the simple categories listed above?*

**Approaches to empathic understanding in everyday communication.** Some readers will already have experienced the following: sometimes the attentive listening of another person is enough to suddenly open up a door to the solution to some complex, unresolved situation. At other times, being empathically understood can help to untangle overly complex thoughts, so that a situation can be seen more clearly. For example, a colleague shares the problems her child is having at school. She is worried about her child's being required to repeat a class and can't make sense of the situation. An empathic response might be: 'You seem worried and unable to think of of a way out... I get a sense you're thinking about transferring to a different school?...So what would it mean to you if you sent Martin to another school?' She can now explore the individual options in a trustful atmosphere and gain more clarity about 'her' problem and behaviour.

**Important issues for everyday communication.** Offering empathic understanding means not using any information received outside that relationship. If someone trusts me and shares something with me, this must remain between us only. Imagine that the colleague who was worried about her child was asked by a third person whether her child was performing well at school. Wouldn't her trust sink rapidly? Would she ever open up again toward the 'empathically understanding' colleague? Empathic understanding must never misuse the other person's trust. There is a responsibility toward the other person that can create closeness – the two people have something in common. Equally, any abuse of this trust will cause distance and withdrawal.

The person sharing must first of all trust. Who are they sharing with? Will that person be able to understand? Will they keep this message to themselves rather than passing it on in the workplace/family, etc.? Is there a danger of over-challenging them?

Everybody is probably familiar with the phenomenon that it is easier to listen to someone if we are interested in their whole life situation, including relationships, themes, events, etc. Interest increases our openness to perceptions and the other person intuitively feels our sympathy. In this sense, after active listening exercises, students frequently reflect that it is easier for them to listen if they have a genuine interest in the *theme*. However, this indicates that they distance themselves from the *person*.

**Everyday empathy is associated with sensing the whole situation.** While it is the core task of counsellors or therapists to empathically understand their clients, this quality should not be expected from a partner all the time. He/she has their own demands, opinions and meanings, and at times will be more open towards our messages and at other times less. Being empathic also means sensing the right moment, and finding the right tone, in which empathic sharing and understanding are possible.

### Invitation to reflect

*Have you ever tried to empathically understand your partner, a family member or friend? How did you feel and what do you think about the result? Do you think you chose the right moment? Were you surprised at the reaction of the other person?*

From counselling practice it is apparent that empathic understanding is a complex process. It doesn't always succeed. Quite often pure empathic accompanying can't help a person to step out of a frustrating experience as long as other aspects or experiences aren't addressed.

**Extending one's perception.** So where is that aspect of empathic understanding which is considered so essential for one's own development? It lies in our precious ability to broaden our perception of any personal situation by being empathic, thus finding out more about it and understanding ourselves as well as others better and better. One might think that empathic understanding is only appropriate in situations in which the other person shares his or her problems. This, however, is *not* the case. Especially in everyday communication, in situations that often remain unnoticed, empathic understanding tends to lead to an improved and more clearly framed relationship. It helps us to perceive the other, where they truly *are*, without long and exhausting explanations, and to react accordingly. What could be more important in communication than comprehending oneself and others within their comprehensive context and extending one's own capacities for better communication and an improved relationship? However, we must not expect that the other person will automatically be able to 'read our wishes' from looking into our eyes. In a dynamic relationship especially, this capacity can require a developmental process that won't happen overnight.

### Synergy of attitudes

As mentioned earlier, the core attitudes are helpful only if they act in a balanced and 'collaborative' way. To live each of them separately could even be taught, since we could build constructs and train people in them. The meaning of person-centred communication, however, is the impression/influence as well as the expression of an empathically perceived, flexibly balanced *relationship* of the three attitudes. Indeed, there is justified criticism for regarding the attitudes separately. For example, ignorance and disregard in effect can be authentic, and manipulative behaviour can be in tune (in other words congruent) with a person's personal strategy. However, the congruence of a facilitator is always embedded in the synergy of all three attitudes. Rogers expresses this clearly: 'For therapy to occur, the wholeness of the therapist in the relationship is primary, but a part of the congruence of the therapist must be the experience of unconditional positive regard and the experience of empathic understanding' (1959: 215). Consequently, since ignorance or disregard, for example, definitely lack positive regard and empathic understanding, they can't be considered helpful even if they are felt genuinely. As another example, consider the acceptance of statements without any consideration or an uncritical agreement just to please the other.

These can't be seen as expressions of unconditional positive regard since they lack genuineness, even though they may have an underlying strategy that motivates such behaviour. According to Rogers (1980: 152), acceptance and empathic understanding are related: a 'consequence of empathic understanding is that the recipient feels valued, cared for, accepted as the person that he or she is'. Thus, empathic understanding allows positive regard to be expressed.

To illustrate the importance of the synergy of attitudes – underlying a *real* personal relationship targeted at mutual understanding and accompanying the client on their way – we include a snapshot of an interview taken from Bozart *et al.* (2002). The excerpt shows Carl Rogers talking with Sylvia about her feeling strong within herself about taking chances.

---

### Example from therapy

**Sylvia:** Reaching out to people and approaching strangers and uh –
**CR:** Taking all kinds of risks that you hadn't before.
**Sylvia:** Some. More, which, I mean I, I don't know about all kinds.
**CR:** Yeah.
**Sylvia:** Quite a few, and it's been exciting and hard.
**CR:** And I guess that leads to a, um, a deeper kind of learning, at any rate a learning that you feel more sure of, I get, I get a sense of assurance in what you're talking about. Assurance in you.
**Sylvia:** Well, yes. Yes and no. And I, I feel more I'm–, like I was saying before, I feel more mature and more, and I'm more aware of my immaturity.
**CR:** M-hm.
**Sylvia:** They're both, uh, a part of each other...And uh, does that make – does that, I guess I'm thinking that it just sounds crazy.
**CR:** No, I don't–
**Sylvia:** To say that I feel more mature because I know I'm how, I know more about how immature I am.
**CR:** Uh-huh. No, that makes a lot of sense to me.

---

### Invitation to reflect

*Can you identify various forms of empathy expressed by the therapist? Can you trace the therapist's expression of acceptance and openness?*

---

Figure 5.2 illustrates the mutual dependence of congruence, acceptance and empathic understanding. The overlap represents the match or congruence

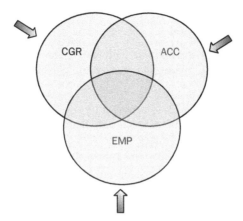

**Figure 5.2** The overlap between three variables of congruence/realness (CGR), acceptance (ACC) and empathic understanding (EMP), denoting the match (congruence) between them

of the three variables. We hypothesize that the larger this overlapping area is, the more developed are the person-centred dispositions of that person – and the more facilitative will their behaviour be for the other as well as for themselves.

The balancing of the three attitudes in every situation, and particularly in stressful situations, is a lifelong task and a motivating challenge that can benefit from experience in relationships. Quite intensively and with full attention, this task can be followed in person-centred encounter groups. The goal is to enable whole-person experiencing in relation to others as well as the whole group.

Person-centred attitudes provide some inner orientation that can be sensed and followed sufficiently such as to indicate a direction in our versatile and multidimensional world. This direction is in tune with nature and our natural developmental tendency, as confirmed by complex research in the neurosciences (Motschnig-Pitrik and Nykl 2003, 2013; Lux 2007, 2010, 2013; Silani *et al.* 2013). At the same time, we regard person-centred attitudes – primarily due to the necessity for collaboration and balance – as sufficiently flexible or dynamic to keep us away from forming rigid behavioural patterns and recipe-like action chains. Rather, each time they challenge us anew to search for our own 'truth' and to learn from each situation. We illustrate this by giving an example from Renate's own experience. It is intended to show that fixed principles and a situated flexibility in life need not necessarily be at odds. The example also shows that moments in which the person-centred attitudes are in tune can set forth something significant and special.

**Example from experience**

Tomas had broken his hand and was surprisingly brave throughout the whole process of recovery. On the evening before the plastercast was going to be removed he said:

**T:** Mum, do I have to go back to school after having been at the hospital at 8 a.m.? School is going to last till 2 p.m. and I don't have maths anyway. Can you imagine, I don't want to attend school for soooo long tomorrow.

**R:** So you don't want to have a long school day tomorrow, but you've had holidays for quite some time – and what should I write to excuse you until 2 p.m.?

**Comment:** in principle, I am strongly against excusing oneself for no clear reason.

**T:** I simply want to come home after the hospital and have some rest.

**R:** Oh yes, you want to have time to play computer games for the whole day; this I don't want to support!

**T:** No, I promise not to play games for the whole day. I want to rest and I could also learn some maths by myself.

**R:** Hmm, so let me think for a while...Are you serious that you want to learn maths? Now, why didn't you do anything for maths during the entire holiday period?

**T:** Definitely, mum, please excuse me from school.

**R:** So, let's sit down now and prepare some maths tasks for you to work on tomorrow afternoon. And I'm going to write a letter of excuse because of your plastercast removal at the hospital and a subsequent X-ray check that I assume you're going to be sent to have.

**T:** [Bringing the maths book] Great, thanks, I really will work on the maths tasks.

**R:** [Opens the book] So, let's see what you could do. What do you think you should learn as the highest priority?

T and R take their time to prepare six tasks. On the evening of the next day:

**T:** [Runs to welcome R at the door] Hey, look here, I solved all the problems.

**R:** Perfect, I'll take a look at once. And how's your hand?

**T:** Look, the plastercast is gone, but I still can't play sports for two weeks, so can you write another letter of excuse for me [smiling]? Here you have all the maths problems!

The subsequent test was – after a considerable period of time – quite good, and we were happy. From that time on, Tom did maths assignments with a lot more self-organization than before. Something had changed. Interestingly, when, two weeks later, Tom had a bad cold, he didn't use it as an excuse to stay at home.

**Invitation to reflect**

*Do you occasionally feel that by staying truthful to your principles you don't experience relationships with their potential quality – be it in your job, partnership or family?*

*Do you think that the scenario above could have had a totally different ending? What if the maths problems had not been completed? What if deviating from principles made them questionable? Would this lead to endless discussion every time?*

We agree that we need to consider all the possible different 'endings' of such a situation since they too do occur. Nevertheless, in our view such situations can be perceived as bringing about personal learning and sharpening one's own intuitions in such a way that the next, or next after next, situation will be resolved in a way that is more satisfactory and more in tune with ourselves.

In the scenario above, something must have succeeded that can only vaguely be indicated in the text. But what is this 'something'? We sense that it is manifold, including:

- The trust in the other person that has clearly been communicated – namely trusting that Tomas would rest and then work on his maths
- The accurate perception, acceptance and understanding of the feelings and sensations of the other person – namely that going to the hospital and then back to school seems too much and that Tomas is in need of rest after the medical procedure
- The genuine expression of fears – namely Tomas would just play games for the whole day – and opportunities at hand – namely the tasks that can be prepared together and then solved by Tomas, and the letter Renate will write

And, indeed, the other person did not misuse what he experienced through the direct communicative exchange including the spoken words and expressed feelings along with the actions (sitting down together and preparing the tasks) in the whole situation, but rather accepted it as supportive for him. Situations and moments such as the one shared above motivate us again and again to choose paths that seem less comfortable, more risky, but which hold a greater chance of personal growth through the increased quality of relationships and collaboration.

## Person-centred communication is relationship-driven

Rogers (1961: 39) clearly expresses his interest in the theme of interpersonal relationships when writing:

> I have long had the strong conviction...that the therapeutic relationship is only a special instance of interpersonal relationships in general, and that the same lawfulness governs all such relationships...My interest in psychotherapy has brought about in me an interest in every kind of helping relationship.

When introducing client-centred orientation, Rogers (1975) emphasizes the pivotal role of a growth- and change-promoting interpersonal relationship. He identifies the uniqueness of the approach being the focus on the process of the relationship itself rather than on the problems or inner conflicts of the client. Furthermore, he points out that the therapeutic approach has turned out to be applicable to all areas of interpersonal relationships in which healthy psychological growth of people is the aim.

Rogers (1961: 201) vividly characterizes the fundamental basis of a relationship in which people grow psychologically by exploring and sharing his own experience in his relationship to his clients:

> I launch myself into the relationship having a hypothesis, or a faith, that my liking, my confidence, and my understanding of the other person's inner world, will lead to a significant process of becoming. I enter the relationship not as a scientist, not as a physician who can accurately diagnose and cure, but as a person, entering into a personal relationship. Insofar as I see him only as an object, the client will tend to become only an object...I let myself go into the immediacy of the relationship where it is my total organism which takes over and is sensitive to the relationship, not simply my consciousness. I am not consciously responding in a planful or analytic way, but simply react in an unreflective way to the other individual, my reaction being based (but not consciously) on my total organismic sensitivity to this other person.

### Conditions of the therapeutic process and consequences for communication

Based on the attitudes of congruence, acceptance and empathic understanding, Rogers (1959: 213) formulated six conditions of the therapeutic relationship. For therapy to occur, it is necessary that these conditions exist:

1   That two persons are in contact
2   That the first person, whom we shall term the client, is in a state of incongruence, being vulnerable, or anxious
3   That the second person, whom we shall term the therapist, is congruent in the relationship
4   That the therapist is experiencing unconditional positive regard toward the client
5   That the therapist is experiencing an empathic understanding of the client's internal frame of reference
6   That the client perceives, at least to a minimal degree, conditions 4 and 5, the unconditional positive regard and the empathic understanding of the therapist

Rogers (1959: 127) stated that these conditions hold for any interpersonal relationship in which psychological growth occurs. Due to their importance, Nykl (2005: 23) formulated closely-related conditions for a congruent relationship that can also be considered as the conditions for optimal communication. The expression 'organismic growth' mentioned in condition 2 means – simplified – personal development:

1   Two people are in contact
2   Both people are in a state of their next potential organismic growth
3   Both people are congruent in the relationship and can symbolize that congruence
4   Both perople are experiencing unconditional positive regard toward each other
5   Each person empathically understands the other's internal frame of reference
6   Each person perceives, at least to a minimal degree, conditions 4 and 5, namely the unconditional positive regard of the other for him/her, and the other's empathic understanding, as well as the symbolized congruence/realness anchored in condition 3

Condition 6 requires that positive regard, empathic understanding and congruence are perceived 'at least to a minimal degree'. This is consistent with Rogers' writings (1961: 35). He writes that if he holds the three attitudes and the other person can 'at least to some degree' experience them, then a constructive personal development will invariably occur. We add that an optimal communication would result in the communication partners' perceiving the three attitudes to the highest possible degree.

In his book *Carl Rogers' Helping System,* Barrett-Lennard (1998: 183) sensitively characterizes 'well-functioning relationships'. In his description he takes into account characteristics that are intimately related to the above conditions, such as the free flow of communication in the relationship, the basic trust pervading the relationship, and the behaviour that mediates mutual acceptance. He adds: 'The significant prevalence of constructive relationships in a social system contributes to the "health" of that system and also benefits from that "health". This holds true for organizations as small as families and as huge as global corporations.'

Careful readers will have realized that a relationship such as the one described above could give rise to a very high degree of personal growth for both partners. Readers familiar with the person-centred approach might even sense the constructive and at the same balanced energy of such a relationship, a relationship in which the whole, the 'we', is a lot more than the sum of its parts.

The conditions stated above, however, do not imply that communication is always smooth. Rather, the relationship as described allows for real encounter, encountering *each other* (Schmid 1994). It also facilitates constructive dialogue (Isaacs 1999). This is because one person can express what is at their disposal – their thoughts and feelings – and be sure that the other person will accept this and, in turn, offer an honest reaction/resonance from their frame of reference. Drawing on both these inner worlds the two people can then move in a direction that is mutually enriching. Such a perceivable constructive sharing effects not only a change in what has explicitly been expressed – the dialogue's subject matter – but also in the connection of the two people at an inner, implicit level.

After having read the manuscript of this book, our colleague Michael wrote an interesting comment that we wish to share: 'Typically, most relationships of readers will not at all be "person-centred", even if they try to live the three Rogers variables. What happens then? Can I let a relationship slide into a person-centred "mode"?' A related comment came from Gisela: 'When reading so many nice "things" about person-centred relationships, I experience more frustration in everyday life since such relationships are so rare.'

We ask: 'Does it make sense to know about person-centred relationships, if in everyday life they are so rare?' What do you think?

In our experience relationships that come close to matching the conditions of optimal communication *are* rare but nevertheless they do exist. Our appreciation and highest respect for them provided much of the motivation to write this book. It takes an effort to offer versatile ways of mediating motivation, inspiration, information and feelings that – based on your decision – you can take up and let unfold in you. However, we must not overlook the fact that each of us lives in a relationship system where one's own, say my, initiative is just one of several influences (referred to as 'attractors' in systems theory – Kriz 2007). The result or fate of my initiative depends on several environmental influences, some of which I can't control. The whole situation, however, can change in the course of time. This happens, for example, when the other has some experience that changes him or her and then takes up an issue that had been unheard and unattended to before. In the context of one's own initiative, while being included in a system, we consider the following quote as providing much insight: 'One can't bring the truth to the other person – rather it is found together' (Trüb 1951: 103).

An attempt at person-centred communication is likely to be promising if the two people frequently feel empathically attuned and mindful of each other and if they are able to mutually be themselves in their relationship. Sooner or later, after a considerable amount of time, the initiative of one will be positively experienced and received by the other. At times, conflicts seem inevitable, but can still offer useful material for future encounters. It all requires a high degree of sensitivity, flexibility, patience and also trust in the process, but can in the end lead to small but significant changes.

Person-centred communication is a person's path toward more sensitivity and continuing experience. It means recognizing and respecting how we can constructively communicate with diverse personalities, where we can meet and in which areas this is not (yet) possible. Besides communicating in the relationship, it is also necessary to understand ourselves in a multitude of situations, and to experience and accept the other as well: both unique beings.

## Co-actualization

We refer to the process of mutually experiencing person-centred attitudes and its potential influence on other people as *co-actualization*. It is a kind of actualization of two or more people including their relationship(s) that builds upon the principle of reciprocity of positive regard (Motschnig-Pitrik and Barrett-Lennard 2010). Co-actualization can spread to other interconnected people and their relationships. It encompasses the whole organismic experience, in particular the level beneath explicit ideas and thoughts. Thereby the relationship forms and unfolds in a self-organizing way – based on the way we interact with and encounter each other. This can be experienced by the relationship partners as well as by other people in their environment. Figure 5.3 depicts the co-actualization of two people and their relationship as well as the potential 'radiation' (continuation) of this process affecting the environment.

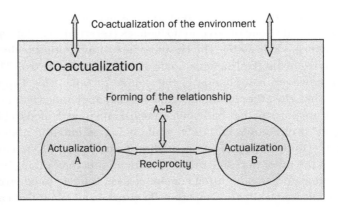

**Figure 5.3** Actualization and co-actualization based on reciprocity in the relationship

Co-actualization strongly resembles the process of an improving relationship as described by Rogers (1959; see also later in this chapter). The fact that the realness or congruence of one person in relationship to another person can support the other to find their 'reality' reciprocally, contributes to the actualization of that person. In this way, both can be facilitative to each other and reciprocally support each other in their respective actualization processes. Co-actualization can create, but does not necessarily result in, moments of meeting.

So how can we imagine co-actualization in practice? Let us look at an example. A conscientious young father (E) who is highly engaged in his job and has an overflowing calendar and a 1-year old son talks to an equally engaged colleague and mother of two children (R).

---

**Example from experience**

**E:** [Just about to leave for the weekend and with the door handle in his hand] This weekend I won't be able to do anything again because I'll have to take care of our boy. My wife is going to a seminar that she needs for the medical training in her specialization. This is the price to be paid when married to a partner who is highly engaged in her job.

**R:** You mean, you have to sacrifice your time and delay things due to your wife's career . . . and this causes you somehow not to feel at ease.

**E:** Yeah, it sure is unpleasant.

**R:** Sure – but I consider it wonderful that you help out so that Erika can study for her specialization.

**E:** Yes, you're right, I really do try hard.

R: And, your boy will love it to have daddy with him for the whole weekend, won't he?

E: Sure, my son and I get along perfectly, that's not the problem. But I simply can't move on with my own stuff. I have one appointment after another and so many important things lying around unfinished. Often, I get things done only after the deadline, such as, for example, the review of the EU project, the submission of our curriculum, etc. . . .

R: Yeah, it sounds really stressful. Constant distractions and appointments and the pile of things that need to get done gets larger and larger.

E: Exactly! But Erika needs the special training and, in addition, she must do the night shifts. Sometimes our parents help us out but this isn't always possible so there are bottlenecks. Yeah, there's no other way; it's just something that we have to go through.

R: Mhm, in my view it isn't easy to make the right decisions: who needs whom at what time and for how long . . .

E: Yes, you said it! So let's go right to it, and thank you for your text that you sent me for the curriculum; this piece I can integrate exactly as it stands.

R: I appreciate that! Yes, and it was cool to chat with you. Now I seem to know you a bit better and also have more insight into my situation, that in fact isn't much different from yours. Cheers and take care!

E: You too, and see you on Monday.

In this conversation, what shines through is how the two people perceive each other and what this means to them. To experience all this in the realness of an interpersonal relationship with a colleague and to personally articulate some issues can help to better understand one's own situation, motivation and responsibility as well as that of one's own partner. How might he feel when taking care of his child? The process doesn't end with the end of the conversation but proceeds and, on occasion, becomes conscious in each of the colleague's minds and may influence perceptions connected to it. Even though the textual 'reproduction' is limited, it should be clear that something changed in the relationship between the two people. In the working climate, mutual respect gains importance, such that, for example, there is more understanding, there is less of a bad feeling when occasionally having to leave a meeting before it ends, there is less extreme stress – and this has the potential to influence other relationships and systems. Perhaps there is even a change in how we experience our own partner.

Can the process of co-actualization also proceed if one partner confronts the other? Does co-actualization happen in moments in which we realize that we did something wrong or have overlooked or neglected something. Do we, in fact, grow or arrive at some insight from such an experience? We think that the process of co-actualization – very much like that of actualization – does not proceed in a linear way but has to overcome hindrances and take detours along the way. The 'inward' perspective of co-actualization is the reciprocal actualization of two or more people and their lived relationship; the 'outward' view shows an improved relationship between the people over a long period of time. This actualized relationship lives on in both/all partners. It can immediately be perceived by others and influence their relationship. It is the *interpersonal* that grows and radiates to the environment. Consider, for instance, the final statement of a participant in an international encounter group who had openly shared a lot in the group. She said: 'Your attentive listening and support for my problem helped me to see some issues more clearly. However, what impressed me *most* in our group and hence will stay with me for a long time was the *way we behaved toward each other...*'. The process that emanated from the individual interactions and the behaviour of the participants toward each other had left a stronger impression on this participant than her considerable progress in personal problem-solving.

We conjecture that person-centred encounter groups provide an extended space for co-actualization. This is because the effects of co-actualizing processes can be multiplied if more people mutually support each other. In such groups the main task of the facilitators is to provide a conducive climate in which all participants can grow personally through mutual sharing, in other words, they can co-actualize.

### The deteriorating and the improving relationship

Since the relationship is so vital for person-centred communication, we are going to consider Carl Rogers' generally specified description of a deteriorating and improving relationship. Even though the original formulation – due to its generic nature – sounds rather theoretical, in our view it captures exactly the essentials. This is why we want to repeat the processes according to Rogers (1959: 236–40). A more easily understandable exposition follows in the subsequent example that should be comprehensible even without knowing the theoretical formulation.

**The conditions of a deteriorating relationship.** For communication to be reduced, and for a relationship to deteriorate, the following conditions are necessary:

1   A person Y is willing to be in contact with person X and to receive communication from him.
2   Person X desires (at least to a minimal degree) to communicate and to be in contact with Y.

3   Marked incongruence exists in X among the three following elements:
   a)   his experience of the subject of communication with Y (which
        may be the relationship itself, or any other subject)
   b)   the symbolization of this experience in his awareness, in its rela-
        tion to his self-concept
   c)   his conscious, communicated expression (verbal and/or motor)
        of this experience.

**The process of a deteriorating relationship.** When the preceding conditions exist and continue, a process is initiated which tends to have these characteristics and directions:

1   The communications of X to Y are contradictory and/or ambiguous,
    containing:
    a)   expressive behaviours which are consistent with X's awareness
         of the experience to be communicated
    b)   expressive behaviours which are consistent with those aspects
         of the experience not accurately symbolized in X's awareness.
2   Y experiences these contradictions and ambiguities:
    a)   she tends to be aware only of B1a, that is X's conscious commu-
         nication[2]
    b)   hence her experience of X's communication tends to be incongru-
         ent with her awareness of the same
    c)   hence her response tends also to be contradictory and/or ambig-
         uous, having the same qualities described for X in B1a, b.
3   Since X is vulnerable, he tends to perceive Y's responses as poten-
    tially threatening:
    a)   hence he tends to perceive them in a distorted fashion, in ways
         which are congruent with his own self-structure
    b)   hence he is inaccurate in his perception of Y's internal frame
         of reference, and does not experience a high degree of empa-
         thy
    c)   because Y is perceived as a potential threat, X cannot and does
         not experience unconditional positive regard for Y.
4   Y experiences herself as receiving at most a selective positive
    regard.

[2]This is a crucial point. If Y is sufficiently open to their experience that she is aware
of X's other communication – described in B1b – then b and c below do not follow,
and her own response to X is clear and congruent. If in addition to her awareness
of all of X's communication she experiences an unconditional positive regard for
X, then this would become an improving relationship, as described in the following
sections.

5   Y experiences a lack of understanding or empathy.

6   The more Y experiences a selectiveness of positive regard and an absence of empathy, the less free she is to express feelings, the less likely she is to express self-referent feelings, the less likely she is to be extensional in her perceptions, the less likely she is to express incongruencies between self and experience, the less likely she is to reorganize her self-concept.

7   Since Y is expressing less of her feelings, X is even more unlikely to perceive Y's internal frame of reference with accuracy, and both inaccuracy of perception and distortion of perception make defensive reactions on X's part more likely.

8   Another characteristic which may exist, particularly if X's communication is primarily of negative feelings, is that those aspects of experience which are not accurately symbolized by X in his awareness tend, by defensive distortion of perception, to be perceived in Y.

9   If this occurs, Y tends to be threatened to the degree that this relates to her own incongruences, and she begins to exhibit defensive behaviours.

**The outcome of a deteriorating relationship.** The continuation of this process results in:

1   Increased defensiveness on the part of X and Y.

2   Communication which is increasingly superficial, expressive of less of the total individual.

3   The perceptions of self and others, because of the increased defensiveness, being organized more tightly.

4   Hence incongruence of self and expression remains in status quo, or is increased.

5   Psychological maladjustment is to some degree facilitated in both.

6   The relationship is experienced as poor.

The theoretical description will be become clearer if we illustrate it with a specific example. Rogers mentions a relationship between a mother X and her child Y in which there is versatile willingness to be in contact.

The mother feels: 'You annoy me because you interfere with my career' but she cannot be aware of this because the experience is incongruent with her concept of herself as a good mother. Her perception of this experience in herself is distorted, becoming: 'I am annoyed at this instance with your behaviour. I love you but I must punish you.' This is an acceptable symbolization of her experience, and it is this which she consciously communicates to the child.

But the child, Y, receives not only this conscious communication. He also experiences (but tends to be unaware of) the expressive behaviours indicating a more general dislike of him. His response may be of several sorts, but its essential characteristic is that it will express the incongruence which his mother's divided communication has set up in him. One possibility is that he will experience himself as bad and unloved, even when his awareness of his behaviour is that he is 'good'. Hence, he will act and feel guilty and bad, even when behaving in an approved manner. This type of response is threatening to the mother, because his behaviours expressing badness and feelings of being unloved threaten to bring into awareness her own rejecting feelings. Consequently she must further distort her perception of his behaviour, which now seems to her as 'sneaky' or 'underhanded' as well as being occasionally annoying. The more this cycle continues, the less acceptance Y feels, the less adequately he can express his feelings, the more difficult it is for his mother to achieve any empathic understanding, the more completely the two are estranged in the relationship, the more maladjusted each becomes (1959: 238).

Turning a deteriorating relationship into an improving relationship is not easy in practice. No matter how intensively we wish to make such a turn, we tend to maintain our own perceptions and to defend them. In this sense, in Carl Rogers' example the mother wasn't even aware of her whole experience and thus perceives the behaviour of her child in a 'wrong', distorted way.

If, however, the mother were open to the 'other communication' of her child (in which case condition 3 of the deteriorating relationship would become obsolete), then – depending on the age of the child – she could react in the following way: 'Hmm, right now I really don't have time for you... this isn't easy for me but it's important... and I very much look forward to being with you in the evening and playing ball with you before it gets dark.' In the case of a very small child, however, the reaction would need to be different.

In his formulation of the 19 propositions of the theory of personality and behaviour, Rogers deals with the cited example and, in particular, addresses potential changes in the mother's attitudes toward her son. Nykl (2005) further elaborates this example.

### Invitation to reflect

*Are you familiar with the process of a deteriorating relationship? How did/do you feel about that process? How does the deterioration express itself? Did you succeed in perceiving the unspoken 'other communication' of the other person, or in experiencing or understanding more of yourself? Did you feel positive regard toward the other person without giving up your self-regard?*

The step toward improvement can mean or require that a person transcends or suspends their momentary state and still stays with the other ('it isn't easy for me but it's important'), at the same time including the other ('...I look forward to being with you'). In this case, growth happens in both people as well as in their relationship (Barrett-Lennard 2005; Motschnig-Pitrik and Barrett-Lennard 2010).

There may be little moments that can indicate the change – a friendly look, the tone of voice, a touch, the recognition of the beginning of experiencing something. It is the symbolization of interest in the person and his or her 'story' in everyday conversation. It is the perception of real endeavour instead of just requiring and valuing results.

Rogers describes the conditions of an improved relationship as follows, whereby in relation to the example, X designates the mother (caregiver) and Y the child in the relationship that has undergone change.

**For communication to be improved.** For a relationship to improve, the following conditions are necessary:

1   A person Y is willing to be in contact with person X and to receive communication from her.
2   Person X desires (at least to a minimal degree) to communicate with and be in contact with Y.
3   Marked congruence exists in X among the three following elements:
    a)  her experience of the subject of communication with Y[3] (which may be the relationship itself, or any other subject)
    b)  the symbolization of this experience in her awareness, in its relation to her self-concept[4]
    c)  her communicative expression (verbal and/or motor) of this experience.[5]

---

[3]This means, for example, that the mother understands that the child is occasionally naughty because it wants more positive attunement and perceives the rejection in the way she behaves.

[4]In the example this means that the mother is aware of her career, her problems and the burden that lies on her, as well as the fact that she can't transfer her problems to her child.

[5]The conscious awareness of her experience reflects itself in her congruent behaviour and her communication.

**Example from experience: communication in a train compartment – an example of an improved relationship**

In a compartment with eight seats, seven are already occupied and lots of luggage makes the space tight. A young woman opens the compartment door and asks: 'Is there a seat vacant?' At least three people respond together, 'Yes.' While they are taking their bags off the seat, her large dog enters the compartment waving his tail and cautiously sniffing at the passengers. At that moment, an elderly gentleman says to the young woman who had just entered, 'But this will not work, moreover, with the dog – is that permitted at all?' Undistracted, self-confidently and at the same time politely, the owner responds: 'It'll be fine, he'll creep under the seat. And he even has his own ticket!' The elderly gentleman doesn't say anything but looks angrily at his newspaper. A young lady sitting at his side says confidently: 'For sure I don't mind the dog!' The situation is strained. The dog continues sniffing for a little while; the owner caresses him on his head and then the dog disappears under the seat without even being asked. Shortly thereafter one pasenger says in a friendly tone: 'Your dog seems to be used to going by train; do you travel often?' The owner responds: 'Right from the first time he behaved like this; that's what he always does.' The other passenger remarks, 'Yes, he looks very smart to me.' People return to their books and papers and there is little conversation. After about an hour, the dog comes up from beneath the seat and immediately creeps underneath another one. The elderly gentleman says to the owner, with a friendly smile on his face: 'He is very well behaved indeed, your dog.' From that moment on, there is a friendly, supportive atmosphere in the compartment. Passengers help each other to take their luggage from the rack and even to slip into their coats. As one person gets off the train and another asks whether a seat is vacant, the 'Yes' comes from seven voices.

In the last example from experience two interactions are particularly significant. First of all, the response of the owner regarding the doubts of the elderly man appear highly coherent. Her words and tone of voice are optimally matched, the confidence that there is a solution is clear, and, at the same time, the man's statement doesn't disconcert her at all. It is noticeable that the owner let the dog sniff the passengers without commanding him to lie down under her seat. We guess readers will sense that, with less congruence on the part of the young woman towards the man or the dog, the whole situation could have had a quite different ending. What happened allowed the man to change his opinion and even openly express his appreciation to the owner. All this brought the travellers into contact and created the change from 'thick air' to breathing freely.

Johnson and Johnson ([1975] 2006: 100) state in their 'social judgment theory' that the:

> *process of acceptance* is based on the individual promoting mutual goal accomplishment as the result of their perceived positive interdependence. The promotive interaction tends to result in frequent, accurate, and open interaction; accurate understanding of one another's perspective; inducibility; differentiated, dynamic, and realistic views of one another; high self-esteem; success and productivity; and expectations for positive and productive future interaction. The process of rejection results from oppositional or no interaction based on perceptions of negative or no interdependence.

**Solution and transformation of conflicts.** Confirmed by the insights from Johnson and Johnson as well as our own experience, we see in Rogers' process of the improved relationship the seed or core to the solution or transformation of conflicts. Since this process builds upon the concurrence of the three person-centred attitudes, the mature and fluent relationship between the attitudes can be seen as a precondition for a constructive way of dealing with conflict. The expression 'constructive way of dealing with conflict' instead of 'resolution of conflict' is chosen deliberately since we think that not every conflict *can* be resolved – but can at least be transformed for the better. Stillwell and Moormon (1997) named their book about a person-centred way of dealing with conflict , *Conflict is Inevitable: War is Optional*.

After having become acquainted with the processes of the deteriorating and improved relationship we add our own thoughts about the transition from a deteriorating to an improved relationship. According to Rogers (1959), the transition is possible if one person is able to perceive aspects of the inner world of the other person despite that person's incongruence. The first person responds congruently and the other person who is being incongruent in that area feels positively regarded. From this we infer that – even in cases of extreme offence to a person – it is the experienced congruent reaction and the positive regard of another person that make the transition possible. This may sound like a paradox, but it can be imagined as throwing a lifebelt to a person who is drowning but still perceiving the rescue operation.

**Relationships within oneself.** According to pluralistically-oriented conceptions such as, for example, those by Barrett-Lennard, Mearns and Schulz von Thun, we unite in ourselves various interrelated parts or compartments. These interact with or act against each other. All approaches share the fact that a healthy 'inner communication' is a precondition for creative problem-solving. It is in accord with person-centred communication, 'applied to' ourselves, to integrate the individual parts accordingly in different situations, to perceive all sensations acceptingly, to take them seriously and to conduct a real 'inner dialogue' (Rodenstock and Beutel 2008). A constant suppression or rejection of some inner part tends to cause that part to occasionally take charge and cause dissonances and incongruence. Barrett-Lennard (2005: 53) notes that relationships to and within ourselves are strongly related to our relationships with others, 'Even when occupied consciously with ourselves, inner conversations resemble those we have had or anticipate with others.'

**Invitation to reflect**

*Do you occasionally have or conduct inner conversations? Which values do they have for you? Do you let other people, whom you consider significant for you, participate in your inner conversations?*

In his chapter 'Persons or science' Rogers (1961) provides us with an example of 'inner communication' that he engaged in over many years. His main question and the subject of his 'inner communication' was the (im)possibility of reaching coherence in himself between his self as therapist-person and his self as therapist-scientist. As therapist-person, he lived a real interpersonal relationship that at its best moments had a strong subjective influence; as therapist-scientist, he wanted to act as objectively as possible and hence needed distance. The acceptance of these two sides and conducting (even in written form) an inner communication led him to a higher level of cognition/insight than each of the starting positions that he had held initially. Interested readers should look at Rogers (1961: 222), which gives the result of his 'inner encounter' that, in a nutshell, accepts subjectivity as the starting point for subsequent objectified research.

Summarizing, we see the goal of 'inner communication' as experiencing more of ourselves, better approaching our inner core, finding our direction and thereby getting along with and mitigating ambiguities. In other words, building a relationship with ourselves in which we can rely on ourselves despite not being univocally united but rather accommodating diversity.

## Person-centred communication is development-process-oriented

Rogers characterizes the fluency of the life process as: 'Life, at its best, is a flowing, changing process in which nothing is fixed' (1961: 27). He considers the actualizing tendency as the motive for the development of every organism, hence also the human being. In the last decade, Jürgen Kriz built on findings from interdisciplinary systems theory to support some of Rogers' thought regarding the actualizing tendency (Kriz 1998, 2007, 2013).

## Actualizing tendency

As already indicated, the actualizing tendency can be seen as a motive for our (communicative) behaviour. Let us consider its definition as given by Rogers (1959: 196):

> This is the inherent tendency of the organism to develop all its capacities in ways which serve to maintain or enhance the organism... It involves development toward the differentiation of organs and of functions, expansion in terms of growth, expansion of effectiveness through the use of tools, expansion and enhancement through reproduction. It is development toward autonomy and away from heteronomy, or control by external forces... It should be noted that this basic actualizing tendency is the only motive which is postulated in this theoretical system.

In his book *On Personal Power*, Rogers (1978: 240) provides examples illustrating that the actualizing tendency is also present in lower creatures and even in plants and controls their actualization of potentialities. Such organisms are self-organizing and, under normal conditions, develop toward their optimal functioning and away from external control. But what does this mean for interpersonal contact and communication? Rogers didn't thnink that he succeeded in creating in a person something that was not already there. However, whenever he provided a facilitative climate, the constructive, directional tendency brought about personal development.

Building upon the attitudes of the facilitator, the facilitative relationship leads to a direction of becoming whereby the path is equally the goal. Rogers (1959: 27) formulated the outcomes of a person-centred climate – as a result of therapy but also outside of therapeutic relationship – in the area of personality and behaviour as follows, whereby the first issue is the essential one and the following issues are just more explicit descriptions of the essential issue. If, while reading, we substitute the word 'client' with the word 'person', then the result is a precise specification of the direction toward which every person tends to develop in the climate of person-centred communication.

## Outcomes in personality and behaviour

These are the changes which are hypothesized as being relatively permanent (and in our example the client happens to be a man):

1   The client is more congruent, more open to his experience, less defensive.

2   He is consequently more realistic, objective, extensional in his perceptions.

3   He is consequently more effective in problem-solving.

4   His psychological adjustment is improved, being closer to the optimum.

5   As a result of the increased congruence of self and experience (4 above) his vulnerability to threat is reduced.

6   As a consequence of 2 above, his perception of his ideal self is more realistic, more achievable.

7   As a consequence of the changes in 4 and 5 his self is more congruent with his ideal self.

8   As a consequence of the increased congruence of self and ideal self, and the greater congruence of self and experience, tension of all types is reduced – physiological tension, psychological tension, and the specific type of psychological tension defined as anxiety.

9   He has an increased degree of positive self-regard.

10  He perceives the locus of evaluation and the locus of choice as residing within himself:

   a)   as a consequence of 9 and 10 he feels more confident and more self-directing

   b)   as a consequence of 1 and 10, his values are determined by an organismic valuing process.

11  As a consequence of 1 and 2, he perceives others more realistically and accurately.

12  He experiences more acceptance of others, as a consequence of less need for distortion of his perceptions of them.

13  His behaviour changes in various ways:

   a)   since the proportion of experience assimilated into the self-structure is increased, the proportion of behaviours which can be 'owned' as belonging to the self is increased

   b)   conversely, the proportion of behaviours which are disowned as self-experiences, felt to be 'not myself,' is decreased

   c)   hence his behaviour is perceived as being more within his control.

14  His behaviour is perceived by others as more socialized, more mature.

15  As a consequence of 1, 2, 3, his behaviour is more creative, more uniquely adaptive to each new situation, and each new problem, more fully expressive of his own purposes and values.

The developmental tendency inherent in each organism is directed toward some developmental goal. As a consequence of that directedness of the developmental tendency toward a developmental goal, we deduce that every other directive control on a person's development undergoes the risk to deviate from that person's own developmental tendency. This argument underlines the benefits of a non-directive way of communication in which each person can develop according to his or her inherent direction. But in that case can we not develop toward being irresponsible egoists? We believe that this is not the case since we come equipped with a basic need for positive regard and this need is reciprocal. If others feel positively regarded by us, we ourselves feel positive regard. This pleasant experience counteracts irresponsible egoism. Furthermore, as living beings we depend on relationships with others which is why our congruence must include a social component and direction.

To be able to fully exploit their personal potential, each person needs access to all their inner resources – feelings as well as cognitions. In this context we observe that our culture and knowledge society might contribute to a stronger emphasis and demand on our intellect than on our capacity to feel and to empathize. Feelings tend to be ignored at the cost of an increase in intellectual knowledge. They shift to the background, and tend to be less and less available. In extreme cases this leads to alienation, in that we consistently distance ourselves more and more from our origins. This is why we favour a balanced integration of intellectual growth with emotional development, particularly in schools.

### The process-continuum, changes in the method of communicating

The above-mentioned consideration is important for communication in particular since a holistic expression in which body language, mimics, gesticulations and spoken words are in harmony contributes a lot to understandability and transparency. Rogers (1961: 125–59) identified seven characteristic phases of a person's development toward full, holistic expressiveness which are set in motion when a person feels accepted or confirmed by at least one significant other person. He emphasized that the phases involve milestones on a continuum, that the transitions are fluent and that the phase in which a person resides depends only to a very small degree on the subject/field of communication and on environmental influences.

The seven stages we briefly deal with here are arranged on a continuum spanning from rigidity and fixity of the self-concept to flowingness and a 'being in motion' quality. As already mentioned, in each instant of time, every person resides at some point on this continuum.

In the *first stage*, a person is not willing to talk about themselves, just about external things. In the *second stage*, a person's expression starts cautiously moving toward parts of the person itself; however, problems are perceived as lying external to the person. For example, a person residing on level two might say: 'Disorganization keeps cropping up in my life' (Rogers 1961: 133). In the *third stage*, people talk about themselves, however self is seen as an external object. Whenever feelings are addressed, the person exclusively refers to *past* feelings. In the *fourth stage*, people describe their momentary feelings but in the form of external objects. For example, a person might say: 'It discourages me to feel dependent because it means I'm kind of hopeless about myself' (Rogers 1961: 137). People in this stage tend to discover personal constructs and start questioning their validity: 'Does this necessarily hold in any case?' The *fifth stage* is characterized by the free expression of feelings as in the present. People can explore them and discover new experiences instead of being dominated by constructs. For example: 'I expected to get a severe rejection – this I expect all the time... somehow I guess I even feel it with you... It's hard to talk about because I want to be the best I possibly can be with you' (Rogers 1961: 139).

In the very crucial *sixth stage* feelings that had previously been 'stuck' can be experienced with immediacy and richness and are accepted. People are able to live their subjective experience. This full experiencing is often accompanied by physiological loosening and is expressed by body language. Moistness in the eyes or spontaneously giving a friend a sincere hug are frequently evident. According to Rogers, in the crucial moment of integration, the phrase 'internal communication' is no longer quite correct, for 'communication between different internal foci is no longer necessary, because they become *one*' (Rogers 1961: 148). In the *seventh stage* feelings are perceived with immediacy and richness of detail. The experiencing of feeling can be used as a referent and each situation is experienced in its newness, not as some past event.

For interpersonal communication, the advanced stages mean that situations are experienced in a quite complete and *differentiated* way. Since perceptions are not distorted by conditions of worth, suitable, often better decisions can be made in complex situations – the person is also able to act in a way that is appropriate to a given or new situation. The path from stage to stage requires time and energy and leads along stony roads. This is indicated by the dashed lines in Figure 5.4. Even though the lines in the figure are straight, we don't want to give the impression that in real life such paths lead so straightforwardly to the goal. Rather, the figure is intended to illustrate the developmental tendencies in various dimensions and to invite readers to decide for themselves whether they want to move in the direction of the goals at which person-centred communication is targeted.

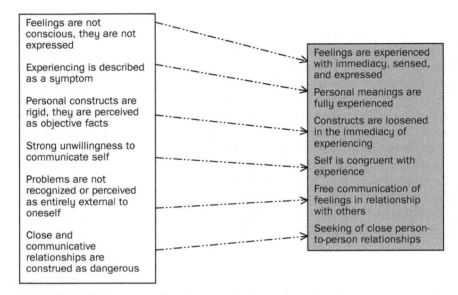

**Figure 5.4** Individual dimensions in the process-continuum that lead from stage 1 (left-hand side) to an area of high maturity (right-hand side, properties of the 'fully functioning person'). The process-continuum was described by Rogers (1961, 1983), and the figure is our simplified illustration of a lifelong process

**Invitation to reflect**

*Did you try to position yourself on the process-continuum? Do you tend to trust your feelings? Do you attend to them consciously? Do you express them exceptionally, occasionally or regularly? Are there people or situations that motivate or block you in expressing your inner world? What are those people or situations like and how do you feel in their presence? What do you think/ sense about expressing feelings at work?*

## Consequences

What are the consequences of person-centred communication? They certainly differ from person to person and from context to context – and they keep adapting and floating rather that staying fixed. Not every person comes equipped with the same qualities. Moreover, our communication is influenced by the immediate environment of our family as well as the wider context of friends and colleagues at work. Nevertheless, we can identify some tendencies that Rogers (1961) mentioned and that are confirmed by our own experience. Let us start with family life and then move on to the study and work environments.

## Expression of feelings

When they become more open to experiences, and hence more conscious of themselves, people tend to perceive and express their feelings and meanings more clearly and in a less 'encoded' way. This concerns both negative feelings such as unwillingness, anger, envy and disappointment, as well as positive feelings such as liking, softness, positive attunement and love. Parents, children and partners begin to express these feelings that they genuinely sense in themselves instead of hiding them and waiting until they accumulate and find their own way to surface. Even though it may seem that the expression of such feelings might cause problems, the opposite seems to be the case – relationships tend to gain in quality and immediacy rather than deteriorating. Alternatively, people become properly aware of how big the rift is between them and can consciously decide to work on their relationship, not do anything, or separate.

## Self-determination

The more clearly we are able to perceive and to express our inner world, the more we accept this in the other. In this way we are more open to the idea that each person can possess his or her feelings, values, goals and meanings, and that they may well differ from ours. It becomes easier for us to listen acceptingly without closing ourselves to the experience of the other or attacking it. There is more readiness to accept the other as an independent personality. Rogers (1961: 326) suggested that children would be more likely to develop into responsible, self-determined people if they grew up in a person-centred climate. They could express their feelings and even if at times their behaviour was rejected they wouldn't need to *deny* their feelings. Their parents would also express their feelings that would frequently be different from those of their children and would also tend to differ from parent to parent. A child would grow up with respect for his or her own feelings but also for those of others. His or her behaviour would find an adequate balance between his or her own feelings and those of the other person and the child would not need to hide behind a façade. He or she would be relatively free from the 'musts' that burden many of us.

Regarding the effects of a person-centred climate on families, Rogers (1961: 327) writes:

> The family circle tends in the direction of becoming a number of separate and unique persons with individual goals and values, but bound together by the real feelings – positive and negative – which exist between them, and by the satisfying bond of mutual understanding of at least a portion of other's private worlds.

**Invitation to reflect**

*What do you think/feel about the direction of the development in families as described in the quote by Rogers? Is it a desirable direction in your view? How would you characterize the direction in which a family might develop optimally?*

*For those who are members of a family: how close or far is the family you are part of from the direction you consider optimal?*

## Creativity

The higher expressiveness of people and their access to inner as well as inter-personal resources leads to a higher level of creativity in a person-centred climate. This has been confirmed in tests for creativity and also comes to the forefront in the way people approach tasks and problems and are able to engage with them and express themselves (Rogers 1983; Sollárová 2005). For example, Sollárová (2005) reports that students who had attended person-centred courses had significantly better results in creativity tests than students who had been instructed in a directive manner. She adopted Guilford's testing model in which verbal aspects of creative thinking were assessed via the completion of hypothetical situations, such as 'What would happen if there was no alcohol?'

## Interpersonal relationships and collaboration in teams

In courses in which students perceive a person-centred climate they find it easier than in other comparable courses to build interpersonal relation-ships and to collaborate in teams (Motschnig-Pitrik 2013). The number of dropouts in courses that are facilitated in a person-centred way tends to be extremely low, sometimes even zero. Students reflect that the stronger direct contact and open communication significantly contribute to getting to know each other better and – time permitting – collaborating more intensively. At the end of person-centred courses students frequently find high value in the contacts and friendships they have made in the course of learning together. In a few cases students don't like the person-centred approach because they come to class with a totally different attitude; equally, many students say that they wish the course had not ended.

We enjoy similarly constructive and cooperative relationships as well as a high level of engagement in our academic work group in which person-centred communication is prevalent and attracts several masters and doctoral students. It is only fair to say, however, that our quite open communicative style is not free of occasional conflicts which pose challenges to be overcome and used as a source of experiential learning.

### From expert/boss to counsellor/facilitator

Empowerment and appreciation of each individual as a person with unique competences and potentials allows hierarchic power structures to dissolve and gradually develop into teams with members having approximately equal rights. Such a transformation is more likely if it springs from a senior person in the hierarchy. Each person is included according to their potentials and competences and carries co-responsibility. However, for such an organization to function properly it first of all needs well-functioning communication between all concerned.

**Decision-making and conflict management.** In order to make unanimous decisions, all concerned need to be listened to and understood. This can be a long and tedious process, however, the involved persons tend to stand fully behind such decisions in which they have had a say. Furthermore, teams tend to learn from experience and person-centred communication to make decisions more efficiently. In a similar vein, a person-centred approach to conflicts requires that the conflicted partners profoundly understand themselves and each other, and the circumstances and environmental influences present at that time (Stillwell 2013). In addition, mutual acceptance and occasionally some readiness to 'jump over one's shadow' is needed – in other words, one's own personal growth. At times it can be important to learn – through communicating in a person-centred way – that, at a given point in time, some conflicts do not have a (real) solution and we need to live with them and not allow ourselves to be compromised or enslaved too much by them. Let us look at a conflict situation in a partnership (compare also Stillwell and Moormon 1997).

**Example from therapy**

Karin likes to plan in advance while Martin is much more spontaneous. Both are attracted by the differences in the other and grant each other independence. They often get into conflict and experience breakdown in their relationship. For example, while Martin wanted to buy new stereo equipment that he had just discovered, Karin thought the equipment had to fit with the style of the apartment and had to be chosen and integrated carefully. This caused a conflict and a compromise of the kind 'This time we'll follow your wants and next time mine' could be considered a fair deal and would likely help to avoid further argument, but it didn't really contribute to improving the relationship between them. Each will likely sigh at having to accommodate the other; such a compromise will reduce their enjoyment in what they do together.

How high is the cost of avoiding a conflict? Is it so high that each solution suffices to re-establish peace and tolerance? While a fast solution via compromise is often well suited to solve a conflict, this tactic can also lead to a chronically compromised position – one of isolation and loneliness.

It can be assumed that conflicts arise due to the different needs of the partners. The question is how they get resolved, which conflicts make sense and which are senseless. The assimilated attitude of respect can help to solve conflicts without reproach and justification: listening to each other and accepting the other. Even if the resolution in a particular situation may look similar to the one described above, something different actually happens. The position of the other can – and in effect is very likely to – loosen up and not harden. The other will be more strongly accepted in his or her way and follow up situations are likely to be addressed and solved in a more composed and suitable manner. It is not to be assumed that future situations will be free of conflict, however, their solution will no longer pose an ever-growing burden.

## Higher sensitivity, more conscious and complex perception

Through the increased openness to one's own awareness and a real interest in other people, established patterns of thought are loosened and perception tends to be sharpened and extended. As a consequence, the environment tends to be perceived in less biased and multifaceted ways. More appropriate solutions for emerging problems and tasks can be sought. Instead of acting too impulsively, the environment is granted the necessary time for development. Partners and groups who communicate in a person-centred way typically do not push for fast agreements and contracts. Rather they tend to accept the floating processes and ongoing changes as well as the necessity to grow through them.

### Influence and engagement without commandment or dictatorship

Person-centred communication requires high personal engagement and enables processes without imposing them. It is part of a larger whole that can develop but cannot be enforced. This often requires a lot of patience and empathizing without 'success' ever being guaranteed. We were helped by the accumulation of experience and understanding to deal with occasional frustration, accepting it equally as part of the developmental process.

## Person-centred communication transcends culture

In this section our goal is twofold. Firstly, we explore whether the features of person-centred communication that we have described so far apply *regardless of a particular national culture* or whether they depend on our cultural origin. Secondly, we speculate about how far the person-centred way of being might qualify as a kind of '*dynamic meta-culture*' at a level that transcends individual national cultures while trying to be empathically attuned to them and not judging them.

These questions are highly complex and sophisticated and hence might be considered to be outside the scope of a book for practitioners. Nevertheless, in our time of intercultural mix and entanglement, such questions appear existential such that we hope our readers will excuse the highly sketchy style and superficial stance we take and will find ideas that they consider worthwhile to follow up and reflect upon personally.

### Intercultural validity

Do the features identified in this chapter characterize person-centred communication across cultures, or are they primarily tuned to western cultures? What about Asian culture in which openness tends not to be appropriate on many occasions? What about numerous conflicts between nations that demonstrate a lack of proper understanding on both sides?

Certainly, the features of person-centred communication should not be confused with a 'silver bullet' that immediately solves all problems. This is because person-centred communication does not exist 'in a test tube' but rather resides in real people like you and me, who enter and co-create relationships based on mutual expectations, demands and often mental models or valuing conditions of which we/they may not be aware. Indeed, person-centred communication is often a non-linear process toward the goal of mutual understanding that, when reached, tends to reward us with a feeling of pleasure, indicating the 'proper' direction of moving forward.

### Invitation to reflect

*Think of a colleague, friend, or relative who originates from a culture different to yours. What can you learn from him or her about yourself? What makes the two of you different to each other and in what respect do you feel enriched or constrained in that relationship?*

In relationships with a high degree of diversity among partners, mutual understanding tends to require more effort and patience. This is because we don't 'implicitly' share the 'same' meanings for words, have different native languages, tend to expect a different amount of context in statements, might have a different sense of time, come equipped with a different degree of emotionality, practise different greeting habits, etc., etc. In such relationships, in particular, active listening, transparent expression and careful checking of understanding are indispensable (Lago 2011).

In the authors' experience, from Rogers' three attitudes, acceptance and a desire for deep understanding hardly ever meet reservations from international participants. This is not always the case with openness. Interestingly, when talking to Asian students about their attitude toward openness (e.g. in the course of a seminar in Austria) they tend to respond that it is something they need to adjust to but it feels OK and certainly more honest than suppressing your opinion, as is customary in their country.[6] While it might be too risky to generalize, such statements appear to confirm Rogers' perspective that appropriate openness – of course combined with acceptance and a quest for empathic understanding – is essential for the positive development of interpersonal relationships.

On a more scientific basis, currently there exist various sources and indicators that speak in favour of the intercultural validity of person-centred communication. Let us consider a few of them:

- Rogers' theory of personality and behaviour (1951) doesn't include any culture-specific preconditions. Indeed, broad parts of the theory – basically all those for which a relationship to neuroscience can be identified – were found to be consistent with

[6]Part of the challenge is that in some cultures errors must not be admitted due to severe punishment if an error is made.

the findings of neuroscientific studies as reported by Damasio (2000, 2003, 2012) and studied in the context of the person-centred approach (Motschnig-Pitrik and Nykl 2003; Sheldon *et al.* 2004; Lux 2007, 2013; Motschnig-Pitrik and Lux 2008; Silani *et al.* 2013).

- The person-centred approach has made its way onto all continents, both practically and scientifically. Intercultural, person-centred workshops are taking place all over the world (Rogers 1980; Lago and McMillan 1998; Wood 2008) and could even position themselves in international peace work (Rogers 1980). Another example confirming the intercultural dimension of person-centred communication is a recent coaching model for use in multicultural environments that has been developed in South Africa on the basis of positive psychology and the person-centred approach (Van Zyl and Stander 2013). On a theoretical level Nykl (2005) elaborates the links between the person-centred approach and other renowned theories that have had international resonance, such as Vygotsky's theory of the higher and lower mental functions.
- Furthermore, Klaus Heinerth's work on the developmental conditions for infants appears to be interesting in the context of the intercultural relevance of person-centred attitudes. In the course of a research workshop in Vienna, Heinerth reported that infants receiving too little empathy and acceptance tend to develop personal and neural disorders (Heinerth 2001). This indicates that empathy and acceptance are needed for the healthy psychological development of human infants.

Thus, person-centred attitudes can be considered as the core of understandable, intercultural communication (Fischer 2005). Because it respects diverse subjective realities, person-centred communication gets along with the pluralism of our society and considers its acceptance a gain more than a loss (Steenbuck 2005). A precondition, however, is a flexible, reliable inner valuing process that, in each new situation, helps us to decide, communicate and act in resonance with ourselves.

## A dynamic meta-culture for relating?

Carl Rogers, his team, and the community that evolved from their 'heritage' have researched and described the features of facilitative interpersonal attitudes and relationships and left it up to us to keep them alive and developing in our ever-changing, increasingly intercultural society.

What has been said so far indicates that while personal expression may differ from culture to culture (and in fact from person to person depending on their inner world at each moment), the characteristics of person-centred communication apply *regardless of specific cultural background*. It thus seems appropriate to consider person-centred communication as an unfolding interactional resource of qualities, a sort of *'meta-culture'*, in the sense of a most promising candidate for a culture-transcending, overarching level of interpersonal relating (Lago 2011; Motschnig-Pitrik *et al.* 2013). This level exists beyond or side-by side 'traditional' cultures – and hence must not ignore them but rather respect them – and emerges when actually living the assumptions and theories of the person-centred approach. In an article on the person-centred approach to constructive international communication, Colin Lago (2013: 211) summarizes the capacities needed for enhancing communication as: 'The capacity of being real and fully present, of fully accepting the other, of striving for a respectful understanding-seeking stance towards the other without giving up on one's own ideas and values', and, furthermore 'not only being fully open to others but also being open to the possibility of being changed by the encounter'. This demands 'a deep sense of security' in the practitioner and 'implies a willingness to take interpersonal risks without being able to predict outcomes'. It furthermore 'requires a patient capacity to listen deeply to others and to be committed to the process of communication rather than any specific outcome [as well as] a deep trust in the other's motivations and capacities'. Overall the 'approach', when embodied and practised by sincere committed people has the potential to offer added value to any (international) communication or event.

The appreciation of the person-centred approach across all continents and numerous nations and religions confirms this statement: in a nutshell, with his work, Carl Rogers and his team opened up a path toward a 'we' that has the capacity of being enriched by and enriching others regardless of national culture.

---

### Improving intercultural understanding

A small step toward better intercultural understanding can be achieved through a variant of an exercise on active listening in triads:

Students of different nationalities form triads such that in each triad there are participants from at least two different nationalities. Then, the *speaker* shares how he or she perceives their own nationality and what he or she thinks that the peculiarities of their nationality are. The *active listener* accompanies the speaker while the *observer* observes how the conversation develops and how well the listener accompanies the speaker. Then, the roles are exchanged so that every participant takes on each role.

In the second round, students share what they had known and thought about the other nationality and their potential experiences so far with people from that nationality. Again, each participant takes on each of the three roles of speaker, listener and observer. Then, experiences from the exercise are shared in the plenum with special emphasis on any changes in perception about one's own or the other nationalities.

## Summary

In this chapter we recalled the basic assumption regarding the nature of the human being and summarized the well-specified theory underlying the person-centred approach as derived from its home-field of psychotherapy and counselling. Then we took up Rogers' hypothesis – namely that his theory would equally hold for any interpersonal relationship in which the growth of the partners was aimed at – and carried it on to the areas of interpersonal communication and international communication. This happened by sketching the kind of communication which would be implied by a person-centred way of being and subsequently inviting readers to reflect upon some of our, as well as their own, communicative situations. Essentially, if the goal of communication is to thoroughly understand the other, share with him or her, make oneself understood by the other and meet him or her at eye-level with respect to the other, then person-centred communication might prove highly effective. In that case it would be beneficial to both or all partners and moreover improve their relationship. If however, the goal is to dominate, control, manipulate, judge or threaten the other, person-centred communication would definitely be misplaced.

# PART II
## Practice

# 6 Person-centred communication in counselling and psychotherapy

*How can I provide a relationship which this person may use for his own personal growth?*

(Rogers 1961: 32)

---

**In this chapter you will learn about:**

- The particular features that characterize person-centred therapeutic relationships and communicative exchanges between client and therapist
- The commonalities and differences between:
  - individual and group psychotherapy
  - therapy groups and encounter groups
  - the therapeutic relationship and non-therapeutic relationships such as between teacher and student or between partners
- Frequent habits or patterns that stand in the way of having facilitative, person-centred communication in everyday exchanges and what problems such rigid patterns can cause

---

In this chapter we aim to provide some insight into person-centred psychotherapy by highlighting its specific communicative aspect and delineating it from other relationships, while at the same time never leaving the scope of the conditions of the therapeutic process (see Chapter 5 or Rogers 1959: 213). Rogers noted repeatedly that the same conditions hold for any interpersonal relationship in which growth is the goal. However, he reformulated the conditions for interpersonal relationships (1959: 235–40) such as not to provide ground for unnecessary discussion and thereby again confirmed his scientific foresight. First let us turn to his view about communication:

The point which is most likely to be misunderstood is the omission of any statement that the therapist *communicates* his empathic understanding and his unconditional positive regard to the client. Such a statement has been omitted only after much consideration, for these reasons. It is not enough for the therapist to communicate, since the communication must be received, as pointed out in condition 6, to be effective. It is not essential that the therapist *intend* such communication, since often it is by some casual remark, or involuntary facial expression, that the communication is actually achieved. However, if one wishes to stress the communicative aspect which is certainly a vital part of the living experience, then condition 6 might be worded in this fashion:

6. That the communication to the client of the therapist's empathic understanding and unconditional positive regard is, at least to a minimal degree, achieved.

(Rogers 1959: 213)

Rogers makes clear that communication can proceed intentionally and unintentionally; it happens along multiple channels, and includes the actual experience together with the radiation of the experienced feelings. Therefore an authentic reproduction of the momentary climate and relationship is almost impossible. Nevertheless, such reproductions are essential for learning as part of personal development as well as for greater theoretical understanding. However, in this chapter we are going to focus on the relationship whose aspects can reveal something about communication.

Let us begin by sharing a few sentences about the tough path Carl Rogers took to confirm his theories in research and practice and to get them acknowledged.

After finishing his studies, Rogers worked with delinquent children for 12 years. Gradually he realized that he couldn't comply with the system that was in place at that time and which required extensive diagnoses (up to 80 pages) and counselling amongst psychologists about how the child was to be treated. A few decisive cases finally convinced Rogers that completely different options existed. Whereas in the beginning he would ask how to treat the patient, he changed the question to: 'How can I provide a relationship which this person may use for his own personal growth?' (Rogers 1961: 32). The treatment focusing on 'objects' changed toward a communicative exchange in which a trustful relationship could unfold.

While at first universities didn't ascribe high psychological value to Rogers' views, he was offered a professorship at Ohio State University in 1940 and could research his concepts with students who were eager for knowledge. However, he stood against two powerful streams, behaviourism and psychoanalysis. Also, he was clearly told that a psychologist could never do psychotherapy. But things were about to change. Rogers didn't seek a fight but rather collected facts through researching psychotherapeutic interviews, something that was strongly opposed in psychoanalysis at that time. His publications reached the public and turned prevalent views upside-down. Later, it became apparent that the attitudes he had postulated for therapy were also important and even vital in other interpersonal relationships aiming at growth, relationship improvement and better communication. Rogers was also intrigued by group processes and gradually achieved appreciation throughout the whole world.

For us it is a particular honour to address here the oft-occurring question about the distinction between facilitative relationships in therapy, encounter groups and other situations. This is because misunderstandings can arise if postulating that the same conditions (except for condition 2) hold for relationship situations in which a step towards psychological adjustment (Rogers 1959: 206) happens, as they hold for the therapeutic process which aims at the resolution of incongruence on the way to psychological adjustment.

## The person-centred therapeutic relationship and process

This is a special relationship between two people, the therapist and the client. The therapist is congruent in the relationship, regards the client positively, and tries to understand him or her empathically while actively listening. Once the client perceives the trust in the relationship (this can happen in the first hour but can equally be a long process), once they understand they are accepted in all aspects of their self as well as empathically, they start to become more open and the feeling that they might be threatened through being judged ceases. They can then explore their experiences and feelings and inquire into their self (Rogers 1951: 510–11).

The seemingly simple conditions of the therapeutic process that Rogers postulated (1959: 213) and our modifications for general interpersonal relationships have already been described in Chapter 5. These conditions need to hold if psychological growth and consequently a step towards psychological adjustment is to happen. Rogers refers to the valuing process increasingly becoming an organismic one (1959: 210). In therapy this process is understood as self-experience and as the dissolution of incongruence or rigid psychic constructs, or as the process of becoming aware, revaluing and assimilating denied experiences in the self. During such processes of self-experiencing, clients also assimilate the therapist's positive regard toward themselves (the clients) and thus strengthen their positive self-regard (Rogers 1951).

In the following we're going to describe some important aspects of the therapeutic relationship which are anchored in the conditions of the therapeutic process.

## Non-directivity

A particularly important aspect of person-centred psychotherapy is the less regarded and understood *non-directivity*. It doesn't express itself only in the therapist's utterance 'mhm' as an expression of acceptance and understanding of the client, but in the fact that there is no analysing and just a little explaining such that the 'dead ends' of the relationship are avoided. Of course, non-directivity also protects the client from being overburdened with too many painful discoveries. Non-directivity, importantly, gives the client the chance to benefit from the relationship, gain their own experiences, gather their own energies and build and activate their potential for meeting the requirements of everyday life.

The following example from therapy illustrates the difference between directive and non-directive therapist responses.

---

### Example from therapy

**Directive:** You were angry with your brother; that was not good; you must learn to accept your brother.

**Non-directive:** You were angry with your brother, weren't you...You're saying, you should not be angry with him because he's got a positive side too...Just let go of your anger...Now I clearly feel your emotion [or] I would like to feel your anger...You felt he misbehaved totally...And his other side indeed matters to you...So you can be angry and also appreciate your brother, can't you?...So how do you feel now you have expressed both your feelings toward your brother?

---

Each sentence, however, needs to be adjusted to the immediate situation, and it is important to attend carefully to the modulation of one's voice (Lewis *et al.* 1959). Non-directivity implies accompanying the client's feelings, the confrontation of seemingly contradictory feelings, their disentanglement, the perception of their meaning and their appropriate communication – all this without setting up any kind of rules but instead targeting the client's self-experience.

Non-directivity is a special skill of the person-centred therapist, and requires considerable experience. It is an ability that is in part learned but also based on empathic understanding. It is quite rare in *everyday* life and hardly recognized by the other person – even though it increases the vitality of life.

Non-directivity also bears in itself the habit that the client's hidden feelings and emotions (residing below the threshold of consciousness) are addressed only once a certain readiness from the client's point of view can be sensed.

### Situational acting

Acting in response to a particular situation is related to non-directivity (Nykl 2005). It is a kind of acting based on the empathically understood situation such that the other person is motivated to an instinctive or intuitive perception of the situation and a corresponding reaction. It is therefore a similar phenomenon to non-directivity.

An example of situational acting would be to act on something or make a comment instead of giving a lengthy explanation to achieve the same result or to clearly articulate one's wishes, or to let an unfolding experience mature (in oneself or in others) and not destroy it by explanations or other means.

### Emotions

Now we arrive at another peculiarity of person-centred psychotherapy: the therapist focuses on the client's emotions and feelings rather than on the content of his or her statements. This is because the perception of the undistorted meaning of the feelings (self-experience) in the climate of a person-centred relationship leads to the gradual ordering of all psychic processes and the wisdom of the whole organism is included in the experience (Nykl 2005). This is exactly what stands at the centre of Rogers' unshakeable belief regarding the constructive human capacities, oriented towards socialization – his belief in the genuine, constructive, organismic experience leading to socialized behaviour.

From the perspective of the neurosciences, person-centred psychotherapy directly reverses the wrong conditionings in the limbic system, as described by Gerhard Roth (2009: 165). However, we feel this can't be achieved – or would be very hard to achieve – by taking a directive approach (Nykl 2005). It is assumed that new, adaptive limbic neural structures are generated that support more of the conscious, balanced control in the self (Rogers 1951: 510–11).

### Example from therapy

In a group a client was grieving about a friend who had passed away. To him, the last touch of hands was important, and he didn't want to forget it. Another participant said that this would never be forgotten. This comment was fitting but nevertheless directive and wouldn't have to be accepted in any case at that moment. It could have been phrased differently: 'You choose not to forget it.' (This confirms empathic understanding of his experience. If this is the case, he would nod or agree in some other way, perhaps he would cry.) Later, once the inherent depth decays, the acceptance 'This is something one would never forget' could comfort and motivate him.

### Don't look for the distortion

A person-centred therapist tends not to look out for distorted experiences and to reduce them, or even cut them off, but rather regards and strengthens the undistorted so that the wholeness of the client's self can reorganize itself.

### Positive regard

A well-known feature of a psychotherapeutic relationship lies in the fact that the therapist accepts all aspects of the client's self (Rogers 1951: 517–18), however the client always remains responsible for his or her actions. Initial doubts of critics who argue that clients will get stuck or even confirmed by the acceptance of their ingrained way of feeling, acting and communicating must be countered by the fact that research has proved not only clients' psychological recovery but also their social adaptation (Rogers 1951: 520). This lies in the whole climate of the relationship, in the intertwining of the three therapist attitudes towards the client (acceptance, empathic understanding, congruence in the relationship). The congruence in the relationship plays an important role in that it provides some free space for the therapist to appropriately symbolize his or her feelings regarding the different aspects of the client's self and to interact appropriately (if really meaningful and necessary!). Here the therapist's authenticity complements itself with the positive regard and empathic perceiving and evaluation of the whole situation (and within it also the relationship).

### Example from therapy

During the last few minutes of her therapy hour, a client suffering from depression shared about her relationship with her father. She said that she felt helpless and very disappointed because he did not respect her. He did not listen to her even when she felt enthusiastic or happy about something and interrupted her in the middle of her talk. It was impossible for her to express her anger or hurt because she feared getting into a fight. The therapist said: 'As soon as he interrupts you, your feeling of happiness is gone … perhaps you can tell him just this.' She responded that if her father would – unexpectedly – apologize, she'd feel obliged to continue sharing.

**T:** But your enthusiasm wouldn't be there any more.

**C:** [Nods]

**T:** Now so many feelings come up in you, is that right?

**C:** Yes, but how can I react in such cases?

**T:** Perhaps this way: 'OK, I accept your apology, but I'm angry and I can't just continue now.'

**C:** Oh! Then my father would say that I'm odd, reacting unreasonably over nothing.

**T:** And that confuses you . . .

**C:** Yes.

**T:** Then the only thing you can do is to accept it, perhaps this way: 'Yes, OK I don't take that away from you [referring to the father's opinion that she is odd], but it [referring to the fact that the father was not interested in what she had to say] made me angry.'

**C:** [Surprised] Aha.

**T:** And this is the point where it is necessary to end this conversation [because any continuation is likely to lead into meaningless argument or a fight].

Finally, the client had touched her problematic relationship with her father. However, this example was intended – in the first place – to show how a way of communicating that is free of positive regard (namely the father's way) can 'chase the other into the corner' and thus contribute to the development of depression.

### Invitation to reflect

*What do you think about this therapeutic scenario? Would you have responded similarly or chosen a different approach? Why?*
*What do you think is the primary cause of the client's depression?*

In the last example from therapy it can be seen how in such a relationship, characterized by habitual attitudes and methods of communication, the other person (here the client) can be forced onto the defensive, which then becomes a very difficult position to escape from and remain independent.

In conversations, Ladislav has often experienced the way in which clients are helpless in such situations and suppress their feelings or react inappropriately. Out of this helplessness depression can arise and a tendency toward aggression can be activated.

### Understanding empathically

The most important factor in the therapeutic process is the therapist's 'talent' for empathy, thereby expressing his or her positive regard towards the client. Empathy of course doesn't mean just repeating what the client has said, but the perception and facilitative symbolizations of what the therapist feels or empathically understands about the client's inner world based on their exploration of it (it is primarily *their* meaning, *their* feelings). At the same time the therapist's empathy contributes to the precise perception of the whole situation including the client's experience and behaviour. Sometimes the therapist may experience their own sense of being lost, at other times they may perceive aspects of the client's world that he or she isn't aware of yet, or sense an urge to provide an unnecessary explanation. However, often the client's experience is a conglomeration of feelings and the therapeutic 'art' is to address the central issue and not turn down innumerable blind alleys.

But how can a therapist empathically understand and express the client's central feeling and later his or her further feelings about what has been shared? What is pivotal in the client's personality and their problems? How can the therapist address the meaning of their feelings in a non-directive way? How can they follow up on the concrete content of what has been shared? Is there anything that can overburden the client right now? These are questions that junior therapists often ask when initially standing behind the 'closed door' leading to the therapeutic relationship and process.

There are several other 'doors' that need to be opened on the path towards becoming an empathic psychotherapist. What is empathically received must not be used against the client, not even with a premature attempt at an explanation. This natural principle, implied by the whole context of Carl Rogers' theories, must not be confused with ethics – it is the therapeutic process that is the issue at hand. It is the therapist's empathy and intuition that tell them what can be facilitative in a given situation and how they can stay in the relationship. What is an ethical consideration, though, is for example, the fact that therapy is no place for making appointments for private activities, in particular not intimate meetings. This would lead to a different relationship and would hinder the therapist's congruence.

Empathic understanding and the therapist's life experience are of the utmost importance in person-centred therapy when compared with other therapeutic models. The person-centred therapist should/must understand the client phenomenologically, which means in their whole being, including their psychological problems, which are different in each clinical category but are subjective in every person and significantly form their personality.

## Therapeutic relationship

Whereas several problems have similar roots, it is surprising and at the same time interesting and natural that each client is completely different and the therapist will experience his or her essence and peculiarities as time progresses. A therapist's empathy should adapt to their clients, their clients' problems and their reception of empathic understanding. If a client doesn't manage to perceive their own feelings or to experience and show them and the therapist's addressing them doesn't reach them, the therapeutic process is very painful and moves forward very slowly. The more fixed are the client's perceptions of themselves, such that they almost don't admit their organismic valuings, the longer the process will take.

All this is inherent in the person-centred approach and shows the personal demands on the therapist and the therapeutic relationship. It also shows that the therapist will always be surprised by how different (and at the same time how alike) people are. The therapist will experience over and over again how important the congruence in the relationship is and that in this context interpersonal intimacy must not be compromised.

## Congruence in the relationship

The decisive factor of the therapeutic relationship is the healing congruence in that relationship that also embraces empathy and acceptance (Rogers 1959: 215) but never makes the therapist the 'expert'. The deep meaning of this condition as well as the meaning of all the other aspects of the relationship can only be experienced through the reactions of the other person – the client.

This attitude, which can be referred to as the 'therapist's personality', includes also his or her congruent (authentic, real) experience that is not guided by strict, mental constructs but meets the situation and relationship in a fluent, facilitative and intuitive way.

Compared with everyday life, in therapy the congruence in the relationship is simpler since there are less mutual commitments; on the other hand, however, it is notably more difficult due to other aspects. The therapeutic relationship is a very personal and close one, but has definite limits – crossing these would make the therapeutic process a lot more difficult. For example, a slip into small-talk will disturb or even destroy the momentary therapeutic process. Likewise, giving naïve advice can be the cause of feelings of guilt on the part of the therapist that in turn cause incongruence. The same can happen if the therapist feels threatened or uneasy (Rogers 1959: 214).

### Complex interplay

In therapy all the aspects mentioned so far are important and it is hard to highlight one or the other, such as sensing and addressing the client's pivotal feeling or non-directivity. The therapeutic process requires that all aspects be 'formed' depending on the relationship and situation.

### Example from therapy

Towards the end of the therapy hour a daughter (as client) said that, finally, she had managed to tell her mother what burdens her in their relationship – always a particularly difficult conversation. The daughter said that she had blamed her mother for several issues, but it worked out well. The mother thought that maybe she could have raised the daughter (and her brother) differently. The daughter felt relieved – but that was all.

What the daughter really wanted was a change in her relationship with her mother, a breakdown of the barriers that both had established. Not the anger, not a wish to be at war, but a desire for a better relationship. She asked: 'How can one address such an issue without blaming?'

A second conversation with the mother came to an end without the essential feelings having been addressed. The daughter could have saved the situation, however, perhaps by saying: 'All this is history and has passed, perhaps each of us can manage to take a small step ... we like each other, don't we? We value each other and our relationship.'

### Invitation to reflect

*How would you proceed in such a case? How might you react without blaming? If you are a psychotherapist, would you react differently in an everyday conversation with similar content? Do you think the client's own initiative would be important?*

To further illustrate the complex interplay of these aspects in a therapeutic relationship, we now provide an excerpt from Carl Rogers interviewing 'Ritchie' in a demonstration interview at the 'Living Now Workshop' in La Jolla, CA, recorded in 1983, transcribed by Will Stillwell and Antonio dos Santos (and translated into several languages).[1]

---

[1] The authors thank Will Stillwell for granting them permission to include an excerpt from the interview. The complete interview in the form of a video tape with subtitles in Chinese, French, German, Russian and Spanish is available from CSP (Center for Studies of the Person).

The situation in the interview is as follows: Ritchie had been successful in his technical job for 20 years but wanted a change, so he studied counselling and wanted to become a counsellor. However, he was quite fearful and undecided about whether he would be a good counsellor. In the interview he shares his inner world with Rogers (while the other workshop participants are listening in the background).

### Example from therapy

**Ri 20:** [Nods his head, whispers] Right. [full voice] I'm not **competent**, I'm not **up** to it, and, and other things um, maybe I'm not **sincere** enough, [**Rogers:** Um hum.] or uh, or making enough **sense**; so many things I think I evaluate myself that way.

**Ro 21:** Um hum. It's really frightening if, if people would find out what you're really **like**... and that you don't measure **up**, perhaps you don't measure **up**.

**Ri 21:** Yeah, I think that's true. Y' know, and it's, it's a funny thing that it happens with a lot of people, even people, uh, that I don't **care** about that much, maybe. [**Rogers:** Um hum.] [...] One of the things coming, thinking about **today** was, y' know, same thing, will I, y' know, [**Rogers:** Um hum.] be a **disappointment**, [**Rogers:** Um hum, um hum.] y' know, will I have enough content?

**Comment:** Here Ritchie starts making a connection between his previous experience and the current situation in the interview. Apparently he feels safe enough to explore his current feelings. Rogers picks up on this important aspect.

**Ro 22:** Will you, will you be a good enough client, huh?

**Ri 22:** [Soft laugh] {audience laughs lightly} You know, it's funny, I thought about that. Heh, I thought that, heh, imagined I'm worried about failing [laugh] about being myself. [**Rogers:** Um hum, um hum.] Um... That feels sad, [**Rogers:** Um?] kind'a. That feels a little sad. Y' know.

**Ro 23:** Can you say more about that sadness? [nine seconds' silence] [**Ritchie:** blinking rapidly] I'm not quite clear what it is that feels sad.

**Ri 23:** [Blinking rapidly] Yeah, I don't know I just felt my eyes getting sad, a little bit. I don't feel it now, but I just feel like it... make...

**Ro 24:** For a moment there, it just seemed **sad**.

**Ri 24:** Yeah. Like how **unfortunate** y' know. You're afraid of being yourself, you're afraid of being a failure like yourself.

**Ro 25:** Um hum. It really is **sad** to think that you're being fearful of being, **who** you are and **what** you are.

**Ri 25:** Yeah. Even allowing myself to fail. [**Rogers:** Um hum, um hum.] I don't know what would happen if I failed. [**Rogers:** Um hum.] Y'know, like it's so credible.

**Ro 26:** You're just, entertaining that thought that, 'even if I fail, would that be so **awful**, would it be terrible'?

**Ri 26:** That's what I said, 'so what' [(laughs]. [**Rogers:** Um. So what.) Yeah. That's what I say here, [laughs] anyhow. That's what I'm thinking now, y'know...okay. [seventeen seconds' silence] Y'know it seems to me an awful lot of in, evaluation here. [**Rogers:** Uh hum.] Even sometimes in situations where I shouldn't have to uh, evaluate myself. Y' know.

**Ro 27:** Always judging, judging, judging, and, never giving yourself very high marks.

**Ri 27:** Yeah. It seems to be the truth.

**Ro 28:** [Ten seconds' silence] So that in your own eyes, you're really, most of the time, not too much of a person. A person with many [**Ritchie:** clears throat] flaws, many
...

**Ri 28:** [Seven seconds' silence] Yeah. I think somehow...yeah, I think, that's true and then I think that uh, somehow I am a person.

**Ro 29:** Somehow you are...?

**Ri 29:** I am a person.

**Ro 30:** Somehow you **are** a person.

**Ri 30:** Yeah, that can count, [**Rogers:** Uh hum, uh hum.] for a lot of the **time**. Y'know.

**Ro 31:** Sometimes, you can really see yourself positively. 'I, I, I'm a **person**, I'm, I'm **some**body.'

**Ri 31:** Yeah, and my opinions **do** count, an' they're just my opinions. [**Rogers:** Um hum.] Um...I feel like in the, right now the last few minutes, I've been uh, been trusting what's going on. [**Rogers:** Um hum.] Y'know um, when there was a pause, not wondering what I'm going to say...y'know, um...

**Comment:** Interestingly, Ritchie turns to exploring how he feels in the current situation and what that might reveal to him. Rogers responds exactly to this essential experiential message.

**Ro 32:** Somehow you've been able to, **trust** yourself a little more, in uh, these last minutes.

**Ri 32:** Yeah. Yeah. I kind'a, came in with the idea to try to trust myself. [**Rogers:** Um hum, um hum.] So...uh...

**Ro 33:** So one thing you wanted to have happen was to, **experience more trusting** of yourself and, not being quite so **harsh** on yourself.

**Ri 33:** Yeah. That's the part I'd like to get rid of, the **evaluative** part [**Rogers:** Um hum.] because, it seems to me that when I have been comfortable with share, to share with some individuals that uh, and just let myself be **spontaneous**, that way just came out right. [**Rogers**: Um hum, um hum.] Y'know, [**Rogers:** Um hum.] and it felt...

**Ro 34:** Not always just looking over your own shoulder or something, and just be **spontaneous** and **real**, why, seems though that works pretty **well**.

**Ri 34:** Yeah, it felt good. [**Rogers:** Um hum.] In contrast to trying to measure, trying to be **honest**, trying to really be honest, and yet **measuring** that honesty.

**Ro 35:** Um hum, Um hum. Um hum um hum. Always sort of, two people present, one person doing something, the other person judging how well you're doing it.

**Ri 35:** [laughs] Yeah. Uh . . .

What is fascinating is that Ritchie's current experience in the interview and hence his relationship with Rogers became pivotal in his personal insights. Rogers provided the proper atmosphere and his presence in the relationship, in which Ritchie felt motivated to explore his doubts, problems and experience as he trusted himself more, and felt the positive organismic experiential effect of being honest and spontaneous, without giving up all of the evaluative part of himself. For Ritchie, the personal/relational momentary experience – what felt good in the interview – came to be the guide for a future, more congruent way of being.

## Groups in person-centred psychotherapy

Psychotherapy also includes therapeutic groups that have certain advantages but also disadvantages in comparison with individual settings. The advantages of groups include the fact that clients hear the problems of other people and can benefit a lot from this. They can participate in the conversations and thereby try out their own empathy. They can also receive feedback regarding their own communication and how others perceive them. They hear different views regarding their own and others' problems and they experience their own reaction and the reaction of others. The experience of being accepted as a person by the group is much more powerful than being accepted by the therapist only. Also, some behaviours such as the negation – or explanation – strategy or fleeing into generality can occur in a group but remain concealed in individual therapy. The climate in the group is influenced by all the personalities of the participants. A group can be powerful but it is not always predictable, in particular if the participants have personality disorders.

Groups of clients with mental disorders are small, having about three to seven members, which means that each person can receive the therapist's attention as needed. Such groups tend to meet every week for one and a half hours, and the same conditions hold for the therapeutic process and relationship as in individual therapy. Most clients, however, don't want group conversation because they prefer to have the therapist to themselves and are burdened with their intimate problems. These clients lack the trust that they will really be understood in the group and so choose individual therapy. The next example from therapy illustrates that, from the point of view of the therapist the acceptance of a person into a group is an important decision because the communication problems and attitudes of some people are not appropriate for certain types of group.

---

**Example from therapy**

A mild-mannered client suffering from depression wanted to join a group. But she couldn't integrate herself, she was anxious and she put the others down. Each time there was tension. The conversations in the group were rather harmful to this client. She feared the reactions of the participants whom she had provoked. Later, in individual therapy it became apparent that she had a strong personality disorder and even on a one-to-one basis progress was very slow.

---

We believe it is best to first experience a client in individual therapy and estimate how his or her modes of expression, problems and personality might fit in with a group.

## Person-centred communication in instruction

The person-centred attitude of the teacher to pupils or the professor to students doesn't differ from that of the facilitator. However, the symbolizations are or can be distinctly different when dealing with children, adolescents or students. The teacher's empathy is directed primarily to what the school or study experience is like for every single pupil or student (Rogers 1980: 307). Rogers (1983) referred to this complex phenomenon as *learning in freedom*.

In a class, however, there are various peculiar constraints; there is an institutional hierarchy and a given curriculum. The difference between person-centred and traditional instruction will become apparent in the way in which students are included into the processes, how the teacher/instructor behaves towards the students and how he/she communicates with them. The difference is also in how the teacher manages to empathically understand the students even in terms of their personal problems and thus remain himself or herself.

As will be illustrated in Chapter 11, courses on person-centred communication can be designed to leave room for students to express themselves on more personal levels including the potential sharing of their worries and problems. In such courses, all kinds of interactions, games and exercises that are compatible with the person-centred approach can be proposed and tend to work very well. It is the active inclusion of students that matters along with the approximate mediation of the meaning of the person-centred direction (Motschnig-Pitrik and Nykl 2007).

The demand on the course instructor/teacher regarding person-centred attitudes is significantly lower than on the group facilitator or therapist. Part of the instructor's/teacher's attitude lies in their natural gift, which nevertheless can be enhanced and improved over time. In our view, this happens most effectively by participating in encounter groups. For many teachers this can be a quite challenging but worthwhile experience, but it should never be compulsory: teachers must *want* to participate.

## Other relationships

It cannot be said that the demands regarding person-centred attitudes in facilitative relationships in everyday situations are fewer than those in encounter groups or in teaching. In this case, the relationship depends on the everyday situation as well as the personality of both people. The steps towards growth are – as in encounter groups – characterized by the quality of the relationship and often mutuality is essential. There are situations that – while they proceed – in one case require just a slight and in another case a highly evolved constellation of all the aspects that have been described as constituting therapy.

In a non-therapeutic, everyday relationship, in most cases psychological growth is not in the foreground and the issues tend to focus on work, entertainment, raising children or the relationship itself. Here everyday life pulses with innumerable mutual demands and obligations that are accompanied by habitual and often ingrained attitudes, communication and closeness or distance. We all know how complicated this can be. In this book much has already been said about the conditions necessary for a path towards maturity and a psychologically adjusted relationship-life.

Hence we focus here on some aspects of everyday life that do not support a facilitative climate, that tend to cause bitterness in a relationship. These are endless criticizing, improving, comparing, always wanting to consult, to know better, to reproach, to justify oneself, to explain unnecessarily, to be prejudiced, to be always in opposition, to slip into generality, and a great, great many more. The flow of a personal message and the momentary relationship is interrupted abruptly by the other person; he or she jumps in with his or her own experience or some well-intended advice. The relationship and communication is also burdened by rigid attitudes, personal fears, games, such as hiding, habitually inappropriate expressions and the drive for punishment. All this does not fit with person-centred conditions and can often clearly be seen in the communication between group participants in the early phases of the group process.

The next example from experience is Ladislav's own.

---

**Example from experience**

In a hospital, a young client who was in an acute psychotic state wanted to enter the nurses' room. She had no place there of course, but she didn't understand that. A nurse stood in the doorway and told her not to enter, but was ignored. I happened to be walking by and knew the client. I spoke with her to provide a distraction, and suggested that we might walk a little together. She agreed and the situation was resolved. The nurse could have said: 'You'd like to come in but...' and with a glance to the corridor invite the client to go for a walk with her, which wouldn't need to last for more than a few minutes since people in acute psychotic states and under medication tend to have short attention spans. They can be as stubborn as they are easy to distract.

---

Our habitual way of behaving tends to be completely unconscious. Habits and structures of perceiving and communicating can be extremely deeply ingrained, with the consequence that meaningful communication becomes impossible: 'It seems nearly as difficult to accept a perception which would alter the self-concept in an expanding or socially acceptable direction as to accept an experience that would alter it in a constricting or socially disapproved direction' (Rogers 1951: 506).

Each of us is on our own path towards making relationships tolerable or perhaps even good and pleasant, and is continually arriving at new insights from our own experiences. However, in order not to construct rigid and distorted new rules and perspectives, it helps to experience a climate that differs from the usual, familiar one and much has been said about this already. But even the new will not easily escape the existing, solid structures, since under their pressure the new is rendered to the self only step by step and this is often quite a lengthy process.

Whether communication in an everyday relationship functions well or badly, there are many situations in which mature attitudes – whose interplay is referred to as 'psychological adjustment' – can help to meet the demands of life in a straightforward and humane way. This applies, in particular, to families and the development of children.

**Invitation to reflect**

*Who in a family should start seeking a path towards better communication and personal adjustment – the child or the parents?*

## Summary

In the everyday world, as in therapy, each relationship is unique. The same holds true for the three attitudes that Carl Rogers postulated for therapy. A good and improving relationship helps one to master one's own life and moreover gives others a chance to develop in the direction of psychological adjustment. This growth provides the opportunity to experience better and better relationships or to more quickly understand and resolve inherent and often seemingly insurmountable problems.

It is undisputed that each relationship includes communication, such that a person's wants, feelings, empathic understanding, sympathy or antipathy can or must be communicated, and that this communication is characterized by their attitudes and experiences, which reflect their personality. There is no doubt that an adjusted communication has the potential to prevent or heal psychological problems.

# 7 Dialogue

*If you want to reach your target fast, walk on your own. However, if you want to get far, then take a friend.*

(shared by Andreas Holzinger)

**In this chapter you will learn about:**

- The meaning of the term 'dialogue' in different contexts
- The characteristics of dialogue according to David Bohm
- The four practices of dialogue according to William Isaacs and how they connect to the person-centred approach
- How dialogue according to Bohm relates to the person-centred approach
- The continuum between dialogue and discussion and how it is traversed in two sample conversations
- The preconditions of having dialogue and how they relate to person-centred theorizing
- What potential effects dialogue can bring about

Throughout history, the term 'dialogue' has had different meanings and definitions. In literature, science, religion, politics, computer science and organizational development, the term is used to emphasize diverse aspects of the communication between two or more people. While, for example, the juxtaposition of a thesis and antithesis determines a dialogue for finding a solution at a higher level, the dialogue in drama aims to present individual views or roles. Central to this chapter is the notion of dialogue according to the physicist David Bohm (1996) who emphasizes the deepening and intensifying of a conversation by thinking together. Hence it seems justified to clarify the meaning of the term 'dialogue' before we take it up in the context of person-centred communication.

At the PCE 2006 conference, Peter Schmid started his presentation about therapeutic dialogue by saying 'We are dialogue' (from the Greek '*dia*' = through, '*logos*' = the word, sense, meaning). This impacted on me (Renate) deeply. To assume the beginning of every relationship is a form of dialogue is something really worthwhile and yet challenging in itself (Schmid 2002, 2013). So let us continue by following up the meaning of dialogue as 'the flow of meaning'.

According to the neuroscientist Damasio (2003, 2012), fluent physiological states enable unhindered access to inner resources and furthermore accelerate the flow of thoughts. Hence, they let us reach new territories, which can't be accessed through rigid paths of thought and behavioural patterns. When in dialogue in our relationships, we don't remain on the same spot but look for movement in the relationship with others and the environment. If the situation is blocked or some obstacle appears such that flow and dialogue are interrupted, new orientation is sought with the aim to re-establish the flow of dialogue. If people encounter each other without any blocking element between them, they can be open to their experience:

> If the spirit of the dialogue is present, the picture or image . . . is of a *stream of meaning* flowing among and through us and between us. This will make possible a flow of meaning in the whole group, out of which may emerge some new understanding. It is something new, which may not have been in the starting point at all. It's something creative. And this shared meaning is the 'glue' or 'cement' that holds people and societies together.
>
> (Bohm 1996: 7)

Not every conversation is a dialogue, as anyone can easily attest. Often trivialities are discussed, experiences are over-analysed, or everyone wants to express himself or herself without ever listening to the others. But what exactly is the difference between a normal conversation or discussion and a real dialogue? Here are some thoughts regarding the experience of dialogue in the sense of 'flow of meaning' in the context of person-centred communication.

## Dialogue and its relationship to active listening

### What is it that brings about the quality of genuine dialogue for me?

First of all, it is the time that I'm willing to spend on this special kind of intensive communication. Time in which I don't want to think about anything else, time that will be devoted to concentrating fully on the other and myself such as to perceive his or her thoughts, feelings and statements as fully as possible and let them affect me. In other words, I fully delve into the stream of what is in me and between us at the given moment. However, this stream doesn't come into being without my contribution, and equally not without the contribution of my partner or partners. It is also influenced by the fact that I have contributed to triggering it.

Coming back to the conversation, I consider it essential to stay with the other long enough to support that person to express as many of their meanings as possible in a clear, transparent and understandable way, regardless whether I agree or not. I am pleased by agreement but find more challenge in different perspectives, looking beyond my own horizon and seeing issues from different perspectives, to 'sense into them' and start understanding them better.

While the other person is sharing, my own opinion or meaning forms itself and gradually pushes to be expressed. It feels good if the other person offers me some space or at least realizes and notes my desire to contribute. For example: 'There is one more thing I'd like to add, is that OK?' If he or she doesn't realize I'm ready to make a contribution I can wait, interrupt cautiously, or occasionally make a brief note in order to save a thought and be able to listen better once again. Throughout the whole process it is important for me to voice my concern constructively, if possible with a connection to what has been said before or the whole situation or otherwise clearly delineated as something new that is in my heart at this point in time. But I have also learned to wait and to trust the process even more, with the risk that my thoughts will remain unexpressed for the time being if the conversation turns to a different topic.

I feel support and enrichment if others respect me as a being in the presence and opinion of whom they are interested and to whom they listen mindfully, and possibly also react or respond. The latter, however, is not immediately necessary since person-centred encounter groups have 'taught' me to remain patient and to learn that a response or a reference will come whenever the time is right. On the whole it seems supportive to me if all participants contribute to the dialogue, share something and also take something with them such that the dialogue turns out to be something mutual or versatile. This may not necessarily be the case for each 'segment', but over time everyone should take part in order to allow something to grow that all the participants have in common.

What I value particularly highly in dialogue is that – together with the dialogue partner(s) – we openly 'lay things on the table' such that we can uncover them, shift them around and deal with them together. We share them and co-own what is there. It is liberating not to have to consider and experience everything alone but to do it together with someone who, metaphorically, 'drifts in the same stream'; someone who supports observing, organizing and experimenting with thoughts, issues and ideas, and who is willing to let them form without immediately calling for consequences and concrete actions. These, however, can follow as soon as both or all of us are ready for them. Before that, we exchange what we sense about the one or the other alternative, what it means or doesn't mean to us and where we locate any difficulties. Each accepts the other as a full partner, as what he/she is, as someone being on the same level of human existence but coming equipped with different experiences and trying to give their best in the common process, to exploit their potential, whatever that might be at the given moment. Such a process is a mental peak performance, often a delight: something comes into being, matures, and we sense it and own it together in a fluent relationship without ever taking hold of it.

### Invitation to reflect

*Perhaps you remember a conversation in which you articulated yourself well and the other party listened well, such that you could experience something meaningful? Do you often participate in such conversations? With whom do they work out best? What, in your view, is the reason if they don't succeed?*

## Ideal image and reality

The description given above should not prompt the illusion that dialogue is 'daily bread'. I suspect it happens quite rarely. It tends to accumulate in conversation with people who have person-centred attitudes, in advanced phases of person-centred encounter groups and also in talks with open-minded, engaged managers and organizational developers, to name a few examples. Why is dialogue so rare? From the countless reasons a few stand out: impatience, instantaneous valuing, not listening, putting positions before genuine interests, resting in oneself, not getting across prefabricated decisions, opinions, constructs of the mind, and thinking in strict hierarchies. Unfortunately, there are no quick fixes for such hindrances, in particular since we know that they are rooted in deeply-held attitudes and/or organizational structures (Isaacs 1999). Nevertheless, I do hope that knowledge of the basics and interconnections of promotive communication, coupled with well-developed person-centred attitudes, will help to reduce the rift between ideal image and reality, step by step. The paths to this target are so versatile that they are to be looked for in the respective situation and occasionally they are indeed discovered there.

### How is dialogue related to active listening?

Attentive, active listening forms the basis for dialogue. However, in addition there is the element of a stronger reciprocity, symmetry and often a shared third thing that rests outside of the personalities of the dialogue partners. Often some joint concern underlies the dialogue, such as the design of a course, the planning of a primary area of work, organizational development, problem-solving, etc. The attention that one person is receiving is granted by the other; we collect and deliberate each step together. We listen actively and, vice versa, are actively listened to.

In the course of a genuine exchange each person should have the chance to bring themselves into the process and to be taken seriously. As with active listening, we don't listen solely to words and their factual content but also to the deeper meaning, the feelings, and the whole situation. Additionally, *all* the relationships – be they between persons or things, themes, concerns, ideas – take their space. Throughout the dialogue, the dialogue partners are in a symmetrical relationship, having equal rights. In dialogue, the empathic, respectful listening is being more intensively complemented by transparent, congruent sharing and often also by some shared concern that reaches beyond personal growth.

Godfrey Barrett-Lennard (1998: 360), a former PhD student of Carl Rogers and his former colleague and close co-worker in Chicago writes:

> Yet, one-way listening, of whatever depth and impact, lacks the mutuality found in some complete natural dialogue. A two-way flow in which each closely shares *and* listens, that is, a *symmetrical* dialogue, must involve a somewhat different inner process. This process would seem to depend on an easy fluency in running two closely linked, interweaving channels at once: close listening attention to the other while also forming and expressing one's own thought and feeling; and an inner building toward a next response as one is reading further signals and sensing below the surface of the other and self. There is no fear in easy and full dialogue, either of inability to express and communicate self or of implying any lower valuing of the other when not concentrating on them wholly. To the contrary, valuing and trust is implied in sharing from self and caring to be known.

Barrett-Lennard (1998: 360) thinks that person-centred processes have brought complementary dialogue (as for example between client and counsellor, student and teacher) to new qualities and depth. The symmetrical, personal dialogue presents a challenge for further development. One goal therefore is to develop the dialogue between relationship partners and group participants in such a way that it is mutually supportive: 'In a training context, the achievement of depth and fluency in such dialogue might be considered an advanced stage of learning, building on mastery of component features, especially, empathic listening and capacity for congruent expressive communication' (1998: 360).

When I talk about dialogue in this chapter and don't explicitly mention some other meaning, then the reference is to the symmetrical dialogue being characterized in this section. In any case, the above-mentioned 'flow of meaning' and the mutually supportive nature of dialogue are centrally included. In the next section I am going to elaborate on the characteristics and considerations regarding 'dialogue' in the sense of David Bohm and highlight some differences between dialogue and discussion.

## Bohm's theory of dialogue

### Dialogue practices

According to William Isaacs (1999: 80) there are four practices that constitute the key elements of a capacity for effective advocating and exploring in Bohm's dialogue. Isaacs posits that the four practices, namely *listening, respect, suspending* and *articulating* or *voicing* form the basis of the ability to engage in dialogue. Intriguingly, each of these practices requires underlying attitudes as well as skills. Isaacs views each as something that can be developed if we actively and repetitively put effort into it. This is why the close relationship between the four practices and the person-centred core attitudes is of such interest.

The practices of *listening* and *voicing* strongly resemble the respective qualities that were presented in Chapter 4 of this book, even though in the person-centred approach the influence of congruence, acceptance and empathic understanding is more prominently present. *Suspending* emphasizes the putting aside of one's own thoughts in order to achieve openness for what the other person shares. So, does it have a corresponding or related construct in the person-centred approach? Suspending is not the same as openness to experience according to Rogers, which means that *each* stimulus, regardless of whether it is initiated inside or outside of the organism, can flow freely in the nervous system without being distorted or pushed back by the defence system. It follows that openness to experience includes stimuli that originate within the organism whereas suspending necessitates the putting aside or postponing of one's own thoughts. In my view, Rogers' construct of openness to experience can rather be viewed as a *precondition* to suspending. Let me explain: we tend to be in a process of perceiving several stimuli in an undistorted way. If, in addition, we aim to fully and exactly understand another person and his or her opinion and meaning, and respect that person, we will tend to put our view to one side for some time, to suspend it, in order to be able to more fully attend to the other person. This is why, to me, the practice of suspending is fully consistent with communicating in a person-centred way, and I even consider person-centred theory to provide a more precise characterization and in-depth derivation of those attitudes and processes which underlie the practice of suspending.

The meaning of Isaac's practice of *respect* is strongly related to acceptance or unconditional positive regard in the person-centred approach, and illuminates further perspectives. Respect – in accord with acceptance – means seeing a person as a whole being, to legitimate them, to regard and support the potential they carry within them and to honour their boundaries. An intriguing consideration is that respect also necessitates the readiness to encounter the problem that comes from outside in one's inside – to perceive or own it as a part of oneself. Underlying this thought is the insight that we can perceive only something that we carry in ourselves since otherwise we would lack any connection to it (compare also Rogers 1951, propositions XI and XII). This aspect joins respect with empathic understanding in the sense of the *readiness and ability* to sense part of the inner world of the other person *as if* it were one's own. Damasio (2003) describes the neural pathways underlying this process.

I'm deeply impressed by a quote that Isaacs passed on in the context of respect when quoting Peter Garrett, who conducted dialogues with imprisoned dangerous criminals. Readers may themselves sense the intimate resemblance of the humanistic view of the person as described in Part I of this book and Garrett's insight:

> The impulse behind intentions is pure, even though the intention may be distorted and the impact not what was intended. Inquiring deeply enough to reach the original impulse will always reveal wholesomeness. This provides the confidence to enter the loudest confrontation and the darkest territory without fear that it will get forever worse.
>
> (Isaacs 1999: 121)

### Advocacy and inquiry

According to Argyris (see Senge 2006: 233), in a dialogue, advocacy and inquiry are in balance. We advocate our view as clearly as we can, without sticking to it. We say openly what we think and why we think that way. During inquiry we encourage others to question their own conceptions and engage ourselves with what we don't know or understand as yet.

Even though the terminology and the emphasis differ between the dialogue scholars and those following person-centred principles, the resemblances, such as mutually supportive sharing and the consequent development of the relationship, can't be overlooked. Let me elaborate more on this issue.

## Characteristics of dialogue

Ellinor and Gerard emphasize the necessity of diversity 'for the power of dialogue to unfold. Dialogue gains depth and the opportunity for learning from the diversity within it while simultaneously providing a way for that diversity to be honoured' (1998: 281). Furthermore, dialogue is seen as one of the most effective ways of dealing with crises, overcoming destructive misinterpretation, liberating creativity and accompanying cultures in transformational processes (Bohm and Peat 2000: 240).

Bohm and Peat emphasize further characteristics of dialogue that – in my view – strongly correspond with the objectives of person-centred communication. In particular, the way of communicating in person-centred encounter groups (to be described in Chapter 11) shares many of the directions or concerns formulated by Bohm and Peat. In both settings – person-centred encounter groups and dialogue groups – a central issue is the loosening of rigid mental structures. This loosening or reorganization enables a creative stream of thought to be set free. A difference in the tendency of encounter and dialogue groups concerns their focus. Encounter groups emphasize the dissolution of emotional constructs followed by an increased flexibility in the realm of feelings, such as to allow new meaning to unfold. Dialogue groups, complementarily, focus on achieving more flexible thought processes by loosening rigid patterns of thought. However, insight from human social and natural sciences repeatedly confirms the interconnections between feeling and thought and the necessity of a holistic perspective. Based on this consideration, the overlaps between dialogue and encounter shouldn't surprise us. In both settings the unhindered flow of thought and feelings isn't forced by anything. Bohm and Peat (2000: 247) write:

In a true dialogue there is the possibility that a new form of consensual mind, which involves a rich and creative order between the individual and the social, may be a more powerful instrument than is the individual mind. Such consensus does not involve the pressure of authority or conformity, for it arises out of the spirit of friendship dedicated to clarity and the ultimate perception of what is true. In this way, the tacit infrastructure of society and that of its subcultures are not opposed, nor is there any attempt to alter them or to destroy them. Rather, fixed and rigid frames dissolve in the creative free flow of dialogue as a new kind of microculture emerges.

Interestingly, and very much in the spirit of the person-centred approach, for Bohm and Peat (2000: 271) the context of dialogue has a personal component as much as a sociocultural one:

> The context of dialogue should include not only discussion relevant to the sociocultural level but also discussion of the life and problems of the individual, and of the cosmic context . . . the essential need is for the 'loosening' of rigidly held intellectual content in the tacit infrastructure of consciousness, along with a 'melting' of the 'hardness of the heart' . . . The melting on the emotional side could perhaps be called the beginning of genuine love, while the 'loosening of thought' is the beginning of awakening of creative intelligence. The two necessarily go together.

As attentive readers will have realized, the word 'discussion' slips into this quote. In my view it should better be substituted by 'conversation' or 'exchange'. Our ingrained habit of using language imprecisely poses a difficulty in achieving communication of high quality and living it (Anderson and Cissna 1997: 69). For example, we use the word 'learning' to denote a balancing act between totally different processes and meanings. It ranges from pure receptive learning, such as rote learning, to significant or experiential learning encompassing personal growth that can't be taught (Rogers 1961; Nykl 2005). If one person thinks of one meaning and the other has the other one on his/her mind, mutual understanding is strongly endangered. The recognition of the deviations through tentative suspending and consequent expanding of one's meaning in the sense of dialogue seems to be the only way to reach clarity.

## Dialogue versus discussion

Ellinor and Gerard write: 'Dialogue occurs when people are trying to learn from one another, to understand from a larger perspective rather than defending and justifying from a personal perspective' (1998: 20). Hence, dialogue facilitates arriving at an extended perspective that can lead to the expansion of personal views. The authors furthermore provide a continuum between dialogue and discussion, shown in Table 7.1.

Bohm states that the essence of dialogue is not to analyse things, to win an argument, or to exchange opinions. Rather, it is to suspend your opinions and to look at them, to listen to everybody's opinion, to suspend them, and to see what all that means. In this scenario sharing could proceed without hostility and we

**Table 7.1** The discussion/dialogue continuum (Ellinor and Gerard 1998: 21)

| Dialogue | Discussion |
|---|---|
| Seeing the *whole* among the parts | Breaking issues/problems into *parts* |
| Seeing the *connections* between the parts | Seeing the *distinctions* between the parts |
| *Inquiring* into assumptions | *Defending/justifying* assumptions |
| *Learning* through inquiry and disclosure | *Persuading, selling and telling* |
| Creating *shared* meaning among many | Gaining agreement on *one* meaning |

would be able to think together in a way that is impossible if we need to defend our opinions. In a dialogue, ideas flow between people. Somebody gets an idea, somebody else takes it up, another person adds to it, rather than

> each trying to persuade or convince the others . . . Everybody is quite free . . . It's a harmony between the individual and the collective, in which the whole moves towards coherence. So there is both a collective mind and an individual mind and the flow moves between them.
>
> (Bohm 1996: 31–2)

**Example from experience: the transition of a discussion into a different 'conversational sphere'**

In the first part of a person-centred encounter group at the University of Vienna, one participant who had studied for one term in Amsterdam talked about the use of marihuana in his student community. Rapidly, even before the participant could talk about himself, a discussion developed around the theme of 'legalization of marihuana' in which group members participated actively. One student said: 'This couldn't even be imagined in our country,' while another responded: 'Why not? People from Amsterdam don't come from Mars, or do they?' Then somebody said: 'But look, we have a totally different culture!' and 'Without illegal business many more people would become homeless.' The students seemed to find it entertaining to voice their pro and contra opinions without establishing any deeper connection to each other. As a facilitator I couldn't find anything worthwhile in this interaction since we couldn't solve the legalization problem anyway.

Suddenly it occurred to me that I'd be very interested in what effect a legalization would have on the individual participants, in particular on the student who had initially shared his experience from Amsterdam. So I asked him: 'What would a legalization of marihuana in Austria mean for you personally?' He responded: 'For me? For me it wouldn't make any difference, my mother would certainly get mad if she found out that I'm taking drugs.' This caused a perceivable shift in the group. Suddenly participation was no longer just fast and intellectual. Participants became interested in each other, the function of parents, the ways they had been raised, and in particular the strict way their parents had imposed themselves to regulate their offsprings' behaviour. Many talked at a very personal level about how they perceived strictness and rules and how these finally did (not) influence their behaviour and their relationship with their parents. For example, one participant shared: 'Once I was a bit older I always used to decide myself whether a prohibition made sense. If not, I simply ignored it.' Thereupon a female student asked: 'How, then, did your father react?' The response: 'Well, there was some punishment but after a while they gave up on imposing meaningless prohibitions. [pause] The good thing was that I could talk to them and tell them why some prohibitions didn't make sense to me and most of the time they understood. We could talk about it.'

I had a rich experience resulting from this sharing in this group and it has influenced my behaviour with regard to my own children. I feel I can draw from more than one perspective and this is something I appreciate highly.

### Invitation to reflect

*How do you perceive the development of the conversation? Would you call the second part (after my question) a dialogue? In your view, how is it and how is it not a dialogue?*

### How an effort to have a dialogue ended up as a discussion

Although I didn't want it, recently I happened to slip from an effort to conduct a dialogue into a discussion. The first implication from this is that in order to conduct a dialogue there needs to be at least two dialogue-attuned people who, in a particular situation, are willing to search together. If one of them wants to reach a resolution fast it is almost impossible to keep the dialogue going. The reason for this could be that the result of a discussion is easier to grasp cognitively such that we are tempted to choose this faster direction.

**Example from experience**

I wanted to initiate a dialogue in order to develop an idea about how and where to spend our holidays such as to let solutions evolve that would satisfy the wants of the individual family members as far as possible. Retrospectively, my enterprise couldn't have been successful since I didn't have the most essential preconditions for a dialogue – namely the full attention and readiness of both partners – on my side. Here is what happened.

Herbert is sitting at his computer in the evening. I take a seat at his side, watch him for a while and then ask:

**R:** Herbert, do you have a moment or are you concentrating on something important?

**H:** It's OK, what's the matter? [looks up briefly]

**R:** I'd like to exchange thoughts with you regarding our holidays, just sense a bit in advance what wishes are there. Do you already know what you want to do in the summer?

**H:** I haven't thought about is so far, but I assume we're going to travel somewhere, aren't we?

**R:** Yes, this is also what I'd want. I thought about a trip to the sea, Niko wants that so much, since he hasn't been there, you know. On the other hand, in July and August it's quite hot and crowded during the high season. I myself could also imagine going to Carinthia for two weeks. Or we could arrange for some combination. What do you think?

**H:** If you prefer to go to Carinthia then we'll go to Carinthia. In any case, I'm going to have holidays for two weeks in one go.

**R:** And what is it that you'd prefer?

**H:** If you don't want to travel to the sea, why then should I say what I prefer?

What certainly did *not* happen was collecting, sharing and sorting out alternatives in the form of a dialogue, as I had intended. Instead, the conversation immediately went straight at arguing for a solution. I assume that, depending on your own experience, you will find reasons why the dialogue didn't succeed. Experiences such as the one shared above prompt me to underline the fact that dialogue can't be 'enforced' and blaming isn't an appropriate reaction if that dialogue doesn't come about. Interpersonal dialogue needs a stress-free atmosphere and at least two people who are willing to share openly and to mutually attend to each other such that they reach a sufficient degree of understanding. Each one risks change, or – in other words – has the chance *to be* changed. Neither party can be interested in a fast solution *only*.

## What we need for successful dialogues and congruent relationships

### Preconditions for dialogue

So far I have talked about the various characteristics of dialogue, such as spontaneity, listening, openness toward the opinions of others, respecting the other and so on. In the following, I collect these and complement them with further aspects, in order to propose a preliminary formulation of the preconditions for dialogue in the sense of person-centred communication. The question of whether all of the preconditions are necessary and whether they are enough for a dialogue to happen must remain open at this point.

**Proper atmosphere.** An atmosphere with sufficient time and space and one that is free of disturbance is needed.

**Openness of the intention, concern or question.** The intention, concern or question that motivates people to conduct a dialogue is known and sufficiently open. Here I consciously avoid the term 'theme' since it is too strongly connoted with something factual. If – besides the sharing and creation of new insight – there is a goal, the paths to reaching that goal must be sufficiently open. New ideas are welcome, surprises are appreciated.

**Willingness to share freely.** People share freely in the context of the intention/concern/question of the dialogue. They are motivated and willing to listen to each other and to share their opinions, feelings, meanings, etc. Thoughts and information flow freely.

**Congruence within scope of the intention/concern/question.** Every person is sufficiently open and congruent in the relationship to the dialogue partners as well as to the intention/concern/question of the dialogue and, furthermore, is able to express this clearly and understandably. This expression contains both the factual content as well as the felt meaning. Each person provides space for the open expression of the other/s and supports it actively. They are willing to be changed in the context of the dialogue's intention/concern/question, which means suspending their momentary view. For this it is beneficial to tolerate ambiguity and to be able to live with it for some time. The transition to a new level can lead people through insecure, unknown territory.

**Respect.** Each person feels respect toward the other persons(s) as well as their opinions, in particular if they differ from their own view. A short phrase to succinctly denote this is 'prizing of otherness'. Furthermore, each person, in turn, perceives at least to some degree that they and their opinions are prized. This, however, does not mean that a person necessarily agrees with others' opinions. But it certainly means that others' statements must not be judged prematurely. A genuine non-judgemental attitude is needed.

**Empathic understanding and voicing of the whole situation.** Each person endeavours to understand the given situation and in particular the other person(s) as deeply and thoroughly as possible. This implies not only understanding the others' words but also their concerns, feelings, meanings, thoughts, ideas, implications, etc. Each person, in turn, feels understood at least to some degree and at the minimum perceives the others' effort to understand them. Everyone clearly articulates in which areas they perceive coherence and in which there exist differences.

**Presence – potential for transcendence.** Out of the full presence of the dialogue partners and the accompanying process there emerges a 'We' which is in constant flow, keeps changing and provides resources and motivation that go beyond the sole 'I' or the 'You' (Barrett-Lennard 1998; Motschnig-Pitrik and Barrett-Lennard 2010).

Some readers might miss the frequently mentioned element of diversity as a necessity for dialogue. In fact, viewed objectively, new insight can stem *only* from different views. This holds true if the primary objective of the dialogue is to gain new knowledge. Nevertheless, based on my own experience, I think that a new level of understanding, namely a deeper, more convinced, safer one, one that has more weight, can emerge from a dialogue whose primary objective is participants' sharing or co-constructing meaning. Providing the partners in a dialogue are honest, confirming opinions – expressed through different words and voices – has the potential to form a shared meaning field that unites individuals and strengthens the mutually-held meaning. The effect of transcending oneself – reaching a different level of thinking or consciousness – will, however, hardly happen in a dialogue where there is a strong consensus among participants.

## Relationship between dialogue and person-centred psychotherapy

In his book *On Becoming a Person*, Rogers describes the relationship between psychotherapy and good communication as follows:

> The task of psychotherapy is to help the person achieve, through the special relationship with the therapist, good communication within himself. Once this is achieved he can communicate more freely and more effectively with others. We may say then that psychotherapy is good communication, within and between men. We may also turn this statement around and it will still be true. Good communication is always therapeutic.
>
> (Rogers 1961: 330)

In this sense Rogers puts forward his necessary and sufficient conditions (1959) for the process of psychotherapy and adds that they hold for each interpersonal relationship in which personal growth is likely to happen. Based on Rogers' conditions, Nykl (2005) formulated conditions for any interpersonal relationship (see also Part I of this book) to bring about personal growth. The above-mentioned preconditions for dialogue thus also resemble Nykl's conditions for a congruent relationship, which he also refers to as *conditions for optimal communication*. While the preconditions of dialogue include these conditions, they go beyond them in order to better capture the phenomenon of dialogue. This is because dialogue includes personal growth but it doesn't come in the first place but is rather a welcome concomitant. Dialogue focuses more on creating new knowledge and meaning, on community-building, planning of enterprises, finding creative solutions, organizational development, etc. in which promotive attitudes and social competences are needed. Interestingly, qualities like tolerance of ambiguity (Steenbuck 2005) and fast recovery from frustration (Rogers 1961) have been shown to improve when people hold person-centred attitudes.

## What dialogue leads to

**New insight.** Due to openness and the increased flexibility of thinking and feeling as well as the provision of ideas, opinions and thoughts, all partners in a dialogue have the potential to derive inspiration and new insight. This applies to the realm of thinking as well as those of feeling and behaviour.

**Dialogue as a way to increase congruence.** I have observed that some of the preconditions for dialogue resemble the conditions for the therapeutic process (Rogers 1959) while others go beyond it. The second condition of the therapeutic process, namely the other person being incongruent and fearful, is missing completely. The overlap between the conditions on the one hand and the omission of the incongruence condition on the other isn't arbitrary. Even though in effect almost nobody is completely free of conditions of worth, defence mechanisms and rigid mental models, we assume that people participating in a dialogue don't have strong incongruences such as prejudices, defences or protection systems in the scope of the dialogue's intention/concern/question. If that were the case, the probability of a dispute developing would be high. Under the preconditions described above and due to the unfolding processes and the actualizing tendency, dialogues have the potential to loosen the thought patterns and constructs of the participants and to increase their congruence. This is due to each person developing toward his or her optimum as long as a facilitative atmosphere is provided, as was postulated above. In this process we recognize another example of a shared actualization – in this case strengthened by thinking together – that can be subsumed under the phenomenon of co-actualization.

**Dialogue as a way to build and improve interpersonal relationships.** There is an intimate connection between the phenomenon of a dialogue and the people who participate in it. Barrett-Lennard (1993: 12) uses the metaphor of a stream to describe the dynamics of an active relationship:

> Each participant in an active relationship may be considered to have two interwoven streams of consciousness. One of these, the 'I stream', reflects their individuality and distinctive positions in the relationship. The other, 'we stream' is an expression of their joint being and runs through the experience of all participants. The voice of this 'we/us' consciousness speaks *through* each member but not from them singly. The referent and source of this voice is not *a* self but a twosome – or larger emergent whole – with its own presence, a presence which exists in intricate relation to the I/me selves of each member.

Given every relationship starts with being in dialogue, every partner is free to continue it or to break it up. The relationship becomes explicit through dialogue and each 'We stream' emerges from the 'I streams' of the partners, 'speaks' through them, and impacts upon them through reciprocal interactions. True dialogues are optimal 'playgrounds' for the reciprocity of congruence, acceptance and empathic understanding, with no defined ending of the 'game'. The joy of participating in the 'game' is immanent in the game itself, not for its own sake, but for the new discoveries and developments in the game and its ever-improving quality.

**Dialogue as a potential for transcendence.** Is transcendence necessary? My recent thinking about transcendence reached new territory absolutely 'by chance' – namely through my interaction with a wasp. Let me share this next example from experience with you.

**Example from experience**

A buzzing wasp distracted me and I was thinking about how to get rid of it without killing it. As the wasp reached the window I quickly drew the curtain behind it and opened the window part-way, hoping the wasp would fly in the direction of the sunlight. As after a while the buzzing ceased, I looked to see whether the wasp had definitely left but unfortunately this was not the case. The wasp was sitting on the glass pane, tired from its effort to get through the glass. I thought for a while: 'This is a really tricky situation for the wasp. The frame that surrounds the pane of glass is much darker than the pane.' The wasp would have to cross this dark frame in order to regain its freedom. For this act the wasp didn't seem to be equipped well in its current position. So I turned on the artificial light in the room, lured the wasp towards it and switched off the light. From its new position the wasp flew directly through the slot of the open window into the garden and I could concentrate again on writing my chapter.

What this encounter with the wasp made so clear to me was that sometimes we are caught in our thinking or acting much like the wasp was. Only a change in perspective, or a state that appears unfavourable for some time (the wasp would have to pass over the dark frame) brings us forward, if we allow for it. Thank you, buzzing wasp, you clarified my thinking and granted me a significant experience!

And who knows how often we are caught in our own systems, our frames of thought, and also our intuitions that tend to be useful in general but not in each and every instance. The shared questioning of events and thoughts, coupled with openness to versatile experience sometimes leads us out of this frame.

## Summary

Confirmed by my own experience I attribute to a 'true' dialogue a real opportunity to arrive at new revelations, resolve conflict and manage difficult situations or transform them gradually such as to make them less intense and threatening. Well-developed person-centred attitudes – in the context of dialogue, better interpersonal attitudes – as well as the capacity for self-exploration are important personal preconditions for the capability to conduct a dialogue. Simultaneously, for a dialogue to succeed these attitudes need to be accompanied by the partners' genuine interest in the other(s) as well as the intention/concern/question of the dialogue, the willingness to share, mature voicing skills, clarity of expression, empathic understanding of the whole situation, and properties such as sustaining tension, having a high level of flexibility and a tolerance of frustration and ambiguity. Furthermore, experience in and knowledge of group processes is beneficial (Rogers 1978; Schmid 1994). Balanced person-centred attitudes provide the foundation upon which everything else can be built, if we provide the opportunities and welcome the new that has emerged between us.

# 8 Online person-centred communication

*The foundation of democracy is universal suffrage. Universal suffrage makes every man a ruler.*

(Rogers 1951: 387)

**In this chapter you will learn about:**

- The potential for and constraints on communicating online and ways of working with or around them

- The meaning of person-centred attitudes in the context of online communication and ways in which they are helpful

- Person-centred online communication by following two brief case studies

- Ways of understanding personal experiences with email

There is no doubt that with computer-mediated communication the direct contact between the communication partners, their immediacy, is compromised. Nevertheless, this kind of communication is often practical and allows us to be in contact with others – although in a restricted form – more frequently. In some cases the medium of the computer (network) even helps to overcome barriers, for example between people of high rank and those with a lower rank in organizational hierarchies. Systems open up, hierarchical levels become blurred and emails that need to be processed fast invite informal communication. As another example, consider people who are very tall, small, attractive, unimpressive, of different origin, age, etc. In an online forum – that may, for instance, be set up in an organization to collect information on a new project – all have an equal amount of space and an equal 'voice'. A multitude of prejudices don't even come up. We can only refer to what we receive through the restricted channel. While most often this is a disadvantage, in some cases it can turn out to be beneficial since potential (often not conscious) prejudice doesn't come into play.

Nowadays there exist numerous studies on several aspects of computer-mediated communication. I only mention some here to provide access points and ideas for interested readers. Analyses of the strengths and weaknesses of various media can be found under the keyword 'media-choice theories', whereas settings and practices for computer-supported collaboration are subsumed by the terms 'e-collaboration' and 'e-moderation'. Furthermore, the term 'e-learning' captures a broad variety of aspects of computer-mediated communication in the context of formal as well as informal learning.

In this chapter I (Renate) am going to focus on how computer-mediated communication, informally referred to as 'online communication' – based on its specific features – can be brought in tune with person-centred attitudes. I ask: how can I communicate as constructively as possible online, share transparently, expressively and respectfully, and actively listen, or more accurately, 'actively read'?

Let us first look at the specific characteristics, problems and potentials of online communication. In general it has been observed that it is more intensive and less obliging than direct (or face-to-face) communication. In email, expressions such as 'Your words touched me, I look forward to seeing you again, with affection...' or 'Love, C' come about faster, but also statements such as 'Think first before writing!' or 'I'm fed up with your constant blaming. If you don't want to understand that...'. The computer's keyboard accepts everything. This makes it easier for some people to write down what they have on their mind. But what can help one to free oneself of burdening emotions and even have a therapeutic effect can be extremely hurtful to the recipient ('flaming'). Hence it seems appropriate to consider which specific effects the medium has that are 'switched' between people.

### Invitation to reflect

*Think about an email or any other online communication that you perceived as particularly effective. What did it trigger in you? How did that come about? Was the content particularly transparent such that the message helped you to move on? Did it address your concern and did you feel included or even understood? Did the author of the message let something of himself/herself shine through?*

*Which messages do you consider painful, tedious, superfluous or even annoying? How does this come about?*

The internet makes it possible to initiate relationships, connect to people, and break up the connection, often without ever directly perceiving the consequences that this has on the online partners. This is essentially different from 'blended' or 'hybrid' communication in which we alternate between face-to-face and online meetings. Since blended communication nowadays is a frequent phenomenon, in this chapter I focus on this mixed, alternating style. Moreover I will deal with so-called *asynchronous* communication in which the partners do not necessarily sit behind their screens at the same time but send their messages at arbitrary points in time. Examples of *synchronous* communication channels are chatting through which people share text or voice messages in some time frame, or messenger systems that allow people to exchange messages through an online channel similar to a phone line.

## Constraints to communicating online

Compared to face-to-face meetings, online communication – in particular the most common, textual form of email – is constrained in the following ways:

- The direct, immediate, social contact, the natural presence of the other person is missing, as is the immediate response. I don't have the chance to perceive the whole, spontaneous reaction of the person to whom I send an email – for example their hesitation, surprise, deliberation, the confluence of various feelings, etc.
- Everything must be expressed in words, fonts (e.g. bold, capitals) and symbols such as emoticons for the expression of feelings (e.g. smileys or a sad face). Often this is tedious and time-intensive, ☹ nevertheless practical, since what is typed persists and one can return to it when needed ☺.
- We can't clarify the precise meaning of a message immediately, but at best can make assumptions. These need to be expressed explicitly to enable clarity. Hence, complex issues can become lengthy and convoluted. It is much harder to avoid or eliminate misunderstandings since in the course of a message we don't receive any signals on what has been understood in which way.
- What was sent can't be unsent. It is hard to take back or adjust statements retrospectively.
- The response can take some time and we often don't know the reason for this. Was the email received at all? Is there something wrong with the content, which is why I'm not receiving any response?
- The state (such as the state of health, mood, workload) of the recipient often can't be known.
- The phenomenon of mood-congruent processing doesn't usually happen. Mood-congruent processing means that 'themes' that arise from a particular mood (e.g. depressed, bright) tend to evoke

responses or 'themes' in others that stem from the same mood. This has the effect that people tend to be on similar 'feeling levels' and thus are better attuned to each other and can better perceive and understand each other. This doesn't work if we are in different rooms, places or contexts. Even the best video-conferencing system doesn't change this state of affairs.

- Due to the lack of signals from the language our bodies speak, the mimics, gesticulations, the tone of voice, etc., the message becomes harder to understand and its ambiguity increases. This in turn increases the risk of misunderstanding. The saying: 'An image is worth a thousand words' seems very fitting here. In this respect, video-conferencing has some advantages over email.
- Often statements are more impulsive and less mature because the emotional distance does not facilitate tact as naturally.
- Unanswered online messages cause stress. They resemble unfinished processes that call for completion.

Some modern technologies for online communication, such as those that transmit voice and image, have the potential to decrease or increase some of the constraints, but not completely. Expressed in one sentence: the contact is mediated, not immediate, the atmosphere and mood of the communicating partners will tend to differ, the presence is filtered through the media channel and the dimension of special closeness or distance is at best encoded.

## Potential of communicating online

These heavy constraints, however, are counterbalanced by considerable benefits. In our time of internationalization and globalization, online communication media have a particularly high impact: we initiate a contact that can evolve into a relationship. The relationship can live on, be actualized and further developed through online exchanges.

We reach even distant partners in a fast and uncomplicated way.

Often we ourselves can determine the point in time when we wish to respond that is convenient to us, though at other times the pace can be expected to be fast.

We can allow our formulation or response to mature such that we manage to include all our inner voices – even those that call themselves to attention late. We can choose our wording mindfully, delete parts that we don't find fitting, and capture a larger part of our inner world than would be possible in a spontaneous response.

The demand to formulate our response in an understandable sequence of thought occasionally may help us to gain clarity ourselves. While formulating the message, we are in contact with the other person in our thought, yet we're largely free and not influenced by their behaviour. What we write is persistent, it doesn't get lost as rapidly as do spoken words. This aspect is particularly beneficial if we are dealing with ideas/thoughts/opinions with a strong cognitive component.

We are able to add documents to a message, such as articles, presentation slides or links to websites that provide additional information regarding some theme. Subsequently we can share our views or comments on these resources.

Via online contact, for any concern or request we might have we are free to choose those people with whom we most desire to share, and from whom we expect most interest, understanding or feedback, even though it might come to be expressed in a few lines only. These lines, however, are fixed and we can get back to the person who sent them whenever we want.

Recently, I asked some students of business informatics what function or role face-to-face meetings and online media had for them. Below, selected excerpts from the students' 'voices' provide some vivid insight into this ubiquitous theme. The multitude of responses suggests that personal experiences and opportunities as well as the particular situation at hand determine the students' choices regarding the communication medium and setting. I suspect that some of the responses will relate to readers' own experiences. Perhaps, as a reader, you'll get some new ideas on how to use online communication media and may end up choosing your content and expression more consciously and with even more care.

It's simply a totally different feeling to look somebody in the eye when talking to him than to read messages from a screen.

During online conversation slight misunderstandings can arise that would not happen during a normal conversation.

In effect: I couldn't imagine being enrolled in a study and being without online media.

For me face-to-face meetings are more important. However, nowadays both kinds of meetings are helpful and couldn't be sacrificed. Online media are beneficial in particular in situations in which a direct meeting isn't possible due to the distance, time, or things like that. Personally, I tend to be more successful in group meetings in real life than online...Even the webcam isn't the same as a meeting person-to-person.

Of course, online media make contact simpler and, in particular, one can be in contact and cultivate contact with a lot more totally different people.

There are also situations in which I get so stressed behind my PC . . . when many are online and everybody has different requests and needs a response at once. At least I myself don't want to wait for responses, this is why I try to respond immediately and if the telephone rings and I often don't have time anyway and perhaps need to leave, then get stressed. On the phone or in direct meetings things happen one after the other.

With those colleagues with whom we're connected by a real friendship besides our studies I meet regularly in my leisure time. In this case online media are a welcome supplement, they couldn't, however, act as a substitute for personal contact.

In my view it would be extremely difficult to develop relationships without direct meetings, and without online media it would be almost impossible for me to cultivate them sufficiently.

Direct meetings are indispensable in particular for creative tasks (e.g. creating ideas). In emails lots of spontaneity and important interaction get lost, since if I first of all have to write down my ideas, these get – even though unconsciously – already filtered and potentially dismissed. For less creative activities, such as the breakdown of tasks and coordination regarding content or specific questions, in my opinion online media are sufficient.

I think that today's opportunities make communicating easy as never before. Of course, at times the understanding between my communication partner and me takes different directions or the direction gets lost. But since we are relatively used to this kind of communication, we manage, for example, to put misunderstandings out of the way.

Some responses from the students concerned the use of media in teamwork. In this context they wrote:

For teamwork a direct meeting plays a significant role. One can estimate the person's reaction better, how he will react to me if he is in personal contact. It is also easy to find out what the other is feeling at the moment. This has the advantage that I can decide how to optimally react to his feelings.

If one is to work on a new project in a new team, in my view it is essential to meet directly to make personal contact and converse about the project – and teamwork, since a face-to-face meeting with all its aspects can't be substituted by anything different. In direct personal contact, shared views as well as different opinions can be recognized much more directly than would be possible through online media.

From these statements as well as from my own perception it is clear that our time requires that we solve several tasks concurrently, switch fast between processes (email, phone, face-to-face meeting) and promptly adjust to different people and situations. Inner flexibility, a sufficient degree of openness and tolerance of ambiguity are clearly needed.

To express oneself transparently even through a restricted communication channel and to perceive the other person empathically and at the same time content-wise/factually requires personal competences that can be developed, in the first place, in direct interpersonal contact. This also includes being clearly aware of one's own feelings and opinions such as to be able to put them in words and symbols constructively. It furthermore includes the ability to enter the inner world and the mediated outer world of the other person in order to react constructively. In cases where such a disposition is developed as part of the personality, it can, in my experience, also be lived in the context of constrained communication channels, despite being governed by the constraints imposed by the medium (Ploil 2006).

## Online communication and person-centred attitudes

All in all, effective online communication requires the same attitudes but in part also different skills than face-to-face conversation, combined with the complementary qualities of genuine presence and mediated connection. Nevertheless, the mere existence of computers and media doesn't change anything regarding the *central importance* of confluent, person-centred attitudes as the *interpersonal basis* for mutually facilitative communication. The electronic media may well conceal important facets and bring others to the forefront, but the constructive image of the person and the inner orientation toward congruence, acceptance and empathic understanding would, in my view, at least in part show through when being internalized. In that case they can radiate their effect to the recipients. However, at the outset we can't say anything about how an online message would be received.

From my own experience I dare to state that communication partners who are at least reasonably sensitive and congruent will perceive the computer-mediated expression of person-centred attitudes at least to some degree. Even more, they will tend to reciprocate that expression in their responses. Thus I am convinced that it is precisely person-centred attitudes that are particularly meaningful for effective online communication. They significantly contribute to making it more alive and motivating. Furthermore, they protect against misunderstandings. In those cases in which person-centred attitudes, some skill and an inner desire for sharing and co-actualization are present, one may even succeed in creating a good online dialogue that is effective, enables significant learning and is fun. To underlie these perceptions with substance, I invite you to read some excerpts from email conversations and reflect upon them.

### Scenario 1: fluent and precise understanding and addressing the situation

The following exchange of messages is derived from the context of the author's participation in a conference. As a newcomer to the person-centred community (in 2003) it was hard for me to estimate whether a contribution in the field of learning would be appropriate for the conference. Although it matched to the conference theme of 'process differentiation', it only marginally suited the focus of the conference, namely 'psychotherapy and counselling'. This is why I wanted to hear the organizers' opinion and also discover whether the articles would be published.

---

### Online example from experience

Dear PCE 2003 Organizers,

I am writing to check with you whether my active participation at PCE 2003 would, in your view, be meaningful. Let me explain in a few words. I have been interested in the PCA for more than 15 years and actively participated at the Carl Rogers symposium 2002, where I organized a workshop on higher education. As a professor of computer science at the University of Vienna, I gradually make my courses more student-centred. Thereby I follow many ideas proposed by Rogers in 'Freedom to Learn', but also develop my own ones. I'd be MOST interested in an exchange of ideas with the PCA community. In my view, the topic of 'process differentiation' could equally be addressed in the context of teaching/learning. Hence my questions:

1) Could a topic like 'Strategies and experiences with person-centred teaching and learning: the role of the facilitator in a time of the internet' find listeners if presented as a paper, or preferably, find participants who would reflect on their teaching practices, if organized as a workshop?
2) Is there a way to publish an accompanying paper (a case study or experience report encompassing students' reactions), e.g. in the conference proceedings?

Thank you for taking the time to consider my mail. For a (potential) newcomer to your conference series like me it is hard to guess in what direction you are heading, so I appreciate your advice to be able to spend my efforts effectively.

Best regards, Renate Motschnig

Dear Renate,

I got this mail forwarded through our conference office. Thank you very much for it. Although the focus at the conference will be on psychotherapy, I think your proposal is worthwhile to include in the programme. Of course, it is difficult to say if it will attract many participants, but I agree with you that an exchange of your ideas with the PCA community will be interesting and the topic of 'process differentiation' could also be addressed in the context of teaching/ learning at universities or in companies. So, please send us a proposal (e.g. for a workshop)…We would appreciate receiving your proposal ASAP. Regarding the proceedings, we have decided to cooperate on this with the editors of the newly published international journal 'Person-Centred and Experiential Psychotherapies'. Of course there will be a conference book containing the abstracts of the presentations at the conference.

I hope to have informed you properly and look very much forward to meeting you in Egmond aan Zee.

Cordially, R.T. (on behalf of the Congress Committee)

## Invitation to reflect

*What do you think of the response by R.T.? Would you be motivated to submit your contribution to this conference? Are there any aspects you would improve upon in the enquiry or the response? Are there aspects you like in particular? Which are they?*

## Feedback

Since my email contains several different aspects (a brief introduction, the problem, two questions) I tried to provide a clear structure. The main reason, however, for selecting this email exchange as a small case study is the way R.T. responds transparently and precisely to all the questions and facets of the request. His response is careful and empathic, transmitting his full understanding of all my concerns and enquiries. I hope that the same 'message' reaches you as a reader and that you can sense how empathically R.T. responds and how precisely and yet briefly he manages to address my whole situation (without having met me in person).

### Scenario 2: writing constructively and being facilitative and empathic

I wanted to participate in a workshop in the USA. Whereas the workshop fee was reasonable, the prices for accommodation in the hotel suggested by the organizers were far too high for me. Would the organizers be willing to support me in finding more reasonably priced accommodation?

---

**Online example from experience**

Dear Organizers,

I have just received your information letter about the La Jolla Program. Since I very strongly wish to take part (and revisit La Jolla after the 100 years Carl Rogers Symposium) I'd like to learn whether there is the option of less expensive accommodation. In the positive case I'd be thankful for any hints on finding an inexpensive place to stay.

Thank you and kind regards from Vienna,

Renate Motschnig

The first response from Will (cc to Livia) arrived promptly, however, then two weeks passed without any communication.

Dear Renate Motschnig,

Thank you for your reply. La Jolla is an expensive place. I am forwarding your request to Livia, who is coordinating our housing. One option I think of right now is to share a room with a couple of other people (if they are available) and that would drive the cost down to about $50 a night. But Livia will see what she can do.

Yours, Will Stillwell

Two weeks pass and time becomes short so I ask myself whether it would OK to ask the organizers for this additional support. But am I requesting something of them? Not really, I just don't want to let my option pass without making an effort. Furthermore, another question comes up. So I follow up mailing and try to clearly communicate my options and politely take up the offer that was made.

Dear Will Stillwell, Dear Livia,

I'd be thankful for any hint and hope for your understanding,
sincerely, Renate Motschnig

PS. Do you already have participants who cannot speak English very well? I am asking since I have a good colleague whose great wish is to participate in your program. Being originally Czech, he never learned English at school. He has been learning English for the last three years, but it's very hard for him and he therefore hesitates. Do you have a message I could give him? Thanks.

Will responds promptly, explicitly acknowledging that he's going to leave the accommodation issue for Livia and picking up the question. I was and still am fascinated by the way he manages to capture so many facets in his elegant response. Let us trace how this comes about. Firstly, Will briefly describes the situation of the La Jolly Program from his experience including the experiences of other non-English natives, without ever giving advice or in any slightest way trying to manipulate, yet expressing a warm invitation. The colleague is cordially welcomed.

Dear Renate,

Will answering. I am leaving your message about accommodation for Livia to answer, but I want to answer you about your Czech colleague. Over the years we have had many La Jolla Program participants whose native language is not English. Almost all our public conversations are carried on in English. I want to make this generalization: sometimes non-English natives struggle very hard to understand impromptu conversation in English. Sometimes we slow down for them. Sometimes they ask us to repeat, and we do. Sometimes they are very tired after a day of attending in English. Sometimes they come to believe that core emotions are most important, and that their imperfect understanding of the English content is less relevant.

It will be an immersion experience for most all of us, and we have wonderful international friendships that develop. Perspectives of life from people of different language-mind-sets have been essential to my personal learning and being.

Your colleague is welcome to attend. Some accommodation will naturally happen for his lack of English skill. His own humour and ambition to participate, in the end, will determine his happiness at the Program.

Yours, Will

Now Livia's response, which is astoundingly full of trust and support.

Dear Renate,

I have just received a communication from Will Stillwell that you would like to attend the La Jolla Program and are looking for a roommate or a less expensive accommodation. I will absolutely work hard to find you a roommate and I also can offer another alternative. My home has an office that also has a bed in it. It is a 10-minute drive from the hotel. I am willing to offer it to you.

I will not be staying at my home but will be at the hotel for the week. The challenge to this offer is finding transportation to and from the hotel (there is no public transportation available). I will find out from Will who has registered for the program who may live near my house so you could drive in with them. Otherwise, I trust there is a way we can work this out. So, Renate, what I am saying is that you should plan to come to the Program and I will make sure you have a place to stay.

Looking forward to being in community with you,

Livia

This requires a huge degree of trust. The offer includes some risk but both sides are willing to take it. Livia first clarifies the situation, how she understands it, and then builds her offer on it. I too had been clear about my situation and tried to express it as clearly and succinctly as possible. Livia also makes sure that she expects that we're going to meet and that potential remaining challenges will be met.

**Invitation to reflect**

*Try to work out why this small case study was selected for this chapter. Do you get a sense that person-centred attitudes are communicated? If so, which ones in particular? Can you find sentences that try to prevent misunderstandings? How do you perceive the respective endings of the mails by Will and Livia?*

## Comparing online and face-to-face person-centred communication

Online communication can be beneficial since it allows for the preliminary decoupling of two or more otherwise entangled processes. We can sequentially follow the process in us and the one in the relationship, while we imagine our partner and finally unite the channels by repeatedly switching to and fro between them. This, in my view, can succeed only if we already have some experience of direct communication and use this to imagine as realistically as possible the reactions of our partner. In this case, the decoupling and the consequent 'preparation' or 'conscious construction of the response' can really help. If we take the time, we can offer a response that expresses how we wish to appear, which may help to form the relationship more mindfully.

In a real dialogue, however, the integration of the 'channels' must happen automatically and fluently. It can, moment by moment, be adjusted in response to the reactions of the other person. It tends also to be supported by one's own body language, gesticulation, mimics, voice, etc. Here, again, we see how the integrated functioning of diverse channels of expression tends to support our response, given that we are sufficiently congruent.

## Some observations and insights from the author's personal experience

- For me it is helpful to imagine my communication partner. What do I know about him/her? In which state might the other person reside when reading my message? Did he/she just return from holiday and likely sit moaning in front of an overflowing mailbox? Is he/she too busy to even read long emails, not to mention respond to them carefully? Will he/she understand our (expert-)language?
- I refrain from writing emails if I am in a bad mood. The danger of overreacting is very high and the damage is hard to repair later. Writing the message spontaneously is OK, this tends to help me clarify my view, but the hitting of the 'send' button is the sensitive issue in the process. Can it wait until the next day or at least for a few hours? How does the message read then? Attention, each email – unlike a spoken message – can be forwarded or opened repeatedly. Viewed outside the direct context, many issues often look far more tragic than they were meant to sound in the heat of the discussion.
- It can be personally revealing, for example, to ask oneself: 'Why am I that angry, what does this trigger in me? How do I feel about this response? How/where do I feel my great joy? Where in this context are my primary interests? What is beneficial or hindering for my interests?' If you feel like it, you can also try to sense into yourself and focus on your feeling in order to get to know yourself better.
- When reading responses, the basic attitude of 'the facts are friendly' (Rogers 1961: 25) turned out to be very helpful for me. I came to think that from every sharing I could learn something, be it only what I would never write myself. Moreover, personal independence and the ability to rely on one's own experience as the highest authority can be a useful relief from disappointments that probably happen more frequently than in face-to-face communication. Responses let you wait, don't arrive at all, are written in a style that demonstrates dominance, or they're causing more work than expected. An inner balance and composure tend to be supportive in managing the stress that thousands of emails undoubtedly cause.

- Personally I find emails particularly 'to the point' if senders articulate their concern transparently and say everything that matters in not too many highly expressive words. They can let some personal message shine through, this speaks to me and lets me feel, well, there's a human being sitting behind the screen, whom I want to understand as well as possible. Furthermore, I find it helpful to learn about specific circumstances if they facilitate the understanding of the situation. For example, 'Best regards, just leaving for the train station' lets me better make sense of the unusually brief 'SMS style' of the message and every doubt that the sender may be offended by something disappears. Also a note like: 'I got your mail, I'll be back to you as soon as I can' doesn't take much effort and can reduce doubt and stress on both sides. However, it may be that I know this person is over-busy and there's an unspoken agreement on mutually accepting longer response intervals.
- I've observed that an appropriate degree of meta-communication, which means the mentioning of aspects that concern communication itself, has the potential to significantly facilitate the understanding of messages. For example, if a sentence starts 'Somewhat exaggerating, I see the situation such that XY would be interested only in . . .', then a clear image can be transmitted that, nevertheless, is to be taken 'with a pinch of salt' only.
- The necessarily brief style requires us to 'draw clear images'. This, however, must not be misunderstood. Here is another example in which I found the expression in brackets charmingly helpful in understanding the whole statement. A journal-editor with whom I had already had some email contact wrote: 'Please let your critical eyes (this is meant as a thankful compliment) pass over the whole again – we would publish the piece as it is.

## Summary

Online communication has its characteristics as much as face-to-face communication does. One of them is that an email response tends to be more of a conscious act than a fast, spoken response, which in turn provides a richer repertoire of expression channels. On the other hand, online communication is more informal and simpler than organizing a face-to-face appointment and thus allows one to increase one's number of contacts. When communicating online we need to pack person-centred attitudes into words, symbols or acts and they have to or can be perceived and 'unpacked' in turn. If these additional coding/decoding processes function at both ends, we can communicate constructively and maintain our reciprocal relationships.

But can attitudes be packed into words without experiencing direct contact with the other person? Even though I suggest that this is not possible in the full range, experience confirms that people communicating online can – to a considerable degree – perceive congruence, acceptance and empathic understanding. Consequently, besides serving the purpose of exchanging information, online communication can also be seen as a means of contributing to personal growth. This can be perceived in particular in arrangements in which online communication is used to bridge the gap between person-to-person meetings in which immediate expression using the full repertoire is possible. However, personally I consider an overemphasis on online communication a danger that could lead to a retardation of our capacity to communicate immediately, intuitively and spontaneously, and to ignorance of our very real need for interpersonal contact.

# 9 Person-centred communication in writing

*I would willingly throw away all the words of this manuscript if I could, somehow, effectively point to the experience which is therapy. It is a process, a thing-in-itself, an experience, a relationship, a dynamic . . . If this book serves as a large signpost, pointing to an experience which is open to our senses of hearing and sight and to our capacity of emotional experience, and if it captures the interest of some and causes them to explore more deeply this thing-in-itself, it will have accomplished its purpose.*

(Rogers [1951] 1995: x)

---

**In this chapter you will learn about:**

- The ways attitudes are expressed and become apparent in writing
- Four features that significantly contribute to understandable writing
- Stylistic elements in writing generally
- Some stylistic elements in the writing of Carl Rogers

---

As much as understanding and being understood are priorities in a person-centred conversation, person-centred sharing through writing aims toward a maximum possible, complex and encompassing perception and understanding of what is being shared. This is a real challenge since 'the true, the genuine, real meaning of a word can never be expressed in words, because the real meaning would be the thing itself. If one wishes to give such a real meaning he should put his hand over his mouth and point' (Rogers [1951] 1995: ix). Hence, each effort to capture the living (communication-) experience using words means risking a single-sided reduction of complex phenomena. We're aware that we can't completely remove that risk. Interestingly – though not surprisingly – the depth of sensing into oneself and empathizing with the other tends to reflect itself in written expression. One can expect that a person with more of these capacities would be more transparent in his or her expression, and would also manage to present him-/herself better, address the other appropriately and express caring or regard.

**Invitation to reflect**

*Do the personal and/or person-centred attitudes of your acquaintances and relatives express themselves in writing? If so, how do you recognize the connection?*

When using a generally understandable, transparent language both authors of this book assume the risk of not being regarded as scientific or knowledgeable as other authors who use lots of scientific vocabulary. This, however, is counterbalanced by a high probability that the book will be received by a wider readership. Hence the desire has been to take the risk and express 'things' that are important more transparently and directly, with appreciation for the reader.

Before turning to explore Carl Rogers' style of writing in his scientific works, I (Renate) would like to pass on some generally applicable and broadly accepted guidelines for more comprehensible writing. While following the guidelines tends to significantly contribute to improving comprehension, in my view it does not guarantee that the resulting text will be perceived as sensitive, motivating and fluent. Hence, above all, I advocate staying flexible and empathically perceiving each respective situation.

## Understandability according to Langer, Schulz von Thun and Tausch

In the search for properties that allow a text be perceived as more or less understandable, Langer *et al.* (1981) conducted several studies and discovered four specific features ('the Hamburg concept of understandability', originally: *'Hamburger Verständlichkeitskonzept'*). For each text, these four features allow one to assess its degree of understandability. In the following, I present the guidelines that Langer *et al.* derived from their research and which were also implemented in an online tutorial (Kroop *et al.* 2006). Interested readers (who read German) can find a more detailed summary and the applied implementation of these rules in Schulz von Thun ([1981] 2002).

**Simplicity – avoid complexity.** Simplicity means to descriptively clarify the theme using short, easily understood sentences. Simplicity is by far the most important property of understandable writing. Don't use foreign words. If they can't be avoided, explain them as simply as possible. Speak to your readers in clear text.

**Structure, order – avoid confusion.** Here the guiding sentence is: 'I'm supporting the reader so that they can orient themselves and maintain a perspective of the whole document.' *Structure*: the structure relates to how the text is arranged. This includes, especially in longer text, an indication of how the text is constructed. Paragraphs, headings and notes help to structure the text thus making it easy and clear to understand and navigate. Important segments should be highlighted. *Order*: the logical structure and the correct sequence of arguments helps establish inner structure. Clear indications of related thoughts and cross-connections help to better grasp relationships between issues.

**Brevity, conciseness – avoid verbosity.** Expressed in one sentence: 'Lots of information with fewer words, brief and bounded, limited to the essential.' Although a 'telegram style' occasionally can be beneficial, in general it is not the best solution. However, lengthy writing tends to become convoluted; the reader's grasp of the essential message(s) can get lost and the reader's attention declines quickly. The text should be as long as needed but not longer than required.

**Additional stimulation – avoid intruding boredom.** Additional inspiration or stimulation serves to address the reader not just intellectually but also affectively. His or her senses are triggered to engage with the input. Learning and the mediation of information become meaningful if they reach the whole person – and this can also be fun. Diverse stylistic techniques can be employed to make the text more expressive including examples, sharing personal experiences, adding line drawings, images and characters who talk using direct speech are just some examples. All this can add spice to the 'mental dish'. Nevertheless that same rule holds true as with cooking: too much seasoning destroys the original taste of the food.

### Invitation to reflect

*If you'd like to deepen the information you've just received and find out where you are on the four dimensions, then take something you have written and apply the four criteria to it. Which ones does your writing cover well? Where do you find room for improvement?*

*What do you like in writing that motivates you to continue reading?*

Science is governed by the ideal of objective truth which must be valid independently of the person who discovers and presents it. Nevertheless, according to Langer *et al.* (1981) it is permissible to connect scientific information with aspects of oneself: why is precisely this content important to me? What was the process that led me to discover it? What meaning does the result have for me? Each scientific report holds a component of self-revelation – and it is not unscientific to include it. Personally important content can be transmitted vividly if we allow our own personality some voice. The meaning for the reader can be enhanced by purposeful connection between the factual and the personal, the intellect and the feelings.

The above information on the guidelines might appear different when compared with the rest of this book, because I tried to follow them fairly strictly. In the remainder of the book, however, we have both tried to minimize the risk of a single-sided reduction of complex 'communicative matter'. This also explains the frequent use of words like 'tend', 'often', 'can', etc. and of subjective statements ('we', 'I').

## Characteristics of Carl Rogers' writing

Since we both feel that Carl Rogers' writing includes the reader (and we certainly feel addressed and included by him), and since he manages to reach and touch a wide audience through his scientific work, I want to illuminate some elements of his own writing. This is intended to complement the perspective on understandable writing presented above.

### Invitation to reflect

*Try to identify stylistic elements in works by an author whose writing speaks to you. Can you give examples? What results do your friends/colleagues arrive at if they are asked to do the same, and what do they consider particularly engaging in books or articles they have read? Do you emulate stylistic elements from authors who speak to you?*

At the beginning of his articles and books, Rogers tends to introduce readers to the context of the situation and to the conditions that frame it. Then he describes how he deals with the situation, what goes on in himself, what he considers, what are the alternatives and what are the advantages and disadvantages presented by the solution he has chosen. In this way, he includes readers not only in the findings he has described but also in the whole process and lets them partake in it from the beginning. For example, Rogers (1980) introduces his book chapter on 'Experiences in communication' by explaining that it grew out of a talk on the theme of communication that he had been invited to present at the California Institute of Technology. Throughout the phase of collecting references he wasn't satisfied with his procedure and he also discarded the idea of giving a demonstration. Then he indicates that the chapter will show how he tried to communicate with the audience instead of just talking *about* communication.

Another stylistic element, namely describing various alternatives and then picking one of them, has already been exemplified in the previous paragraph – instead of talking about communication or demonstrating it, Rogers chose to communicate with the audience. In what follows readers discover his explanation for this choice. Rogers states that pure 'knowledge about' isn't what matters; instead there's a determined search for experiential knowledge.

I consider Rogers' style as essentially *non-directive*. He shares his own experiences and findings without imposing them on us or presenting them as absolute truths. Frequently he calls upon his readers to decide for themselves what they want to take from his experience and what to question.

Rogers often demonstrates his statements by means of concrete examples, the inclusion of interviews or by letting others 'talk'. He shares a lot of himself, both from his scientific and his personal life. In other words, he shares himself as a living example and there is an enormously high degree of openness in his messages. Not many are willing to share their very personal experiences from their marital relationship in scientific books.

Rogers puts forward questions that he poses to himself after having expressed something. This indicates reflection and self-exploration and underlines the fact that multiple perspectives are invited. It motivates us to read not only passively, but to inquire into the positions given and to *position ourselves*, which means 'listening' to our own thought and evaluation processes.

Rogers also includes us explicitly in the objectives and intentions of his writing. For example, 'if this and that happens, then the chapter/book will have accomplished its purpose' (for a concrete example see this chapter's introductory quote).

Viewed as a whole, in Rogers' writing there is a convinced, often inquiring and inviting but never prescriptive or instructive attitude. It is consistently non-directive. Rogers' openness, depth of reflection and self-perception are remarkable. As readers we feel considered, included and accepted.

## Summary

Numerous examples illustrate that, in person-centred accounts, attitudes or other value-orientations are revealed. There is no doubt that we owe it to our readers to write as understandably as possible. To be clear about the goals and purposes of any particular messages is a precondition for conveying them to others in a way they can follow by being more engaged. It is well worth considering how a seamless transfer can be accomplished and how the message can be put into words coherently and understandably. In this context, Langer *et al.* (1981) discovered that simplicity, structure, brevity and additional stimulation are those features that most prominently support understandable writing.

# PART III
# Experiential learning

# 10 Communication in person-centred technology-enhanced learning

*Changingness, a reliance on process rather than upon static knowledge, is the only thing that makes any sense as a goal for education in the modern world.*

(Rogers 1983: 120)

**In this chapter you will learn about:**

- Significant, whole-person learning
- Attitudes necessary to facilitate this kind of learning
- Further elements that support significant, whole-person learning
- Ways in which technology can contribute to enriching learning processes
- Online reaction sheets supporting multiple perspectives in the organization of experience and the development of a class community based on honest feedback
- The process of reflection as a step in significant learning

Considering the educational goals of the European Union, it is important to understand that the situation Rogers (1983: 120) identified as completely new is becoming increasingly important:

> We are, in my view, faced with an entirely new situation in education where the goal of education ... is the facilitation of change and learning. The only man who is educated is the man who has learned how to learn; the man who has learned how to adapt and change; the man who has realized that no knowledge is secure, that only the process of *seeking* knowledge gives a basis for security.

Person-centred communication provides the basis for the interpersonal approach in significant, person-centred learning processes. These aim at facilitating *whole-person* learning – in the sense of integrating intellect, skills, abilities, attitudes and feelings – and *significant* learning – in the sense of leading to changes that are perceived as significant by the learner. The person-centred technology enhanced learning (PCeL) developed at the University of Vienna is targeted at complementing person-centred immediate presence with technology. This is done in a way that allows students to develop not only in their respective subject area but also along the interpersonal dimension. It can be achieved by providing online learning resources for those areas that have a high percentage of intellectual content. In this way, face-to-face time is set free for intensive sharing between learners and instructors, more appropriately called facilitators. In these slots used for sharing – be it a group discussion, the elaboration of a topic in small teams or an interactive presentation – person-centred attitudes are expressed as transparently as possible such that they tend to be experienced.

In this chapter the most important concepts and processes are going to be summarized and illustrated using examples, students' reactions and course results (from courses not including encounter groups). Furthermore I (Renate) will show how innovative learning technology can be used to provide space for person-centred communication, significant learning, reflection and new insights derived primarily from experience.

## Person-centred learning

According to Carl Rogers, 'The organism reacts as an organismic whole to this phenomenal field' ([1951] 1995: 468). Well-grounded scientific studies (Rogers 1961, 1983; Aspy 1972; Barrett-Lennard 1998; Cornelius-White 2007; Cornelius-White and Harbaugh 2010) confirm that learning is most persistent if it addresses all three levels of development – our intellect, (social) skills and attitudes – in a person-centred climate (Motschnig-Pitrik and Nykl 2004; Nykl 2005). In Rogers' words: 'Significant learning combines the logical and the intuitive, the intellect and the feelings, the concept and the experience, the idea and the meaning. When we learn in that way, we are whole...' (1983: 20).

Rogers (1983: 121) consistently highlighted the vital contribution of the interpersonal relationship to the facilitation of meaningful and significant learning that encompasses personal development:

> We know... that the initiation of such learning rests not upon the teaching skills of the leader, not upon scholarly knowledge of the field, not upon curricular planning, not upon use of audio-visual aids, not upon the programmed learning used, not upon lectures and presentations, not upon an abundance of books, though each of these might at one time or another be

utilized as an important resource. No, the facilitation of significant learning rests upon certain attitudinal qualities that exist in the personal relationship between the facilitator and the learner.

According to Rogers (1961: 37, 280), psychological growth in a person-centred climate encompasses (among others) the following areas:

- Higher acceptance of self, increased self-confidence, more self-direction
- Higher acceptance of others
- Better understanding and sensing of self and others
- Becoming the person one would like to be, more balanced, having less stress
- Higher flexibility and more openness both to what is going on inside and what is going on outside of oneself
- Adopting more realistic goals and improving the ability of coping with the problems of life

Readers familiar with the person-centred approach won't be surprised to find that the preconditions for person-centred learning are the teacher's or facilitator's core attitudes of congruence or realness, acceptance or respect, encompassing empathic understanding of the learner's whole person (Rogers [1951] 1995, 1961, 1983). If learning is to be experienced as significant, the learners need to perceive these core attitudes to some degree. In addition to these preconditions, I consider the following elements to be essential for supporting significant learning (Motschnig-Pitrik 2006c; Tausch and Tausch [1963] 1998).

**Team-/groupwork.** The facilitator supports collaborative problem-solving in teams or groups. This means that the facilitator creates an atmosphere that is conducive to sharing in teams and groups, solving problems and tasks, and learning from and with each other. This leads to intensified contact and communication (Motschnig-Pitrik and Santos 2006; Motschnig-Pitrik and Figl 2007).

**Participation and self-organization.** The facilitator respects learners' ability to self-organize and self-initiate. This means that facilitators provide space for learners to bring their own talent and direction into play. They support learners to make optimal use of the freedom provided. The increased variety and magnitude of options in technology-enhanced environments undoubtedly supports this endeavour. However, the implementation depends directly on the facilitator's and learners' attitudes toward self-organization or, in other words, how far they are willing to yield self-organizing processes.

**Reflection, learning to learn.** The facilitator promotes sharing and including experiences that result from the learning process of individuals, teams and groups. This addresses learning at the level of individuals, teams and groups. It is intended to provide offerings that allow learners (and also facilitators) to be confronted with change and new situations, and to manage them in order to learn from them personally and professionally regarding some specific subject matter (Motschnig-Pitrik 2006c).

While person-centred learning has already been studied thoroughly (e.g. Tausch and Tausch [1963] 1998; Aspy 1972; Rogers 1983; Barrett-Lennard 1998) and an encompassing meta-study has been conducted (Cornelius-White *et al.* 2004; Cornelius-White 2007; Cornelius-White and Harbaugh 2010), a thorough integration of novel technologies is posing fresh challenges (Motschnig-Pitrik and Mallich 2004; Motschnig-Pitrik 2005). The following examples are intended to illustrate the synergy unfolding from the integration of presence and the carefully-tuned use of technology. Regarding the accompanying research process I share Rogers' view that science originates in the genuine participation of people who follow their goals and values (Rogers 1961; Hutterer 1990; Haselberger and Hutterer 2013). From subjective immersion there emerges a feeling for direction and constellation. Rogers (1961: 216–17) writes:

> Science has its inception in a participating person who is pursuing aims, values, purposes which have personal and subjective meaning for him. As a part of this pursuit, he, in some area, 'wants to find out.' Consequently, if he is to be a good scientist, he immerses himself in the relevant experience…He senses the field in which he is interested, he lives it. He does more than 'think' about it – he lets his organism take over and reacts to it, both on a knowing and on an unknowing level…Out of this complete subjective immersion comes a creative forming, a sense of direction, a vague formulation of relationships hitherto unrecognized…It is indeed the matrix of immediate personal, subjective experience [in which] science, and each individual scientific research, has its origin.

## Integration of new learning technologies

### Integration of face-to-face and online elements

Instructors/facilitators provide well-chosen resources such as articles, slides, links and references for further study such that they complement the course's subject matter. From these resources students can freely (or after consultation) choose the field in which they want to specialize and elaborate, or complement the resources from the point of view of a particular project they propose. In the course of this work, personal experience, thoughts or applications are included and the existing resources are questioned critically such that some added value tends to result. Students discover strengths, weaknesses and gaps in existing materials and are challenged to propose their own resolutions to those problems for which they don't find satisfactory responses in the literature. Resources such as articles and elaborated project documents are stored in such a way that all students on a course can view them. They are presented and discussed briefly in class. After each unit, further feedback and reactions to the presentations are followed up online. A special potential lies in the fact that sharing starts face-to-face, is continued online and brought back to direct exchange in class again. In this process both the benefits and the disadvantages of face-to-face sessions and the employment of new media can be experienced directly. As a consequence, students can decide more mindfully whether – in a particular situation – they prefer to communicate via the internet or to organize face-to-face meetings.

Another example illustrating the alternation of personal presence and online phases can be observed in capturing students' expectations of a course. In the initial unit, participants share their expectations and fears regarding the course. They are asked to formulate their personal expectations and fears and to upload their written responses to the learning platform. In the next unit participants' expectations are collaboratively summarized to see how they can be realized in the design of further units. Due to the mix of media used, each person has the opportunity to choose, explore and apply the communication medium that suits them best such that individual strengths are furthered.

In a related scenario the results of project work are reflected upon and shared as well as the processes that teams went through during cooperation. In this way, subtleties in communication and teamwork can come to the surface and be explored in a supportive climate.

## More transparency through online spaces

Online workspaces and evaluations provide a high degree of transparency. Projects can be put online and commented upon so that all the participants can learn far more than from their own project alone – given that a proper communicative culture has been established beforehand. A reciprocal online evaluation of the projects and achievements of colleagues confirms that participation and feedback are highly valued. Additionally, this allows one to experience the formulation as well as the reception of open and respectful feedback. As a further step, the online feedback can be shared directly in the next face-to-face unit. As the course facilitator I often realize that aspects and perspectives are being brought up that I had never thought of. In my view it is the variety of perspectives expressed that produces the real added value.

Well-deliberated learning scenarios integrate blended sequences. This supports instructors/facilitators in motivating students to participate actively in a rather self-organized way and thereby to endeavour to understand each other personally, socially, professionally and empathically.

## Reflection and feedback – face to face and online

Reaction sheets – basically free-reaction journals without any given structure – can be seen as one of the most simple, but meaningful, instruments for improving a course, for quality assurance and for improving the relationship between the facilitator and the students, as well as between the students themselves. In these reaction sheets participants are invited to share anything that comes to mind in connection with a workshop or unit of a course. The reaction sheets are written at the end of a course unit and put online on the course homepage where they can be read, but not edited, by other participants. At the beginning of the following unit participants can express themselves regarding the reaction sheets. Students appreciate that their voices are heard, even though it is rarely possible to address all reactions. Students 'voiced' their views regarding the reaction sheets by writing:

> I liked the addressing of the reaction sheets at the very beginning of each unit – this facilitated a fluent transition to the new unit. This is something that really worked well in the last course!

> This unit started by briefly reviewing the reaction sheets. I found this rather good because you can see quite well that the reactions are taken seriously and are considered.

An exciting feature is that even though reactions often converge in one direction, participants tend to highlight different aspects and occasionally also express opposing views. For instance, most students find it worthwhile to present their initial project proposals in class after a short preparation period to get the group's feedback. For some students it was a new experience to have such a spontaneous presentation in class. Others found the initial sharing in the team valuable, yet others liked to get the facilitator's comments promptly or to observe the different approaches two teams had regarding the same topic. But I also read in the reactions that one participant found my quite detailed conversation with one team boring because it wasn't relevant to him. He suggested that it might be better to indicate the task in an earlier unit so that students could think about it and prepare their concepts beforehand. If, in such a situation, I manage to consider some of the voices so as to let them influence the follow-up units – for example, to introduce a task that will be pursued in the next units beforehand, or be briefer in giving comments to individuals – then students tend to be deeply impressed. An atmosphere of belonging together develops and motivates high achievement, a common, shared search for solutions and detailed feedback. Individuals and teams participate genuinely and in turn share their impressions and thoughts in the reaction sheets and in dialogue during class. This allows participants – including the facilitator – to learn from situations that work out well, as well as those aspects that don't work. This learning can also be realized in action and everyone can have an active part in it.

Frequently, the more shy participants submit detailed reactions. The online medium supports them in becoming more present to the group. This seems to contribute to a faster increase in openness, understanding and trust in the group compared to pure face-to-face classes. What counts for grading is less the first deliverable and more the final result, including active participation in direct and online modes.

In order to give readers an idea of the opportunities that simple online reaction sheets provide, here are some excerpts. They refer to a course segment in which students presented the concept of their seminar thesis which was done in teams in a predominantly self-organized way.

Preparing a concept for the seminar thesis was very appropriate. This immediately contributed to the development of a group spirit. One could not only form initial thoughts regarding the topic but also receive others' opinions.

It would have been sufficient to talk about the individual topics with the course facilitator, since, to be honest, the other topics or how they were tackled didn't interest me very much. Hence I'd say that up to the break the course wasn't so interesting for me, but it can't always be so exciting, can it?

I liked it that we addressed the seminar thesis intensively. So each team had the opportunity to form their thoughts regarding the contents of their work. The feedback we got as a response to our short presentation makes it easier to write the thesis, because we know better which direction the whole thing [should] take.

I'm already very excited... and look forward to next Friday.

I was very intrigued by the elaboration of the whole concept within just 20 minutes. In former seminar or similar works one met with the team outside the course and elaborated a concept. This often took a lot of time (travelling to the meeting, finding a time slot...). Scheduling this within the course session resulted in a number of benefits: one had some kind of pressure (time limit of 20 minutes) to produce a meaningful concept. For me this was very helpful. One could immediately share one's elaborated knowledge with the facilitator and get feedback. I considered this very productive since in other courses one often receives feedback only after having elaborated a gross version of the thesis and larger changes in the content require an enormous investment in time.

As pointed out earlier in this book and in many other places besides, giving open and constructive feedback is an 'art'. The reaction sheets offer an outstanding opportunity to experience the giving and receiving of feedback. The online medium provides the option of distance paired with an undisturbed, uninfluenced reflection by each person, while personal sharing requires and contributes spontaneity.

## Reflection and its contribution to significant learning

In everyday language 'reflection' means thoughtful deliberation, observation, thinking or pondering about something, or the deepening of some thought process. *Webster's Dictionary* (1990) provides, among others, the definition: 'The action of the mind by which it is conscious of its own operations; attentive consideration.' In this sense 'to reflect' means to enter one's inner world, to think about some experience, to let something pass in front of your 'inner eye', and at times to arrive at some insight. This can proceed in our thought only, or alternatively also be written down, in order to preserve as much as possible.

However, 're-flexion' also means a transformation. Something of the original experience is changed, be it only the context – the environment, the feelings, thoughts, meanings. This is how some experience gains different perspectives, and hence will tend to be organized in a more versatile, *flexible* way, due to the acquired richness of perspectives.

### Invitation to reflect

*Who hasn't observed that experiences tend to be different in the memory compared to the original event? Try to remember your first day at work or your first counselling experience: how do you feel about it now?*

### What person-centred reflection is (not)

In order to characterize the phenomenon of person-centred reflection and to distinguish it from similar processes, let us start by ruling out what person-centred reflection is not. It certainly is not a strict analysis of some experience and not an ongoing nagging, it is not justifying to oneself, nor inner blaming. Moreover, it doesn't have fixed rules or action patterns but rather means stating consciously: *I accept my experience – it is valuable to me, this is how I felt before; how do I feel now? Having gained some distance, what do I think now? What can I take with me without deriving rigid constructs?* To reflect in a person-centred way means to have an inner exchange with oneself. Optionally others can take part, however, it is essential that the reflective processes proceed in a person-centred climate. Experiences are mindfully received in their entirety – not just as facts or opinions – and fully sensed such that meaning and significant learning can occur.

### Effects of person-centred reflection

What is happening inside of us? We 'naturally' tend to think about situations that are unfinished. We say: 'This keeps me busy.' Who isn't familiar with the situation when someone or something triggers a process in us that continues and attracts our attention repeatedly, as if longing for closure. In effect, unfinished processes consume lots of energy while pushing toward closure, as Lewin and his team found out (the '*Zeigarnik* effect'). We want to gain clarity about something, we want to understand, we want to actualize our potentials. Intermediate states mean 'unfinished business'. If someone or something hinders us in finishing some ongoing process, be it some enterprise or the article we're reading, we tend to have a negative reaction. This can be seen as another indication of the fact that our organism wants to reach closure. I conjecture that the actualizing tendency activates processes that make us want to understand and to gain insight in order to set free the energy that is bound up in trying to do so, and then be able to reinvest it in a new process. We have at least some conscious influence in this circuit in so far as we can 'mark' situations that are important to us as not completely finished by reflecting upon them and exploring them further. The more perspectives we gain, the larger is the probability that some of them won't be totally completed such that they attract our interest when – often arbitrarily – called upon.

When reflecting we recall some experience into consciousness. Since the new context is different – in the vast majority of cases it will be more relaxed and less spontaneous and intense than the original experience, we can perceive and organize the experience under different perspectives and become aware of additional feelings and meanings that originally had been concealed under the intensity of the experience. We regain access to some experience that we already valued internally and can better organize the experience without being so intensively present in the whole happening. The new, relaxed and accepting climate lets us perceive ('symbolize') the reflected situation, including ourselves, more precisely, and helps us to build a stronger connection between our feelings and thoughts. This contributes to a better interconnectedness between individual parts of our organism, which is a clear indicator of mental health (Rogers 1961; Damasio 2003).

With all the benefits of reflecting, we must not forget to mention the danger that lies in distorting our genuine experience with established constructs so that new insight is extinguished. It is vital that reflection proceeds in a relaxed, accepting atmosphere, a climate that is void of fear or the assigning of guilt or praise. Our original feelings remain pivotal. Through reflection they will be accompanied more consciously by our personal direction in that we complement our genuine experience with our thoughts.

According to Rogers (1980: 62) the phase of reawakening or reflecting on an experience is the second of three steps that together constitute significant or experiential learning.

---

**Rogers' three steps to significant learning**

- Living the experience on a total basis
- Rehearing it on an experiential, cognitive basis
- Studying it once more for every intellectual clue

---

Significant learning integrates all the resources that our organism provides in this process. Regarding the three steps to significant learning, Rogers (1980: 62) notes: 'I know of no other way of combining the deepest experiential learning with the most highly abstract cognitive and theoretical learnings...' This is absolutely consistent with Schön's concept of the 'reflective practitioner' (Schön 1983) and his work on 'reflection-on-action'. Indeed, recent approaches to organizational development give reflection and multifaceted perception, or sensing, considerable weight (Senge 2006).

## Summary

This chapter was targeted at providing an impression of the function and value of person-centred communication, reflection and cooperation in the field of significant learning. Research at the University of Vienna shows that students – from their own perspective – tend to benefit most from interaction, team collaboration and practical tasks. In person-centred courses it is exactly those elements that are emphasized. Furthermore, our research and experience confirms Rogers' hypothesis that a person-centred climate promotes significant learning. Thus, the basic tenets of humanistic pedagogy are transferable to the field of modern learning technologies and appear particularly apt in helping learners become active, open, collaborative and reflective participants. The new contribution lies in the thoughtful inclusion of modern learning technologies that support learning processes and form a learning culture that appears appropriate to our time.

## Further reading

Readers interested in PCeL are referred to Motschnig-Pitrik (2004, 2005, 2006a, 2006b, 2006c, 2006d, 2013), Motschnig-Pitrik and Derntl (2005), Motschnig-Pitrik and Figl (2007), Motschnig-Pitrik and Nykl (2004, 2005), Motschnig-Pitrik *et al.* (2007) for further considerations and examples from practice. Studies of individual courses are published as scientific articles, several of which can be downloaded from my homepage (www.cs.univie. ac.at/renate.motschnig). An encompassing collection of scientifically studied and practically confirmed teaching/learning scenarios and examples based on the person-centred approach can be found in the PhD thesis by Michael Derntl (2006). Person-centred learning in management and other non-therapeutic contexts is described in Sollárová and Sollár (2013).

# 11 Person-centred encounter groups

*I still retail the conviction I had at that time: The intensive group experience, the encounter group – whatever you wish to call it – is, when well managed, well facilitated, I think, one of the most significant inventions of this century. I think it has had – and still continues to have – a tremendous impact.*

(Rogers and Russell 2002: 194)

---

**In this chapter you will learn about:**

- The origins of the intensive group experience of which encounter groups are one special representative 'species'

- Characteristic features of encounter groups

- Changes in individuals, relationships and organizations due to participation in encounter groups

- The 15 phases of the encounter group process

- Students' reflections on encounter groups at universities in the twenty-first century

- The differences and commonalities of the process in dialogue groups and person-centred encounter groups

- The opportunities and challenges resulting from international participation

---

Person-centred encounter groups offer a chance to experience person-centred communication and thereby support one in organizing and extending one's inner world. Such groups are also referred to as person-centred, self-experience groups. In this chapter, we first provide a brief overview into this way of encountering through immediate, interpersonal communication and presence, according to Rogers' description of encounter groups (Rogers 1970). Subsequently we turn to our own experiences and students' reactions to our academic courses on person-centred communication in which the majority of time tends to be spent on person-centred encounters. Then the group process in dialogue groups will be compared with that of person-centred encounter groups. Finally, special attention will be devoted to international participants and the phenomenon of diversity in encounter groups.

## Origins

The movement towards an intensive group experience developed at about the same time in two different places and with two distinctly different objectives. Prior to 1947, Kurt Lewin, a renowned psychologist at the Massachusetts Institute of Technology (MIT), realized that the development of human relations skills was an important but overlooked area of education. The first so-called 'T-group' (T standing for training) was conducted in 1947. In the following decades the newly-formed organization, National Training Laboratories (NTL), continued to develop the T-group, mainly under the influence of industry, managers and executives. This direction developed primarily because industry could afford the cost of intensive group experiences for their top personnel, who were taught to observe the nature of their interactions with other members in order to better understand their own functioning and to better cope with difficult situations.

At about the same time (1946), Carl Rogers and his team at the University of Chicago were involved in training personal counsellors for the Veterans Administration. They felt that no amount of cognitive training would prepare them, so they experimented with an intensive group experience. The 'trainees' met for several hours each day in order to better understand themselves, to become aware of their attitudes, and to relate to each other in ways that would be helpful and could carry over into their counselling work. This was an attempt to integrate experiential and cognitive learning in a process which had high value for the individual. This process provided many deep and meaningful experiences for the participants and turned out to be so successful that the staff continued to use the procedure in summer workshops. The concepts were gradually further developed to include various orientations and forms (Natiello 2001).

## Characteristic features of encounter groups

According to Rogers (1970: 6):

- The group tends to be small (8–18 participants – there are, however, reports about quite successful large groups as well), relatively unstructured and choosing its own goals and directions.

- The group experience often, though not always, includes some cognitive input – some content material to be presented to the group or some particular direction to focus on.
- In almost all instances, the leader's responsibility is primarily the facilitation of the expression of both feelings and thoughts on the part of participants. The group leader and the members focus on the process and dynamics of immediate personal interactions.

## Frequently occurring tendencies

Rogers (1970: 6–7) formulated a set of hypotheses which tend to be held in common by all intensive groups:

- A facilitator can develop a psychological climate of safety in which freedom of expression and reduction of defensiveness tends to occur. In such a climate, many of the immediate feeling reactions, meanings and thoughts of each member tend to be recognized and expressed more freely.
- A climate of mutual trust develops out of this mutual freedom to express genuine feelings, both positive and negative. Each member moves toward greater acceptance of his/her total being – emotional, intellectual and physical – as it *is in the moment*, including its potential.
- With individuals less inhibited by defensive rigidity, the possibility of change in personal attitudes and behaviour, in professional methods, in administrative procedures and relationships, becomes less threatening. With the reduction of defensive rigidity, individuals can hear each other more clearly, and can learn from each other to a greater extent.
- There is a development of feedback process, such that each individual learns how she/he appears to others and what impact she/he has on interpersonal relationships.
- With this improved communication, new ideas, new concepts, new directions emerge. Innovation can become a desirable rather than a threatening possibility.
- The learnings in the group process tend to spill over, whether temporarily or permanently, into relationships with spouses, children, students, subordinates, peers and even superiors following the group experience.
- After initial uncertainty and tension an atmosphere develops that invites the free expression of feelings, meanings and ideas. However, this tendency can't be perceived through an intellectual approach alone, it requires the personal experiencing of such an open atmosphere.

# Changes after taking part in encounter groups

According to Rogers and Russell (2002: 194), 'a well-facilitated encounter group which relies on the potential that resides in the group is, and continues to be, a very powerful experience for personality change, for behaviour change, for laying the basis for solutions of social problems.' An essential question is whether the group process leads to significant changes in attitudes and behaviour and whether these changes are sustainable and can proceed even after the group experience ends. Here we summarize some changes that Rogers (1970) observed in individuals, relationships and organizations. Further thought and research in the area of person-centred encounter groups can be found, for example, in the following books and articles: Rogers (1961, 1970, 1978, 1980, 1983), Schmid (1994), Barrett-Lennard (1998, 2003, 2005), Lago and McMillan (1999), Natiello (2001), Motschnig-Pitrik and Nykl (2004, 2007), Nykl (2005), Nykl and Motschnig-Pitrik (2005), Cornelius-White *et al.* (2013a, 2013b).

## Individual change

Rogers (1970: 76) saw that 'individuals alter, very measurably, their concepts of themselves, as they explore their feelings in an accepting climate and receive tough and tender feedback from group members who care'. Some people choose a whole new – philosophical, vocational, intellectual – direction for their lives. On the other hand, some participate in encounter groups without being touched, experiencing no significant change. Some *seemingly* uninvolved people, however, show interesting behavioural changes later. Very few individuals seek psychotherapy later in order to work through problems that have surfaced during groupwork, or to continue to grow personally. Summarizing, Rogers considers the encounter group to be 'the best instrument I know for healing the loneliness that prevails in so many human beings. It holds forth a real hope that isolation need not be the keynote of our individual lives' (1970: 127).

## Relationship change

Rogers (1970: 76) explains that he knew people

> for whom the encounter experience has meant an almost miraculous change in the depth of their communication with spouse and children...They are able to share their growing insights, take the risk of expressing their real feelings, both loving and negative, as soon as they themselves have become aware of them.

Rogers (1970: 79) had seen fathers who came home, able for the first time in years to communicate with their sons. He also saw teachers who had transformed their classes

> into a personal, caring, trusting learning group, where students participate fully and openly in forming the curriculum and all the other aspects of their education. Tough business executives who described a particular business relationship as hopeless, have gone home and changed it into a constructive one.

There were situations in which couples faced the hidden differences between them and frequently reached a real reconciliation. In other situations they gained insight that the communication gap between them was so large that they could not bridge it. Rogers writes very openly and thoughtfully that the changes in relationships – while mostly constructive from a personal point of view – are sometimes negative from a social perspective.

### Organizational change

Rogers witnessed situations in which *individuals* were greatly changed while their *institutions* changed scarcely at all. In other situations teachers – as a result of encounter experiences – brought about deeply rooted changes in grading systems, placed students on committees and opened up channels of administrator-faculty-student communication. In another case, interpersonal communication became the heart and core of a business enterprise (Rogers 1970: 79). Summarizing, encounter groups were recognized as fostering independence, openness and integrity but not necessarily unconditional institutional loyalty. Some group participants resigned from their jobs, having decided to work for change outside the institution rather than within it because of the courage gained in encounter groups.

We are intrigued by the high degree to which Peter Senge's (2006) principles of the learning organization with its respective attitudes and competencies correspond to the positive changes that encounter groups bring about in the vast majority of cases. Prominent examples are a more encompassing and sensitive perception of the environment, the loosening of rigid mental constructs, the capacity and readiness for dialogue and many more.

### The group process

Rogers describes the group process as consisting of 15 phases. These, however, are not clearly delimited but rather overlap with each other. There can also be phases that are not reached in a particular group. Furthermore, certain phases can unfold individually for some participants but hardly at all for others. The following description is a shortened summary of Rogers' (1970: 16–40) account.

## 1 Milling around

The facilitator makes clear:

> that this is a group with unusual freedom and not one for which he will take directional responsibility, there tends to develop a period of initial confusion, awkward silence, polite surface interaction, 'cocktail party talk,' frustration and great lack of continuity...Individual A will present some proposal or concern, clearly looking for a response of the group. Individual B has obviously been waiting for his turn and starts off in some completely different tangent as though he had never heard A. [The question arises:] 'What is the purpose of the group?'
>
> (Rogers 1970: 16)

Initially, participants tend to be overburdened with the excess of freedom they are experiencing. Only gradually do they find out that further development requires a certain adaptation.

## 2 Resistance to personal expression

It is the *public* self that members tend to show each other, and only gradually, fearfully and ambivalently do they take steps to reveal something of the *private* self (Rogers 1970: 17). Considerations and thoughts that would reveal an 'imperfect me' tend to be kept back. Many participants lack trust in the group: 'How can one know the group can be trusted?'

## 3 Description of past feelings

As the process continues, the expression of feelings begins to assume a larger share despite the ambivalence about the trustworthiness of the group and the risk of exposing oneself. The executive tells how frustrated he feels by certain situations in his industry and the housewife recalls related problems she had with her children. Typically, feelings are described as being in the past – there and then – even if they are obviously current in a person. It is as if a person describes himself or herself as an object and their gestures and feelings appear to be inconsistent. A person's feelings are often not perceivable by others and this is frequently voiced.

## 4 Expression of negative feelings

Curiously, participants' first expression of genuine 'here and now' feelings often comes out in the form of negative attitudes towards other group members or the facilitator. For example, in a group in which members introduced themselves, one woman refused to do so because she wanted to be known for what she was in the group. Shortly after this, a man in the group verbally attacked her. He was angry because she wasn't willing to cooperate. Frequently, the leader is attacked for his or her lack of giving proper guidance. Why are negatively toned expressions the first feelings to be expressed? Rogers hypothesized that expressing negative feelings was one of the best ways to test the trustworthiness of a group.

## 5 Expression and exploration of personally meaningful material

Following the resistance to personal expression and the articulation of negative feelings it often happens that some individual reveals himself or herself to the group in some significant way. That person has come to realize that he/she can contribute to make something meaningful out of it. Trust is beginning to develop. Participants have realized they can express negative feelings without catastrophic consequences. They know that there is a freedom here, even though it is risky. Some participants dare to reveal to the group some deeper facet of themselves. For example, Sam explores his fear in saying:

> The first time I realized that I could *frighten* someone – It really, it was a discovery that I had to just kind of look at and feel and get to know, you know, it was such a *new* experience for me. I was so used to the feeling of being frightened by *others* that it had never occurred to me that anyone could be – I guess it never had – that anyone could be frightened of *me*. And I guess maybe it has something to do with how I feel about myself.
>
> (Rogers 1970: 21)

Participants are beginning to share their personal problems, joys, desires, etc. and get support from the group. We observed that they endeavoured to 'accompany' each other in the ways they were used to, such as by giving advice, clues and analyses. The group members also experienced the presence of the facilitator, holding back his/her own such habits and instead focusing on the experiences of the participants.

The example from an encounter group characterizes this phase.

**Example from an encounter group**

One of our participants expressed her stress and misgivings due to her indecision as to what to do once she completed her studies. She shared her worries with the group and asked the members: 'What about you? Do all of you know already what you're going to do once you finish your studies?' Shortly after that the person sitting beside her said calmly: 'Once I've got that far something will come along.' The group members shared how far they had got with their job-related plans and how they felt about it. Even though the participant who had initially expressed her worries wasn't addressed directly, at the end she said that this sharing had helped her a lot.

## 6 Expression of immediate feelings in the group

Sooner or later some members start explicitly bringing into the open feelings – be they positive or negative – they experience toward another group member in the immediate moment. For example, a participant says: 'I feel threatened by your silence.' Or 'I like your warmth and your smile' (Rogers 1970: 23). In the increasing atmosphere of trust, each of these attitudes can be explored.

## 7 Development of a healing capacity in the group

One of the most fascinating aspects of person-centred encounter groups is to experience the manner in which some group members have a natural and spontaneous capacity for dealing in a helpful way with the sorrows, fears and troubles of others. For example, when Joe shared the almost complete lack of communication between himself and his wife, the group members tried to help him find a path to her, each one in their own way. They asked him how he felt if his wife didn't speak to him or how he showed his anger, and whether he felt defensive when trying to avoid conflict.

The next example is from an encounter group with international students that took place at the University of Vienna.

**Example from an encounter group**

The real interest in the person was most evident at the instant when an international student, let's call him Beno, expressed his inner conflict. He didn't know whether he should go back home once he had finished his studies – as was his mother's wish – or stay abroad and gain more experience – as his father said would be better for him. Andreas said to him: 'And so you feel torn between where to go and not clear what you want? Is that right?' Then Marta said, 'And you'd prefer to see more of the world rather than sit around at home?' The facilitator said: 'And still I feel some hesitation on your part and perhaps some fear of being left on your own, but I also feel your courage and enterprising spirit.' Through their ongoing interest in Beno, the group helped him to become more aware of his thoughts and desires, and to organize and express them.

## 8  Self-acceptance and the beginning of change

Gradually group members come to realize that self-acceptance does not block out change but instead can be the beginning of change. If I don't need to fight against something in me, then I have more of my inner resources available to question my attitudes, consider them and change them if necessary. For example, attitudes would be expressed as follows: 'I *am* a dominating person who likes to control others. I do want to mould these individuals into proper shape.' 'I really have a hurt and overburdened little boy inside of me who feels very sorry for himself. I am that little boy, in addition to being a competent and responsible manager' (Rogers 1970: 26).

## 9  The cracking of façades

One of the threads in the continuing group process is an increasing impatience with defences. As time goes on, the group finds it unbearable that any member should live behind a façade. The group wants to know members deeply and so insists on them removing any mask and expressing their current feelings. For instance, in one of Carl Rogers' groups there was a highly intelligent and quite academic man who was rather perceptive in his understanding of others but didn't reveal himself at all. One participant said: 'Come out from behind that lectern, Doc. Stop giving us speeches. Take off your dark glasses. We want to know *you*' (Rogers 1970: 29). (Note: The expression 'façade' or 'mask' is often used without explanation. We think that Rogers included introjections in this expression – i.e. values taken over from others that result in conditions of worth  – Nykl 2005: 51.)

## 10  The individual receives feedback

As the process of interacting in the group continues, members acquire a great deal of information about how they appear to others. Through these experiences – positive as well as upsetting – members become a lot more direct than in everyday interaction. In addition, distorted patterns of thought and learned constructs tend to be addressed directly.

## 11 Confrontation

In this phase the feedback becomes sharper and sharper, so that individual members can begin to confront one another. These confrontations can be positive but are often negative. Readers may feel relieved to know that participants who confront each other heavily during the sessions frequently understand each other at the end of the group better than ever before.

> Norma: (Loud sigh) Well, I don't have any respect for you, Alice. None! (Pause) There's about a hundred things going through my mind I want to say to you, and *by God* I hope I get through 'em all! First of all, if you wanted us to respect you, then why couldn't you respect *John's* feelings last night? *Why have you been on him today?* H'mm?...Any real woman that I know wouldn't have acted as you have this week and particularly what you said this afternoon. That was so *crass!*
>
> (Rogers 1970: 33)

## 12 The helping relationship outside the group sessions

One exciting aspect of the group experience is the many ways in which members assist each other, for example when an individual is struggling to express him- or herself, or wrestling with a problem, or hurting because of some painful new discovery. This can happen within the group sessions or even more frequently during contacts outside the group. As an example let us quote an excerpt from a letter – addressed to the group members – that Rogers received from a young man about a month after an encounter group.

> None of you had to care about me. None of you had to seek me out and let me know of things you thought would help me. None of you had to let me know I was of help to you. Yet you did, and as a result it has far more meaning than anything I have so far experienced. When I feel the need to hold back...then I remember that twelve persons just like those before me now said to let go and be congruent, be myself and of all unbelievable things they even loved me for it. This has given me the courage to come out of myself many times since then. Often it seems my very doing of this helps the others to experience similar freedom.
>
> (Rogers 1970: 35)

A primary characteristic of this phase is that participants talk to each other and make themselves available to one another. Frequently, unforgettable and very candid relationships are formed. Often aspects of the talks and experiences flow back into the group, but freely and without any pressure or predetermined rules.

## 13 The basic encounter

Members tend to 'come into much closer and more direct contact with each other than is customary in ordinary life. This appears to be one of the most central, intensive, and change-producing aspects of group experience' (Rogers 1970: 35). Individuals can grow from such relationships in ways unrecognized thus far. A participant wrote shortly after a workshop: 'Thus real change seemed to occur when feelings were experienced and expressed in the context of the relationship. "I can't *stand* the way you talk!" turned into a real understanding and affection for you the *way* you talk' (Rogers 1970: 36). Intensive I-Thou relationships (using Buber's term here) often bring a moistness to the eyes of the participants.

## 14 Expression of positive feelings and closeness

A part of the group process in which a great deal of closeness and positive feelings arise is when feelings are expressed and can be accepted in a relationship. As the sessions proceed, an increasing feeling of trust is built up out of a realness which includes both positive and negative feelings. One group member tried to sum this up in the following words: '... it would have to do with what I call confirmation – a kind of confirmation of myself, of the uniqueness and universal qualities of men, a confirmation that when we can be human together something positive can emerge' (Rogers 1970: 37).

## 15 Behaviour changes in the group

Behavioural changes occur in the group itself. Gestures change, tones of voice change, becoming more spontaneous, less artificial, with more feeling. Participants show an astonishing amount of thoughtfulness and helpfulness toward each other. A participant writes:

> I am more open, spontaneous, I express myself more freely. I am more sympathetic, empathic, and tolerant... My relationships with my family, friends, and co-workers are more honest and I express my likes and dislikes and true feelings more openly. I admit ignorance more readily. I am more cheerful. I want to help others more.

(Rogers 1970: 38)

Long-lasting changes in the behaviour of group members can be confirmed as well. They strongly depend on the people themselves and on the actual evolution of the group process.

While the description of the group process above can provide a glimpse into that phenomenon it can never substitute for a first-person experience of an encounter group. Viewed from the perspective of a particular person, some phases of the group process may occur for/in that person later, or in a subsequent group, or even only after having gone through some real experience in one's life. Viewed in this way, the description of the group process can be understood as providing a characterization of an individual's change process as well.

In the following section, we provide excerpts from students' reaction journals which they submitted after having participated in an academic class on person-centred communication in the course of their studies of business informatics. The reactions were submitted online and could be read by all participants of the respective classes.

## Excerpts from participants' reaction sheets

One female, rather quiet, participant wrote:

> One could clearly perceive how the trust in the group was increasing and therefore the communication became open and very personal. The climate in the group improved through every session and one could realize the group spirit that had developed. Personally, the group caused me to think about issues that had not been on my mind before. Moreover, the encounter groups helped me to think about certain areas of my life and to gain new insights.

A male participant shared:

> The encounter groups helped me practically train and experience the themes that had been elaborated more theoretically in the preceding workshops – for me a no less important aspect of the class. I think that the major potential of this course lies in the freedom it grants: time for developing trust in a group of people, space for resolving conflicts and openly addressing each theme that came to your mind...The ability to resolve conflict is essential for good communication. Personally, I'm often experiencing that the reason for conflict is a misunderstanding. Therefore it is vital to be responsive to the other and to try to understand him or her...Furthermore I appreciated that we were a colourfully

mixed group with some international participants. The cultural differences were often mirrored in the personal opinions and this helps me to gain a better understanding of some issues.

Another participant described her process of experiencing as follows:

In the beginning of the encounter group I had no idea what would happen. I knew that the group would be unstructured and would proceed totally freely, however since I had never had a chance to experience anything of that kind before I was very excited about what would happen in the first unit. Today, after having spent 25 hours in a person-centred encounter group I come to the following conclusion: I had the opportunity to experience my own and others' communication behaviour and hence to understand it better. I had the opportunity to encounter people of different age, gender, origin and culture and could extend my behavioural repertoire in social situations. Furthermore I have witnessed the development and the growth process of our group. The group gave me the safety to be understood, accepted and respected. In addition, friendships began to develop and the first meetings with participants [outside the group] were already scheduled.

In a more critical reaction we read:

Person-centered communication was an interesting and novel experience. The total absence of traditional lectures and the elaboration of all topics in the group were something I had not had the chance to experience before. However, I would have preferred if the course had been more about factual issues in the area of communication... I sense that the goal of an encounter group is to provide a climate in which one can openly talk about everything. Due to this openness all members of the group can communicate, share and make experiences with each other on a level that is not possible in the world 'out there'.

There are three facts that I consider to be inhibiting when an encounter group is conducted as a part of a course... Factor one is the pressure of participating. Pressure is incompatible with freedom but freedom is necessary for openness. Factor two is that, in my opinion, the roles of facilitator and course instructor appear to be incompatible... Factor three is that I need to fully trust all participants that they will deal with the information they get from me in a trustful way. To gain this trust, in my view, is not possible in the time that was at our disposal.

[Addendum – two weeks later] On a positive note I do value the fact that the thoughts I expressed above are preserved in a reaction sheet. In almost all courses I thought about what I had liked and disliked. However, in those courses nobody had asked me for my input.

One student focused on comparing structured workshops with encounter groups:

The workshops provided me with important theoretical foundations. In my teams also the literature and seminar theses were characterized by a harmonious togetherness and enthusiastic cooperation...In my view the teamwork enriched the course in addition to the face-to-face phases. Retrospectively, however, I come to realize that the encounter groups impressed me more than the workshops and also contributed to a change in my behaviour to a more sustainable degree. I regret a little that it was only four days that we had at our disposal, since in the last unit I felt an urge to continue where we had stopped. Regarding the question of whether we'd participate in an encounter group again it was immediately clear to me that I'd certainly like to be part of such an experience again.

## The group process in dialogue and person-centred encounter groups: a comparison

The process of dialogue groups, according to Scharmer (2000), is strongly related to and consistent with the process of encounter groups according to Rogers (1970). However, the authors employ a totally different terminology for describing the process. Whereas Rogers describes the encounter group process as consisting of 15 phases that tend to overlap, Scharmer talks about transitions from one 'conversational field' into another. However, in both cases it is not a linear sequence of steps that is meant but a tendency in the direction of development, including complex retardations and cycles, depending on the given situation.

The four conversational fields are now briefly described, drawing on their characterization as given in Isaacs (1999). For a more detailed description you can refer to the original literature (Rogers 1970; Isaacs 1999; Scharmer 2000).

### Field I: talking nice – politeness

During the first meeting participants tend not to think about what is under the surface – about unexpressed expectations, tensions and differences. All bring with them a set of learned interactions, behaviours and assumptions that seem self-evident *for them*. They hide what they really think and feel. According to Scharmer, a key feature of this field is the lack of reflection. Similarly, according to Rogers, the process in an encounter group starts with phases (1) milling around, (2) resistance against personal expression and (3) description of past feelings. In Scharmer's first field, as in Rogers' phases 1–3 the 'here and now' is dominated by the past and by habits participants bring with them.

### Field II: talking tough – debate

In this field participants say what they think. Subsurface fragmentation and dissonance arise. People tend to collide and fight about whose meaning has more power. In this field the dominant emotion is anger because participants realize that they won't be able to get all the others to share their view. Participants plead for their positions without suspending or exploring how they arrived at them. It is more important to express one's own point of view than to question it. Isaacs (1999: 266) thinks that, unfortunately, many groups never get beyond this point.

In Rogers' conceptualization of the group process, phases (4) expression of negative feelings and (5) expression and exploration of personally meaningful material, follow. In phase 5, however, there is one of the characteristics of field III, namely talking about and for *oneself* instead of talking in the third person.

### Field III: reflective dialogue – inquiry

It is in this conversational field that a recognizably different kind of sharing begins to take place. Participants shift from 'third person data – stories about other people and other places – to first person data – inquiries about how things look from where I stand' (Isaacs 1999: 272). It is the phase of deliberation about 'What is it that I'm doing?', 'What effect do I have?' and people start to be surprised. Participants start becoming aware of their assumptions and begin to explore them; they examine the rules that have governed how they have operated. Meaning can unfold because the participants are speaking for themselves rather than for others. As a group comes to the point of engaging in inquiry and flow of exchange together, there comes the moment when pressure builds up and another change becomes necessary. Participants begin to realize the extent of fragmentation in the group. The opportunity to give up isolated identity for insight increases so that together the group finds a much wider set of possibilities than would be possible as individuals.

Rogers recognized the following phases in the process of encounter groups that capture several of the characteristics of field III (whereby phase 5 mentioned above fits both fields II and III): (6) expression of immediate feelings in the group, (7) development of a healing capacity in the group, (8) acceptance and the beginning of change, (9) the cracking of façades, (10) the individual receives feedback, (11) confrontation.

### Field IV: generative dialogue – flow

At this point, traditional positions are loosened far enough so that genuinely new possibilities come into being. In this fourth space, participants share the experience of *flow*. This experience often happens collectively and there is often synchronicity: one participant thinks of something and another expresses it. People sense more clearly that they are part of a larger whole and they notice that what they say impacts on everyone. They also notice that it can be difficult to put powerful experiences into words. However, Scharmer thinks that this conversational field is quite rare and that the art of generative dialogue is directed toward the actualization of an intersubjective 'field-intelligence'. By this he means the exploitation of social power sources and potential for action that reach far beyond the existence of individuals.

Rogers uses more modest words to describe one of the most central, intensive and important aspects of the group experience. Individuals 'come into much closer and more direct contact with each other than is customary in ordinary life' (1970: 35) and 'show an astonishing amount of thoughtfulness and helpfulness toward each other' (1970: 38). According to Rogers, the group progresses along the following phases: (12) the helping relationship outside the group sessions, (13) the basic encounter, (14) expression of positive feelings and closeness, (15) behaviour changes in the group.

### Leadership

Dialogue groups and person-centred encounter groups differ significantly on the issue of leadership. According to Scharmer, each conversational field requires particular intervention techniques. For Rogers, the facilitator is an experienced group member and his/her offering of the person-centred core attitudes is pivotal throughout the whole group process. Some of the facilitator's behaviours are more frequent in the beginning while others appear more often at the end of the group process.

### Implications from the comparison

There is a tendency toward reaching the qualities of fields III and IV faster in person-centred encounter groups, due to the stronger emphasis on interpersonal presence. Typically, participants in encounter groups need not tackle some preconceived problem (as is often – but not always – the case in dialogue groups) but are free to deal with anything that emerges in the current moment, anything that the participants themselves consider important. However, this is just a subjective impression because we have not yet participated in *longer* groups led professionally by following the dialogue method.

At this point, another personal experience becomes relevant, one that concerns seminars with PhD students. In this context I (Renate) got the impression that problem-solving conversations – retrospectively, I'd call them 'dialogue sessions' – were very fertile whenever accompanied by person-centred attitudes. The participants tended to pass the initial two conversational fields quite quickly and moved into areas that I'd identify as 'Field III with occasional excursions to Field IV'. The atmosphere was significantly distinct from that in other courses. Let me illustrate this by excerpts from the reaction sheets of students who participated in a PhD seminar that was facilitated in a person-centred manner:

> I regret I haven't been able to communicate the whole problem statement regarding the scenarios...I should have organized the whole thing differently, but I've learned from this...Nevertheless I think that despite the confusion – or even due to the confusion – we arrived at a pretty interesting conversation. For me it was very valuable and it brought me forward in leaps and bounds. Thank you everybody; without you I wouldn't have come to where I am now.

> When reflecting upon the seminar I'm realizing that I caused some puzzlement and I apparently haven't managed to communicate my contribution appropriately. For me, the exchange of experience was important...I hope that in the future I'll be able to share ideas with one or other of you.

> I got the impression that now, at the end of the term, I'm better or somewhat more able to understand colleagues from other disciplines. For me this was an important learning process: at the beginning of the seminar I had perceived myself as quite impatient, I felt impelled to impose my pedagogical perspective onto some subject matter very promptly without even listening thoroughly. All in all I found the last session extremely exciting! I experienced the group as very productive, the conversations very pleasant and I sensed a high degree of positive regard.

In these reactions I appreciate the openness of expression, the personal account students express, the consideration of the group as the context of learning, and the valuing of the seminar experience as such, with the wish to keep in touch in the future. Regardless of the particular kind of group experience, it seems likely that significant learning had taken place.

## International participants and diversity groups

While the focus in the previous section was on comparing the group process in dialogue groups with that in person-centred encounter groups, our spotlight in this section is on international participants in groups and their likely contribution to a special field of experiential learning. This field is connected to nationality and tends to remain unnoticed in groups in which all participants share the same nationality and hence take national or cultural habits for granted. However, this tends not to be the case if at least a few participants are of another nationality and hence some source of difference arises between the group members. This difference, if not valued or judged, can provide fascinating ground for mutual exploration, since participants from different nationalities have the opportunity to interact with people, habits, systems, attitudes and beliefs that are more or less different from their own and hence have the potential to open up their world view. Participants from all nationalities tend to learn from the phenomenon of difference that exists between them, as long it is met with respect, a desire to understand and a willingness to open up and share.

While more thoughtful research on international encounter groups is necessary, the following insights and 'trends' have been apparent in student groups we have facilitated.

### Understanding needs more effort, active listening is harder to achieve but essential

For example, a South African student needed a couple of tries to repeat in her own words what a Czech student had shared about what concerned him at that moment, until the Czech student felt understood. The young woman from South Africa wrote in her reaction sheet:

> Another remarkable point was our dialogue exercise. I was surprised that sometimes it is so hard to paraphrase what your partner said, and it's so extremely hard to explain your mind in simple, understandable words.

### Learning through interpersonal contact and participants' real 'stories'

This is appreciated and tends to be felt as worthwhile by the vast majority of participants. It is clearly understood that it works both ways, meaning that something new about one's own nationality, whether a majority or minority in a group, can be learned through exploring different mind-sets and habits.

After the second block of an encounter group at the Masaryk University in Brno, Czech Republic, a Czech student commented:

> I really like that we are not only Czech people in this group so we have to speak English all the time – also at lunch. This way our soft skills are improving the whole day. I also consider it great that we can listen to the different ideas and experiences from participants from different countries – this way we can learn something new about our own nationality, how others see and perceive us.

### Loosening of national or cultural constructs

Besides becoming aware of habits and typical behaviours, participants start *exploring* them rather than defending them and sticking to them. Let us illustrate this by a sample statement in which another student of the group at Masaryk University reflected the following after a session in which an African student had explored the hard time he was having when trying to talk to people in a supermarket. Instead of getting a normal response, he typically received a dark and startled look which made him feel really awkward:

> First I must say that I like our international mix. I think that this group is unique for discovering ideas, or maybe even making myself (and the others) think about my (their) patterns of behaviour and responses. This is a condition for possible improvement.

Apparently what had happened in that session was that the African student learned that, in a big Czech city, it simply was not customary to talk to foreigners while shopping and that this had nothing to do with his origin, language or personality but was just 'the norm'. The group then talked about how different life might be if people were more outgoing in their country and agreed they might start experimenting with introducing a change, starting at the university!

### Learning about self through listening to the other

Although this dimension is present in any encounter group, it tends to stand out in terms of intensity and variety in international groups. It takes on several forms as the following examples illustrate.

### Example from an international encounter group

A young, attractive and open-minded Pakistani woman with beautiful, long black hair shares in a group session what it means to her not to wear a scarf. On the one hand, she feels rather proud, having dared to leave her scarf in her room or handbag and equally relieved at having got rid of what was a potential barrier between her and her colleagues. On the other hand, she hates the thought of what might happen if a male member of her family saw her with her head uncovered. When the participants ask what would happen, she shares that a strong sense of fury would rest upon her and that she would likely be expelled from her family and religious group. So her move toward integration, which she perceives as the right thing to do experientially, also threatens her and is an enourmous risk. In the group, all hearts seem to beat for her; we admire her courage and I'm pretty sure our attitude toward wearing a scarf has received a broader perspective.

### Example from an international encounter group

A student from Kosovo who appears very impatient all the time finally shares some of his experiences during the war, like soldiers coming to his school and shooting at random. He seems to be torn between staying in Austria where it is hard for him to find real friends or going back into an atmosphere of total uncertainty. Listening to him, some participants start seeing their own 'problems' in a new light and begin to acknowledge the openness and contribution of the student from Kosovo. Finally he 'earns' true appreciation from the group and his 'impatience' is no longer looked down upon, but is seen as a 'natural part' of him that at times attracts attention in the group and then pretty much settles down.

Often it is a relief when international participants come to understand that some 'strange' behaviour of the national majority is due to a cultural habit rather than denial of them as a person of different origin.

### Example from an international encounter group

A student from Argentina who used to hug colleagues as a form of greeting felt that they 'stiffened' when he approached them with a hug. Initially, he thought there was something wrong with him and only gradually realized that hugging is not a usual habit with Austrians. While he had to learn that during his stay, in the encounter group he explored that while intellectually knowing the difference helps a little, experientially he was still missing the closer contact so dear to him in his culture. In the next break he received a sympathetic hug from a student of southern origin.

Even more intensive learning tends to occur in 'diversity groups'. In such groups members are typically from various ethnic groups, for example, some majority group and minority group(s) meet in a workshop format to explore their differences and improve their living together (e.g. in a town or on a campus). Pioneering facilitators and researchers of diversity groups are, for example, Margret Warner (a former PhD student of Carl Rogers) from the Counseling Center of Chicago and Colin Lago from the UK. A famous writer in this area and a former colleague of Carl Rogers was J.K. Wood (see, for example, 2008).

## Summary

Both academic practice as well as research indicate that person-centred encounter groups should have their own space in higher education – far beyond the study of psychology. This is particularly the case if, besides factual knowledge, interpersonal attitudes, relationships and communication can be encouraged. The vast majority of students mentioned that it was the encounter groups that they had perceived as most meaningful out of three elements: structured workshops, online support/materials and encounter groups (Motschnig-Pitrik and Nykl 2005).

Most students react positively to the encounter experience but some go even further and call them the most meaningful experience they had in their studies. On the other hand, there are a few students who can hardly make any use of the freedom they are granted. In some cases they even hinder the whole group's progress in the group process. Hence some factors must be considered in order to properly integrate encounter groups into the context of academic education. These are, for example, experienced facilitators, a well thought-through and transparently communicated concept for the respective courses, curricula with some free space and an open-minded administration that understands the nature and vast potential, but also the possible risks, of encounter groups and then subsequently supports their being conducted. In any case, research results point to the fact that structured, interactive workshops and person-centred encounter groups provide powerful potential to develop those disciplines that Peter Senge (2006) propagated as the 'disciplines of the learning organization'. They promote the constructive advance of both people and organizations.

Rogers saw encounter groups as a particularly powerful means for facilitating the living together of people in situations characterized by tension, without having to resort to the application of power. He and his team offered intercultural workshops and encounter groups for international politicians and hostile peoples such as, for example, the Catholics and Protestants in Belfast (Rogers 1980). For these efforts Rogers was nominated for the Nobel Peace Prize but unfortunately he passed away before he could have potentially been awarded it. Rogers himself thought of encounter groups as 'pilot models' that society can put in place whenever the time is right. He emphasized that encounter groups are in a field in dire need of broad and profound study and research.

# PART IV
# Conclusion

# 12 Personal reflections

**In this chapter you will learn about:**

- Various means of acquiring person-centred communication

- What matters most in developing person-centred attitudes

- The relationship between bodily fitness and keeping up person-centred relationships

- Two different paths the authors have taken to approach person-centred communication

If person-centred communication speaks to you or if you are drawn to the person-centred approach and want your personal development to go in that direction, you're likely to ask: 'What's the best way for me to proceed?' According to the person-centred approach, everyone tends to find their own way toward more congruence, acceptance and a better empathic understanding of their environment. Nevertheless, we can propose some ideas for the purpose of orientation. In any case we believe that *the path is simultaneously also the goal.*

You are currently in the company of a book on the person-centred approach. We have never been able to read such a book quickly, because the reading process always brings to mind our own experiences, which we want to digest, thus slowing us down. Often we have been surprised at how Rogers manages to express something in clear words that we only dimly sensed ourselves. Almost always, such a reading is a vivid enterprise and offers an opportunity to get back in contact with oneself. Often it provides an incentive to sympathize with the experiences and situations Rogers shares with us. Furthermore, it evokes something new each time we revisit his works.

We know that person-centred attitudes – the foundation of person-centred communication – are acquired through direct interpersonal relationships with other people who hold these attitudes – be it by 'nature' or as a consequence of their professional orientation. Person-centred attitudes are contagious. They can carry you along like a mighty stream and not let you go. Moreover, they encompass the need to choose the path – sometimes even the more painful one – to orient oneself more according to one's own complex experience rather than blindly following others or old habits. It is from this stream of experience and thought that this book originated.

How liberating and self-affirming it is to know someone with whom you can *really* share, someone who is genuinely interested and feels the need to meet at eye-level, to communicate transparently and wants to understand you accurately even in situations of conflict. No book can act as a substitute for such a relationship. It can, however, provide inspiration to incorporate what has been read and experienced into one's (communication) behaviour.

Reinhard Tausch (Tausch and Tausch [1963] 1998), among others, introduces the following activities that are known to contribute to the development of person-centred behaviours:

- Participation in person-centred encounter groups.
- Frequent contact with people with distinctly developed person-centred attitudes.
- Watching of audio- and video-recordings of person-centred interviews and subsequent reflection with a supervisor or with colleagues/friends.
- Acquisition of knowledge about person-centred attitudes and activities.
- Physical fitness: the relationship between person-centred attitudes and bodily fitness has primarily been researched by Aspy (1972) in the context of education. Aspy found that his data strongly support the assumption that physical ability is a prerequisite to staying in a constructive relationship over a considerable period of time.
- Regular relaxation exercise.
- Attendance at workshops to develop one's ability to empathize.

From all these, we see the greatest potential from participating in person-centred encounter group.

There exist associations worldwide that offer 'training' in various fields of application of the person-centred approach. Often you can participate in seminars and encounter groups even if you're not enrolled in some 'training' programme. One of our objectives is to complement these offerings and to support the development of highly capable facilitators.

At this end point, we'd like to share our personal paths to a way of being that orients itself to person-centred values. I (Renate) became enthusiastic about the person-centred approach by reading Rogers' books on *Counselling and Psychotherapy* (1942) and *Becoming Partners* (1973). I discovered them 'by chance' more than 25 years ago, at a time when I found it highly desirable to be in constructive relationships. Since my parents separated when

I was 6 years old, I was on a search for something that would support me in improving the quality of interpersonal relationships and in gaining more clarity about what mattered for a long-term relationship and what I personally could contribute. Since I could find the most valuable inspirations in Rogers' books, which supported me in making important decisions, I bought and read more. This author's writings touched me and I felt directly included as never before. Rogers' ideas and his way of expressing himself spoke to me in a way that I felt inherently energized and motivated me to really *be* or live the knowledge and experience I had acquired in my partnership, family and at work. In particular, at the university, I could experience person-centred 'teaching' and learning that continually confirmed in me the vivid and expanding effects of the person-centred approach. However, I also realized that there were situations in which I felt powerless.

In sum, I'm convinced that both the contact and collaboration with congruent people, and my participation in encounter groups – in this field, I owe a lot to Ladislav – significantly influenced my personal path and development. I wouldn't want to change any of it, not even the meaningful but occasionally tough experiences that resulted from the close cooperation and co-facilitation of encounter groups. The variety of perspectives in groups, particularly in international ones, and my tendency to experience something from each one amazes me and fills me with awe as I become aware of the almost endless giving and taking in relationships with others. These experiences have notably changed me and their effect continues. And I don't want to keep them to myself only, as this book confirms.

It isn't easy for me (Ladislav) to describe what motivates me and what – in spite of several misunderstandings – has kept me on this path and how I have changed throughout many years, given I realized that I was changing at all. For reasons that aren't quite clear to me, a tendency to stay with person-centred groups developed in me. I sensed something new and personally important, without even knowing who Carl Rogers was. After many years, I wouldn't call myself a guru in communication who accomplishes miracles in encounters with others; that would be misleading. What is essential to me and brings about a feeling of self-assurance is that I can better recognize several issues, feel irritated less often, and only become angry when I really can 'stand behind' my anger. I do not believe that the path of experience leads only through a soft empathic understanding, but that my empathic understanding and my acceptance help me to better understand several situations, even unfavourable ones, and not to be naïve and dependent. The core of the attitudes that are called person-centred, but equally could exist without a name, can't be learned in a traditional way; they need to be experienced and assimilated in a climate that motivates and activates psychological growth.

# 13 'Thanks!'

**Renate:** I cordially thank Helmuth Beutel and Reinhard Tausch who always showed their interest in my ideas and activities. Helmuth and Reinhard repeatedly devoted their time to sharing in a person-centred atmosphere. In particular, over several years, the professional as well as interpersonal connection with Helmuth has brought sunshine and gratitude into sunny as well as dark days.

Sincere thanks are due to Michael Lux for numerous stimulating dialogues, both face-to-face and online, which gave us the chance not only to explore several aspects of the person-centred approach but also to experience them personally. I very much appreciate Michael's constructive comments on a previous draft of the manuscript, just at a time when I particularly needed help to overcome my own doubts.

I want to thank Peter Schmid for various group experiences, reflections, and sharing of his professional as well as personal being and acting, both in direct contact and in related books, articles and presentations.

Sincere thanks are also directed to my husband Herbert, my sons and my mother, for the time they granted me for interacting with pencil, paper, the computer, Ladislav, colleagues, literature, etc. that contributed to the development of this book. Herbert, Tomas and Niko, I thank you cordially also for your contributions to our life together as a family, with all our needs and all we have in common, as well as all our many differences – and the many intimate experiences that enrich our life together. Some of them found their way into this book. This is one of the reasons that I started to change from my current detailed name in publications 'Motschnig-Pitrik' to the shorter variant of my family name 'Motschnig' (originally my husband's name).

Furthermore, I feel thankful to my colleagues Michael Derntl, Kathrin Figl, Sonja Kabicher-Fuchs and Jürgen Mangler at the University of Vienna. Our experiences and achievement as a team would not have been possible without their collaboration, inherent motivation, openness and empathic support. Thanks, too, for reading the manuscript and returning comments and questions, though responsibility for the contents remain with the two co-authors.

Special thanks are due to Gisela Steenbuck for numerous comments and her transparent sharing of her – not always positive – reading experiences, based on her detailed delving into several chapters of an earlier version of the manuscript. I hope that in the future we'll find further opportunities to put our thoughts and experiences together.

Furthermore, we found the careful comments by Mr Beyer and Mrs Arnold from Klett-Cotta very helpful for stylistic refinement and better comprehensibility. Later, David Ryback devoted a significant amount of his precious time to improve the English style of the translated manuscript and Jef Cornelius-While helped in refining the chapters on dialogue and online communication. We highly appreciate their support and feel grateful for their immersion into our writing!

At McGraw Hill, Monika Lee accompanied us perfectly from the beginning until manuscript submission and suggested some valuable extensions and improvements in the revised English edition. Monika, thank you!

Editor Jon Ingoldby helped us enormously in reworking and polishing the text from Renate's original translation, providing clarification without losing the original meaning and authorial style.

The production team at McGraw-Hill, in particular Sarah Fleming, were supportive and helpful throughout.

My expression of gratitude wouldn't be complete if didn't include my contact with Godfrey Barrett-Lennard, Rogers' colleague and former PhD student. We first met at the PCE conference in 2003 and have stayed in email contact since then. During my one week-long research visit at the Murdoch-University in Perth, Australia, I experienced such a huge 'dose' of person-centred attitudes by Goff, his wife Helen, and their relationship that the week will live on in my memory as an immensely confirming, formative and unforgettable experience.

**Ladislav:** I thank all those who helped me on my path toward becoming more empathic and accepting and often also to better intuitively sense difficult situations. This happened at times through empathizing and accompanying, at times through confrontations. I'm thankful to my former wife, Lenka, for her patience with my studies and my innumerable hours of writing. I'm extending my thanks to my clients with whom I experienced so much. It is a mosaic of indescribably wonderful and varied experiences that opened the door for me to basic insight into the depth of interpersonal relationships. I thank all those people whom I encountered on my path.

Renate Motschnig and Ladislav Nykl
Vienna, September 2013

# Bibliography

Anderson, R. and Cissna, K.N. (1979) *The Martin Buber–Carl Rogers Dialogue: A New Transcript with Commentary*. Albany, NY: State University of New York Press.

Aspy, D.N. (1972) *Toward a Technology for Humanizing Education*. Champaign, IL: Research Press Company.

Bach, G.R. and Wyden, P. (1969) *Streiten verbindet: Spielregeln für Liebe und Ehe* [*Quarreling Unites: Rules for Love and Marriage*]. Düsseldorf: Rowolth Verlag.

Baddeley, A.D. (1999) *Essentials of Human Memory*. Hove: Psychology Press.

Barrett-Lennard, G.T. (1993) The phases and focus of empathy, *British Journal of Medical Psychology*, 66: 3–14.

Barrett-Lennard, G.T. (1998) *Carl Rogers' Helping System: Journey and Substance*. London: Sage.

Barrett-Lennard, G.T. (2003) *Steps on a Mindful Journey: Person-centred Expressions*. Ross-on-Wye: PCCS-Books.

Barrett-Lennard, G.T. (2005) *Relationship at the Centre: Healing in a Troubled World*. Philadelphia, PA: Whurr.

Barrett-Lennard, G.T. (2009) From personality to relationship: path of thought and practice, *Person-Centered and Experiential Psychotherapies*, 8(2): 79–93.

Barrett-Lennard G.T. (2013a) Relationship worlds and the plural self, in J.H.D. Cornelius-White, R. Motschnig-Pitrik and M. Lux (eds) *Interdisciplinary Handbook of the Person-centered Approach: Research and Theory*. New York: Springer.

Barrett-Lennard, G.T. (2013b) *The Relationship Paradigm: Human Being Beyond Individualism*. Basingstoke: Palgrave Macmillan.

Berne, E. (1961) *Transactional Analysis in Psychotherapy: A Systematic Individual and Social Psychiatry*. New York: Grove Press.

Berne, E. ([1964] 1984) *Games People Play*. Harmondsworth: Penguin.

Bohm, D. (1996) *On Dialogue*, ed. L. Nichol. London: Routledge.

Bohm, D. and Peat, D. (2000) *Science, Order and Creativity*. London: Routledge.

Botbol, M. and Lecic-Tosevski, D. (2013) Person-centred medicine and subjectivity, in J.H.D. Cornelius-White, R. Motschnig-Pitrik and M. Lux (eds) *Interdisciplinary Applications of the Person-centered Approach*. New York: Springer.

Bozart, J.D., Zimring, F.M. and Tausch, R. (2002) Client-centered therapy: the evolution of a revolution, in J. Cain and J. Seeman (eds) *Humanistic Psychotherapies: Handbook of Research and Practice*. Washington, DC: American Psychological Association.

Cain, D.J. (2010) *Person-Centered Psychotherapies*. Washington, DC: American Psychological Association.

Cain, D.J. and Seeman, J. (eds) (2002) *Humanistic Psychotherapies: Handbook of Research and Practice*. Washington, DC: American Psychological Association.

Cornelius-White, J.H.D. (2007) Teachers who care are more effective: a meta-analysis of learner-centered relationships, *Review of Educational Research*, 77(1): 1–31.

Cornelius-White, J.H.D. and Harbaugh, A.P. (2010) *Learner-Centered Instruction: Building Relationships for Student Success*. Thousand Oaks, CA: Sage.

Cornelius-White, J.H.D., Hoey, A., Cornelius-White, C.F., Motschnig-Pitrik, R. and Figl, K. (2004) Teachers who care are more effective: a meta-analysis in progress, *Journal of Border Educational Research*, 3: 81–96.

Cornelius-White, J.H.D., Motschnig-Pitrik, R. and Lux, M. (eds) (2013a) *Interdisciplinary Handbook of the Person-centered Approach: Research and Theory*. New York: Springer.

Cornelius-White, J.H.D., Motschnig-Pitrik, R. and Lux, M. (eds) (2013b) *Interdisciplinary Applications of the Person-centered Approach*. New York: Springer.

Damasio, A.R. (1994) *Descartes' Error: Emotion, Reason and the Human Brain*. New York: Grosset/Putnam.

Damasio, A.R. (1998) Investigating the biology of consciousness, *Philosophical Transactions of the Royal Society London*, 353: 1879–82.

Damasio, A.R. (2000) *The Feeling of What Happens: Body and Emotion in the Making of Consciousness*. London: Vintage.

Damasio, A.R. (2003) *Looking for Spinoza: Joy, Sorrow and the Feeling Brain*. Orlando, FL: Harcourt.

Damasio, A.R. (2012) *The Self Comes to Mind*. London: Vintage.

Deci, E.L. and Ryan, R.M. (2000) The 'what' and 'why' of goal pursuits: human needs and the self-determination of behavior, *Psychological Inquiry*, 11: 227–68.

Derntl, M. (2006) *Patterns for Person-Centered e-Learning*. Berlin: Aka Verlag.

Dewey, J. ([1933] 1998) *How We Think*. Boston, MA: Houghton Mifflin.

Ellinor, L. and Gerard, G. (1998) *Dialogue: Rediscover the Transforming Power of Conversation*. New York: John Wiley & Sons.

Faber, A. and Mazlish, E. (1980) *How To Talk So Kids Will Listen & Listen So Kids Will Talk*. New York: Avon Books.

Fischer, V. (2005) Fortbildung und Vernetzung, in V. Fischer, D. Kallinikidou and B. Stimm-Armingeon (eds) *Interkulturelle Kompetenz. Fortbildung – Transfer – Organisationsentwicklung*. Schwalbach/Taunus: Wochenschau Verlag.

Gendlin, E. (1978) *Focusing*. New York: Bentam Books.

Gendlin, E.T. and Wiltschko, J. (1999) *Focusing in der Praxis*. Stuttgart: Pfeiffer bei Klett-Cotta.

Gordon. T. (1970) *Parent Effectiveness Training: The Proven Program for Raising Responsible Children*. New York: Three Rivers Press.

Gordon, T. (1972) *Familienkonferenz [Parent Effectiveness Training]*. Hamburg: Hoffmann und Campe.

Häcker, H. and Stapf, K.H. (1994) *Dorsch Psychologisches Wörterbuch [Dorsch Psychological Vocabulary]* 12, überarbeitete und erweiterte Auflage. Bern: Hans Huber Verlag.

Harris, T.A. (1970) *I'm OK – You're OK*. London: Pan.

Haselberger, D. and Hutterer, R. (2013) The person-centered approach in research, in J.H.D Cornelius-White, R. Motschnig-Pitrik and M. Lux (eds) *Interdisciplinary Handbook of the Person-Centered Approach: Research and Theory*. New York: Springer.

Heinerth, K. (2001) Versperrte und verzerrte Wahrnehmungen: Zum differentiellen Verstehen von Persönlichkeits- und neurotischen Störungen [Locked and distorted perceptions], presentation by Prof. Dr Klaus Heinerth, Universität München. OGWG, 30 November, in Wien.

Hutterer, R. (1990) Authentic science: some implications of Carl Rogers' reflections on science, *Person-Centered Review*, 5(1): 57–76.

Iacoboni, M., Molnar-Szakacs, I., Gallese, V., Buccino, G., Mazziotta J.C. and Rizzolatti, G. (2005) Grasping the intentions of others with one's own mirror neuron system, *Plos Biology*, 3: 529–35.

Issacs, W. (1999) *Dialogue and the Art of Thinking Together*. New York: Doubleday.

Isaacs, W. (2002) *Dialog als Kunst Gemeinsam zu Denken*. Bergisch Gladbach: Edition Humanistische Psychologie, EHP.

Johnson, D.W. and Johnson, F.P. ([1975] 2006) *Joining Together, Group Theory and Group Skills*. Old Tappan, NJ: Pearson Education.

Knoll, L. (1991) *Lexikon der praktischen Psychologie*. Augsburg: Weltbild Verlag.

Kriz, J. (1998) *Systemtheorie für Psychotherapeuten, Psychologen und Mediziner. Eine Einführung*. Wien: UFB/Facultas.

Kriz, J. (2007) Actualizing tendency: the link between person-centered and experiential psychotherapy and interdisciplinary systems theory, *Person-Centered and Experiential Psychotherapies*, 6: 30–44.

Kriz, J. (2013) Person-centred approach and systems theory, in J.H.D. Cornelius-White, R. Motschnig-Pitrik and M. Lux (eds) *Interdisciplinary Handbook of the Person-centered Approach: Research and Theory*. New York: Springer.

Kroop, S., Mangler, J., Hutterer, R. and Swertz, C. (2006) eLearning-Tools zur Verbesserung verständlichen Schreibens, in A. Mettinger *et al.* (eds) *eLearning an der Universität Wien, Forschung – Entwicklung – Einführung*. Münster: Waxmann Verlag GmbH.

Lago, C. (2011) *The Handbook of Transcultural Counselling and Psychotherapy*. Maidenhead: McGraw-Hill.

Lago, C. (2013) The person-centered approach and its capacity to enhance constructive international communication, in J.H.D. Cornelius-White, R. Motschnig-Pitrik and M. Lux (eds) *Interdisciplinary Applications of the Person-centered Approach*. New York: Springer.

Lago, C. and McMillan, M. (1999) *Experiences in Relatedness: Groupwork in the Person Centered Approach*. Llangarron, Ross-on-Wye: PCCS Books.

Langer, I., Schulz von Thun, F. and Tausch, R. (1981) *Sich verständlich ausdrücken* [*Expressing Oneself Understandably*], 2nd edn. München: Ernst Reinhard Verlag.

Lewis, M.K., Rogers, C.R. and Shlien J.M. (1959) *Case Studies in Counseling and Psychotherapy*, ed. A. Burton. Upper Saddle River, NJ: Prentice Hall.

Lux, M. (2004) Neurowissenschaftliche Perspektiven für den Personzentrierten Ansatz, Neurowissenschaften [Neuroscientific perspectives of the person-centered approach], *Gesprächspsychotherapie und Personzentrierte Beratung*, 35(4): 261–7.

Lux, M. (2007) *Der Personzentrierte Ansatz und die Neurowissenschaften* [*The Person-Centered Approach and Neuroscience*]. München: Ernst Reinhard Verlag.

Lux, M. (2010) The magic of encounter: the person-centered approach and the neurosciences, *Person-Centered and Experiential Psychotherapies (PCEP)*, 9(4): 274–89.

Lux, M. (2013) The circle of contact: a neuroscience view on the formation of relationships, in J.H.D. Cornelius-White, R. Motschnig-Pitrik and M. Lux (eds) *Interdisciplinary Handbook of the Person-centered Approach: Research and Theory*. New York: Springer.

MacMillan, M. and Lago, C. (1993) Large groups: critical reflections and some concerns, in E. McIlduff and D. Coghlan (eds) *The Person Centered Approach and Cross Cultural Communication: An International Review*, Vol. 2. Dubliw: Centre for Cross-Cultural Communication.

Marci, C.D., Ham, J., Moran, E. and Orr, S.P. (2007) Physiologic correlates of perceived therapist empathy and social-emotional process during psychotherapy, *Journal of Nervous and Mental Disease*, 195: 103–11.

McCleary, R.A. and Lazarus, R.S. (1949) Autonomic discrimination without awareness, *Journal of Personality*, 18: 171–9.

McCombs, B.L. (2011) Learner-centered practices: providing the context for positive learner development, motivation, and achievement, in J. Meece and J. Eccles (eds) *Handbook of Research on Schools, Schooling, and Human Development*. Mahwah, NJ: Erlbaum.

McCombs, B.L. (2013) The learner-centered model: implications for research approaches, in J.H.D. Cornelius-White, R. Motschnig-Pitrik and M. Lux (eds) *Interdisciplinary Applications of the Person-centered Approach*. New York: Springer.

McCombs, B.L. and Miller, L. (2008) *The School Leader's Guide to Learner-Centered Education: From Complexity to Simplicity*. Thousand Oaks, CA: Corwin Press.

McIlduff, E. and Coghlan, D. (1989) Process and facilitation in a cross cultural communication workshop, *Person-Centered Review*, 4(1): 77–98.

McIlduff, E. and Coghlan, D. (1993) The cross-cultural communication workshops in Europe: reflections and review, in E. McIlduff and D. Coghlan (eds) *The Person-Centered Approach and Cross Cultural Communication: An International Review*, Vol. 2. Dubliw: Centre for Cross-Cultural Communication.

Mearns, D. and Cooper, M. (2005) *Working at Relational Depth in Counselling and Psychotherapy*. London: Sage.

Mearns, D. and Thorne (2007) *Person-centered Counseling in Action*, 3rd edn. London: Sage.

Motschnig-Pitrik, R. (2004) Person centered e-learning in a major academic course: what are the results and what can we learn from them? Proceedings of 4th International Conference on Networked Learning (NLC), Lancaster.

Motschnig-Pitrik, R. (2005) Person-centered e-learning in action: can technology help to manifest person-centered values in academic environments?, *Journal of Humanistic Psychology*, 45(4): 503–30.

Motschnig-Pitrik, R. (2006a) Two technology-enhanced courses aimed at developing interpersonal attitudes and soft skills in project management, in W. Neijdl and K. Tochtermann (eds) *Innovative Approaches for Learning and Knowledge Sharing*. Proceedings of the first European conference on Technology Enhanced Learning, EC-TEL 2006, Crete, Greece, LNCS 4227: 331–46. Berlin/ Heidelberg: Springer-Verlag.

Motschnig-Pitrik, R. (2006b) Web-technologie begegnet personzentriertem Lernen [Web-technology encounters the PCA], *Zeitschrift der GwG: Gesprächspsychotherapie und Personzentrierte Beratung*, 4: 212–20.

Motschnig-Pitrik, R. (2006c) The effects of a blended course including person centered encounter groups on students' learning, relationships, and teamwork. Proceedings of Networked Learning Conference, Lancaster.

Motschnig-Pitrik, R. (2006d) Participatory action research on a blended learning course on project management soft skills. Proceedings of 36th Frontiers in Education Conference, San Diego, CA.

Motschnig-Pitrik, R. (2013) Characteristics and effects of person-centered technology enhanced learning, in J.H.D. Cornelius-White, R. Motschnig-Pitrik and M. Lux (eds) *Interdisciplinary Applications of the Person-centered Approach*. New York: Springer.

Motschnig-Pitrik, R. and Barrett-Lennard, G.T. (2010) Co-actualization: a new construct for understanding well-functioning relationships, *Journal of Humanistic Psychology*, 50(3): 374–98.

Motschnig-Pitrik, R. and Derntl, M. (2005) Can the web improve the effectiveness of person-centered learning? Case study on teaching and living web-engineering, *IADIS International Journal of WWW/Internet*, 2(1): 49–62.

Motschnig-Pitrik, R. and Figl, K. (2007) Developing team competence as part of a person centered learning course on communication and soft skills in project management. Proceedings of 37th Frontiers in Education Conference, Milwaukee, WI: IEEE.

Motschnig-Pitrik, R. and Holzinger, A. (2002) Student-centred teaching meets new media: concept and case study, *IEEE Educational Technology & Society*, 5(4): 160–72.

Motschnig-Pitrik, R. and Lux, M. (2008) The person centered approach meets neuroscience: mutual support for C.R. Rogers' and A. Damasio's theories, *Journal of Humanistic Psychology*, 48: 287–319.

Motschnig-Pitrik, R. and Mallich, K. (2004) Effects of person-centered attitudes on professional and social competence in a blended learning paradigm, *Journal of Educational Technology & Society*, 7(4): 176–92.

Motschnig-Pitrik, R. and Nykl, L. (2003) Towards a cognitive-emotional model of Rogers' person-centered approach, *Journal of Humanistic Psychology*, 43(4): 8–45.

Motschnig-Pitrik, R. and Nykl, L. (2004) Wirtschaftsinformatiker erlernen den Personenzentrierten Ansatz [Students of business informatics develop in the person-centered way of being], *Zeitschrift der GwG: Gesprächspsychotherapie und Personzentrierte Beratung*, 6: 117–25.

Motschnig-Pitrik, R. and Nykl, L. (2005) Was hat Carl Rogers Wirtschaftsinformatikern im Zeitalter des Internet zu sagen? [What can students of business informatics in the age of the internet learn from Carl Rogers?], *Gruppendynamik und Organisationsberatung*, 36(1): 81–102.

Motschnig-Pitrik, R. and Nykl, L. (2007) The application of technology enhanced learning in person-centered education including encounter groups. Proceedings of ICTE'07, International Conference on Information and Communication Technology in Education, Rožnov, CZ, September.

Motschnig-Pitrik, R. and Nykl, L. (2013) An interactive cognitive-emotional model of the person-centered approach, in J.H.D. Cornelius-White, R. Motschnig-Pitrik and M. Lux (eds) *Interdisciplinary Handbook of the Person-centered Approach: Research and Theory*. New York: Springer.

Motschnig-Pitrik, R. and Santos, A.M. (2006) The person centered approach to teaching and learning as exemplified in a course in organizational development, *Zeitschrift für Hochschulentwicklung*, 1(4), www.zfhe.de/index.php?id=169.

Motschnig-Pitrik, R., Kabicher, S., Figl, K. and Santos, A.M. (2007) Person centered, technology enhanced learning in action: action research in a course on organizational development. Proceedings of 37th Frontiers in Education Conference (FIE), Milwaukee, WI: IEEE.

Motschnig-Pitrik, R., Lux, M. and Cornelius-White, J.H.D. (2013) The person-centered approach: an emergent paradigm, in J.H.D. Cornelius-White, R. Motschnig-Pitrik and M. Lux (eds) *Interdisciplinary Applications of the Person-centered Approach*. New York: Springer.

Natiello, P. (2001) *The Person-Centered Approach: A Passionate Presence*. Llangarron, Ross-on-Wye: PCCS Books.

Nykl, L. (2005) *Beziehung im Mittelpunkt der Persönlichkeitsentwicklung [Relationship in the Center of Personal Development]*. Münster: LIT Verlag.

Nykl, L. (2012) *Carl Ransom Rogers a jeho teorie. Přístup zaměřený na člověka [Carl Ransom Rogers and His Theories: Person-Centered Approach]*. Praha, CZ: Grada.

Nykl, L. and Motschig-Pitrik, R. (2002) Eine Theorie zur Vereinigung der Persönlichkeitstheorie von C.R. Rogers mit dem Gedankengut von L.S. Vygotskij [A theory toward the integration of C.R. Rogers' theory of personality and L.S. Vygotsky's body of thought], *Psychologie in Österreich*, 2: 252–61.

Nykl, L. and Motschnig-Pitrik, R. (2005) Encountergruppen im Rahmen des ganzheitlichen Lernens an den Universitäten Wien und Brünn – Motivation, Kontext, Prozesse, Perspektiven [Encounter groups in the context of whole-person learning at the University of Vienna and the Masaryk University in Brno – motivation, context, processes and perspectives], *Zeitschrift für Hochschuldidaktik*, 4: 36–62.

O'Hara, M. (2013) PCA encounter groups: transformative learning for individuals and communities, in J.H.D. Cornelius-White, R. Motschnig-Pitrik and M. Lux (eds) *Interdisciplinary Applications of the Person-centered Approach*. New York: Springer.

Ploil, E. (2006) Personzentriertes Arbeiten im Internet [Person-centered work in the internet], interview in *Zeitschrift der GwG: Gesprächspsychotherapie und Personzentrierte Beratung*, 4: 205–6.

Rizzolatti, G. and Craighero, L. (2004) The mirror neuron system, *Annual Review of Neuroscience*, 27: 169–92.

Rodenstock, U. and Beutel, H. (2008) *Spiegel-Bilder: Kommunikationsförderung bei Gruppen, Paargesprächen und im inneren Dialog mit sich selbst [Mirror-Images: Facilitation of Communication in Groups, Pairs, and in Inner Dialogue with Self]*. Köln: GwG Verlag.

Rogers, C.R. (1942) *Counseling and Psychotherapy – Newer Concepts in Practice*. Boston, MA: Houghton Mifflin.

Rogers, C.R. ([1951] 1995) *Client-Centered Therapy*. London: Constable.

Rogers, C.R. (1959) A theory of therapy, personality, and interpersonal relationships, as developed in the client-centered framework, in S. Koch (ed.) *Psychology: A Study of a Science*, Vol. 3. New York: McGraw-Hill.

Rogers, C.R. (1961) *On Becoming a Person – A Psychotherapist's View of Psychotherapy*. London: Constable.

Rogers, C.R. (1962) The interpersonal relationship: the core of guidance, *Harvard Educational Review*, 32(4): 416–29.

Rogers, C.R. (1969) *Freedom to Learn*. Columbus, OH: Charles E. Merrill.

Rogers, C.R. (1970) *Carl Rogers on Encounter Groups*. New York: Harper & Row.

Rogers, C.R. (1973) *Becoming Partners: Marriage and its Alternatives*. New York: Dell Publishing Co.

Rogers, C.R. (1975) Client-centered psychotherapy, in H.I. Kaplan, B.J. Sadock and A.M. Freeman (eds) *Comprehensive Textbook of Psychiatry II*. Baltimore, MD: Williams & Wilkins.

Rogers, C.R. (1978) *On Personal Power*. London: Constable.

Rogers, C.R. (1980) *A Way of Being*. Boston, MA: Houghton Mifflin.

Rogers, C.R. (1983) *Freedom to Learn for the 80s*. Columbus, OH: Charles E. Merrill.

Rogers, C.R. and Farson, R.E. (1987) Active listening, *Communicating in Business Today*, www.gordontraining.com/pdf/active_listening_article_rogers-farson.pdf.

Rogers, C.R. and Rosenberg, R.L. ([1980] 2005) *Die Person als Mittelpunkt der Wirklichkeit [The Person in the Focus of Reality]*. Stuttgart: Klett-Cotta.

Rogers, C.R. and Russell, D.E. (2002) *Carl Rogers, the Quiet Revolutionary: An Oral History*. Roseville, CA: Penmarine Books.

Rogers, C.R. and Stevens, B. (1967) *Person to Person: The Problem of Being Human, a New Trend in Psychology.* Lafayette, CA: Real People Press.

Rogers, C.R. and Wood, J.K. (1974) Client-centered theory, in A. Burton (ed.) *Operational Theories of Personality.* New York: Brunner/Mazel.

Rosenberg, M.B. (2003) *Nonviolent Communication: A Language of Life.* Encinitas, CA: PuddleDancer Press.

Roth, G. (2009) *Aus Sicht des Gehirnes [From the Brain's Perspective].* Frankfurt am Main: Suhrkamp Verlag.

Ryback, D. (1998) *Putting Emotional Intelligence to Work.* Boston, MA: Butterworth-Heinemann.

Ryback, D. and Motschnig-Pitrik, R. (2013) Successful management with the person-centered approach: building the bridge to business, in J.H.D. Cornelius-White, R. Motschnig-Pitrik and M. Lux (eds) *Interdisciplinary Applications of the Person-centered Approach.* New York: Springer.

Sachse, R. and Elliot, R. (2001) Process-outcome research on humanistic therapy variables, in D.J. Cain and J. Seeman (eds) *Humanistic Psychotherapies: Handbook of Research and Practice.* Washington, DC: American Psychological Association.

Santos, A.M. (2003) *Miracle Moments: The Nature of the Mind's Power in Relationships and Psychotherapy.* Lincoln, NE: Iuniverse.

Scharmer, C.O. (2000) Organizing around not-yet-embodied knowledge, in G. Crogh, I. Nonaka, T. Nichiguchi *et al.* (eds) *Knowledge Creation. A Source of Value.* London: Macmillan.

Schmid, P.F. (1989) *Personale Begegnung [Encounter Person-to-person].* Würzburg: Echter Verlag.

Schmid, P.F. (1994) *Personzentrierte Gruppenpsychotherapie, 1. Solidarität und Autonomie [Person-centered Group-psychotherapy, 1. Solidarity and Autonomy].* Köln: Edition Humanistische Psychologie.

Schmid, P.F. (2002) Was ist Personzentriert? Zur Frage von Identität, Integrität, Integration und Abgrenzung [What is person-centered? The question of identity, integrity, integration, and delineation], in U.A. Isele, *Identität, Begegnung, Kooperation. Person-/Klientenzentrierte Psychotherapie und Beratung an der Jahrhundertwende.* Köln: GwG Verlag.

Schmid, P.F. (2013) A practice of social ethics – anthropological, epistemological and ethical foundations of the PCA, in J.H.D. Cornelius-White, R. Motschnig-Pitrik and M. Lux, M. (eds) *Interdisciplinary Handbook of the Person-centered Approach: Research and Theory.* New York: Springer.

Schön, D.A. (1983) *The Reflective Practitioner: How Professionals Think in Action.* New York: Basic Books.

Schulz von Thun, F. ([1981] 2002) *Miteinander reden 1: Störungen und Klärungen [Talking with Each Other 1: Disorders and Clarifications],* 37th edn. Reinbek bei Hamburg: Rowolth Taschenbuch Verlag.

Schulz von Thun, F. (1989) *Miteinander reden 2: Stile, Werte, und Persönlichkeitsentwicklung [Talking with Each Other 2: Styles, Values, and Personal Development].* Reinbek bei Hamburg: Rowolth Taschenbuch Verlag.

Schulz von Thun, F. ([1998] 2001) *Miteinander reden 3: Das 'Innere Team' und situationsgerechte Kommunikation [Talking with Each Other 3: The 'Inner*

*Team' and Situational Communication*], 8th edn. Reinbek bei Hamburg: Rowolth Taschenbuch Verlag.

Schulz von Thun, F. (2005) *Klarkommen mit sich selbst und anderen: Kommunikation und soziale Kompetenz. Reden, Aufsätze, Dialoge [Being Clear with Oneself and Others: Communication and Social Competence]*. Reinbek bei Hamburg: Rowolth Taschenbuch Verlag.

Senge, P.M. (2006) *The Fifth Discipline, The Art & Practice of the Learning Organization*. New York: Currency Doubleday.

Sheldon, K.M. (2004) *Optimal Human Being: An Integrated Multi-level Perspective*. London: Erlbaum.

Sheldon, K.M., Arndt, J. and Houser-Marko, L. (2003) In search of the organismic valuing process: the human tendency to move towards beneficial goal choices, *Journal of Personality*, 71(5): 835–69.

Sheldon, K.M., Elliot, A.J., Ryan, R.M., Chirkov, V., Kim, Y., Wu, C., Demir, M. and Sun, Z. (2004) Self-concordance and subjective well-being in four cultures, *Journal of Cross-Cultural Psychology*, 35: 209–23.

Silani, G., Zucconi, A. and Lamm, C. (2013) Carl Rogers meets the neurosciences: insights from social neuroscience for client-centered therapy, in J.H.D Cornelius-White, R. Motschnig-Pitrik and M. Lux (eds) *Interdisciplinary Handbook of the Person-centered Approach: Research and Theory*. New York: Springer.

Sollárová, E. (2005) *Aplikacie prístupu zameraného na človeka (PCA) vo vzt'ahoch [The Application of the Person-Centred Approach in Relationships]*. Bratislava: Pegas/Ikar.

Sollárová, E. and Sollár, T. (2013) Person-centered approach: theory and practice in a nontherapeutic context, in J.H.D. Cornelius-White, R. Motschnig-Pitrik and M. Lux (eds) *Interdisciplinary Applications of the Person-centered Approach*. New York: Springer.

Steenbuck, G. (2005) Zur Aktualität Personzentrierter Begleitung und Beratung [On the recency of person-centered facilitation and counseling], *Gesprächspsychotherapie und Personzentrierte Beratung GwG*, 2: 81–6.

Stillwell, W. (2013) Conflict transformation, in J.H.D Cornelius-White, R. Motschnig-Pitrik and M. Lux (eds) *Interdisciplinary Applications of the Person-centered Approach*. New York: Springer.

Stillwell, W. and Moormon, J. (1997) *Conflict is Inevitable: War is Optional*. La Jolla, CA: Center of the Studies of the Person.

Tausch, R. (2007) Promoting health: challenges for person-centered communication-behavior in psychotherapy, counseling and human relationships in daily life, *Person-Centered and Experiential Psychotherapies*, 6: 1–13.

Tausch, R. and Tausch, A.M. ([1963] 1998) *Erziehungs-Psychologie [Developmental Psychology]*, 11th edn. Göttingen: Hogrefe.

Teml, H. (1999) Der Personzentrierte Ansatz in Schule und Lehrerbildung [The person-centered approach in schools and teacher-education], *Person-Centered Review*, 1: 47–55.

Trüb, H. (1951) *Heilung aus der Begegnung [Healing Through Encounter]*. Stuttgart: Ernst Klett Verlag.

Van Zyl, L.E. and Stander, M.W. (2013) A strengths based approach towards coaching in a multicultural environment, in J.H.D. Cornelius-White, R. Motschnig-Pitrik and M. Lux (eds) *Interdisciplinary Handbook of the Person-centered Approach: Research and Theory.* New York: Springer.

Watson, J.C. (2007) Facilitating empathy, *European Psychotherapy,* 7: 61–76.

Watzlawick, P., Beavin, J.H. and Jackson, D.D. (1969) *Menschliche Kommunikation [Interpersonal Communication].* Bern: Verlag Hans Huber.

Webster (1990) *Webster's New Dictionary and Thesaurus.* New Lanark: Russel, Geddes & Grosset.

Wood, J., K. (2008) *Carl Rogers' Person-centered Approach: Toward an Understanding of its Implications.* Ross-on-Wye: PCCS-books.

# Index

**The Handbook of Transcultu**
**Psychotherapy**
First Edition

Colin Lago

9780335238491 (Paperback)
Nov 2011

eBook also available

This fascinating book examines recent critical thinking and contemporary research findings in the field of transcultural counselling and psychotherapy. It also explores the effects of different cultural heritages upon potential clients and therapists.

**Key features:**

- Covers key issues such as: the implications of identity development for therapeutic work; ethnic matching of clients and therapists and working with interpreters and bi-cultural workers.
- Examines ways to overcome racism, discrimination and oppression within the counselling process.
- Provides an overview of current research within this field.

www.openup.co.uk

**AN INTRODUCTION TO COUNSELLING**
Fifth Edition

John McLeod

9780335247226 (Paperback)
August 2013

eBook also available

This bestseller provides a comprehensive introduction to the theory and practice of counselling and psychotherapy. This new edition has been thoroughly updated with new research, examples from practice and case studies. An extended introduction is used to explain the new 4-part structure and help readers to track key themes across each section of the book.

**Key features:**

- Topics for further discussion
- Key terms and concepts
- Suggested further reading

www.openup.co.uk

 OPEN UNIVERSITY PRESS
McGraw - Hill Education

**KEY CONCEPTS IN COUNSELLING AND PSYCHOTHERAPY**
A Critical A-Z Guide to Theory

Vicki Smith, Patrizia Collard,
Paula Nicolson and Rowan Bayne

9780335242214 (Paperback)
2012

eBook also available

This book offers a concise, readable review of the main concepts in the four dominant approaches to counselling and psychotherapy: the psychodynamic, humanistic-existential, cognitive behavioural and narrative.

Using the popular alphabetical format and written in an accessible writing style, this book iseasy to navigate and is designed as a first source for students with an essay on counselling theory to write, a case study to analyse, a belief or assumption to challenge, or a question about someone, e.g. a client or themselves, to explore.

**Key features:**

- Definitions and brief discussions of each concept, with critical analysis of the evidence for and against its validity and value
- Brief biographical sketches of leading theorists, with the emphasis firmly on aspects and experiences which may have significantly influenced their ideas
- Carefully chosen, annotated references for individual follow-up -usually longer discussions and original research studies or reviews of research

www.openup.co.uk